CU01240136

KENDALL'S GLORY YEARS

STEVE ZOCEK

KENDALL'S GLORY YEARS

In Their Own Words

pitch

First published by Pitch Publishing, 2025

1

(pitch)

Pitch Publishing
9 Donnington Park,
85 Birdham Road,
Chichester, West Sussex,
PO20 7AJ
www.pitchpublishing.co.uk
info@pitchpublishing.co.uk

© 2025, Steve Zocek

Every effort has been made to trace the copyright.
Any oversight will be rectified in future editions at the
earliest opportunity by the publisher.

All rights reserved. No part of this book may be reproduced, sold or utilised in any form or transmitted in any form or by any means, electronic or mechanical, including photocopying, recording or by any information storage and retrieval system, without prior permission in writing from the publisher.

A CIP catalogue record is available for this book
from the British Library.

ISBN 978 1 83680 143 6

Typesetting and origination by Pitch Publishing

MIX
Paper | Supporting
responsible forestry
FSC® C013604

Printed and bound in the UK on FSC® certified paper in line with our continuing commitment to ethical business practices, sustainability and the environment.

Printed and bound by CPI Group (UK) Ltd, Croydon, CR0 4YY

CONTENTS

Introduction 7
A Tribute from Athletic Bilbao. 11
Foreword by Martin Tyler 13
Foreword by Jenny Seagrove 15
Mike Lyons. 17
Mark Higgins. 21
Trevor Ross 27
Billy Wright 31
Asa Hartford 33
Peter Eastoe. 35
John Bailey 38
Joe McBride 42
Eamonn O'Keefe 46
Kevin Ratcliffe 51
Graeme Sharp 55
Steve McMahon 64
Paul Lodge 66
Alan Ainscow. 72
Mike Walsh. 76
Alan Biley 80
Mickey Thomas 83
Jim Arnold 86
Mick Ferguson 93
Gary Stevens 95
Neville Southall MBE 101
Alan Irvine 108
Adrian Heath. 116
Brian Borrows 119
Stuart Rimmer .123
Kevin Richardson. 126
Kevin Sheedy 134
Andy King 136
David Johnson .138
Glenn Keeley 143
Terry Curran 148

Peter Reid	153
Derek Mountfield	158
Alan Harper	164
Trevor Steven	170
Andy Gray	179
Darren Hughes	184
Rob Wakenshaw	187
Ian Bishop	191
Paul Bracewell	193
Pat Van Den Hauwe	198
John Morrissey	202
Ian Atkins	204
Neill Rimmer	208
Jason Danskin	213
Darren Oldroyd	216
Paul Wilkinson	217
Gary Lineker OBE	222
Ian Marshall	228
Neil Pointon	231
Darrin Coyle	237
Peter Billing	241
Bobby Mimms	244
Paul Power	249
Neil Adams	254
Kevin Langley	262
Dave Watson	267
Warren Aspinall	273
Ian Snodin	276
John Ebbrell	281
Wayne Clarke	289
Colin Harvey	293
Mick Heaton	297
Graham Smith	300
Jim McGregor	308
John Clinkard	313

INTRODUCTION

HOWARD KENDALL succeeded Gordon Lee as Everton manager in the summer of 1981, arriving from Blackburn Rovers. As a player, he severed his ties with the Toffees in February 1974 when joining Birmingham City, and after a seven-year absence, Howard was back at his spiritual home to take charge of his first game against none other than his old club from St Andrew's. Talk about a coincidence!

He brought with him a trusted member of his backroom staff, Mick Heaton, a man who was reliable and very well respected.

As a player in his Everton days, Howard was part of a trio known as the Holy Trinity in a partnership with Colin Harvey and Alan Ball, a trio still talked about today.

Howard was a member of the Everton side that won the First Division in 1969/70, appearing 36 times in the league out of a possible 42 and registering four goals.

Having a winning mentality, Howard decided to try his hand at management with Blackburn. After a testing start to his managerial career, he took the club on a remarkable run of 14 wins and one draw including a sequence of eight straight victories, which remains Rovers' record.

When he was approached about the vacancy at Everton in the summer of 1981, the club were desperate for someone who had the hunger and belief to bring silverware to Goodison, the Toffees having been starved of success since being crowned league champions on April Fool's Day 1970 after sweeping aside West Bromwich Albion 2-0.

The appointment was met with delight from the Evertonians who once worshipped him in that well-respected midfield.

In his first season, Howard managed to steer the team to eighth in the First Division, 23 points behind champions and neighbours Liverpool. The following season, Everton improved by going one place higher and recording the same points (64) as 12 months before.

In 1983/84, results weren't good with attendances failing to reach 15,000. Those fans who managed to brave the games were getting impatient with the manager and chairman, with calls for them to leave as leaflets were distributed outside the historic stadium. It wasn't a good time to be an Evertonian.

Chairman Philip Carter gave his manager a vote of confidence, and thankfully so.

In the November, the arrival of old heads Peter Reid and Andy Gray seemed to bring confidence into the dressing room. An FA Cup third round win at Stoke in January 1984 saw the story of Howard's team talk when he opened the dressing room window, urging his players to listen to the hordes of away fans who had made the short trip to the Potteries.

An 81st-minute goal by Adrian Heath at Oxford United in the League Cup quarter-final produced a replay won emphatically by Everton.

With these three major factors, was it a coincidence that they led to Everton's success? Who could forget two Wembley finals in 1983, in the League Cup and the FA Cup, the latter in May which brought the first piece of silverware to Goodison since 1970?

From 1984 onwards, Everton started to attract attention around Europe. They broke the dominance of Liverpool, certainly becoming a match for their neighbours in their own right.

INTRODUCTION

Trophies and finals became a regular feature in the football calendar with Wembley being called their 'second home'. They won all three domestic trophies, eventually testing themselves in Europe which eventually they conquered by winning the European Cup Winners' Cup in 1985. Just prior to that, the league championship had been secured, but Everton were denied a treble as the FA Cup eluded them, losing the final against Manchester United. Down to fatigue from winning their European trophy three days earlier in Rotterdam, perhaps?

That season, Everton competed in 63 games in all competitions with the European Cup being on the radar for 1985/86 until a bad night for English football at the Heysel Stadium in Brussels as 39 Italians were killed before Liverpool and Juventus met for the European Cup.

As a result of the circumstances surrounding Heysel, all English teams were banned from European competition for five years.

Everton continued to reach finals, losing in the FA Cup to Liverpool at Wembley in 1986, and were runners-up to the Reds in the First Division that same season.

Twelve months later, Everton snatched the championship trophy from their neighbours with the future looking bright. However, at the end of 1986/87, the club went on an end-of-season tour, and on their return it was announced that Howard Kendall was leaving to join Athletic Bilbao.

This book is about the players who played for Howard from 1981 until his departure in May 1987, a headline that shocked the whole of Merseyside, and the country.

They tell their own story about the man who brought success and happiness to L4.

A TRIBUTE FROM ATHLETIC BILBAO

THE FIRST thing that always comes to mind when we talk about Howard Kendall is how positive he was.

I remember the day he came to Bilbao. He did not understand a single word of Spanish. Of course, not in Basque either. He conveyed the image of happiness, smiling at all times, placing his thumb up when asked for a photograph.

He was a born winner. He came with the aura of having been a champion at Everton where he was idolised, but he was not intimidated when it came to giving some youngsters their debuts with the first team – Rafael Alkorta, Asier Garitano, Josu Urrutia, Andoni Lakabeg – players who gave much to Athletic and to those who transmitted their ambition.

He knew a lot about football and how to lead teams, he understood it very well. He had very clear ideas of what he wanted to do at Athletic. The players appreciated his methods, intense training and always with the ball. And with many laughs and smiles. Always positive.

He also knew how to listen. Although 4-4-2 was his clear style, he relied heavily on his 'second', Txetxu Rojo, and on more than one occasion acknowledged at a press conference the help provided by his assistant in tactical aspects. He was generous.

From the beginning he fitted in with us. His joy, his smile, his ambition, his work, helped him a lot. He made real friends while in Biscay. He played golf, went to Txokos – a typical place of the Basque culture where friends meet to organise dinners or meals of brotherhood; in the past, only men came, but today there are also women – with his team.

The fans also loved him. At his farewell press conference, with tears in his eyes and this time his thumb upside down, he proclaimed that Athletic was the best club in the world and that his next destination would be down. He was deeply loved by the *Athleticzales* (a name for the Athletic fans). For what he said, for how he said it and for its authenticity.

José Ángel Iribar
Legendary former Athletic Bilbao
goalkeeper and manager, the club's all-time
highest appearance maker

FOREWORD BY MARTIN TYLER

IT IS a huge pleasure to write this foreword to the latest of Steve Zocek's splendid contributions to the history of the football club he adores, Everton FC.

The Howard Kendall years fully deserve the recognition contained in this book – a tribute to an intelligent and industrious football man, seen through the eyes of those who won matches and trophies for the Toffees, those who knew him best, those who now share their tales from behind the scenes. These players did not just work *under* him. They performed *for* him.

I was privileged to see this historic time at Goodison Park at close quarters. I joined Granada Television as their football commentator in the summer of 1981, as Howard, a league championship winner with Everton as a player in 1970, was returning to the club. He succeeded Gordon Lee. I succeeded Gerald Sinstadt.

Saturday, 29 August 1981 was a big day in the home dugout and on the television gantry. And on the pitch for several fresh faces in Everton blue. A 3-1 win over Birmingham City was more than just a start to a season. It was the beginning of an era. It was the first indication of the impact of Howard's way, and for a slightly apprehensive young commentator lots of high-class action to describe.

Andy Gray's arrival a couple of years later was an inspired Kendall signing, a daredevil striker who would later show that he could talk the talk as well as walk the walk. Howard gave the Scot his head, and some of his great Everton moments were in the air while I was on the air! I gripped the Granada microphone as he frightened Bayern Munich out of the Cup Winners' Cup and out of Merseyside on that intimidating evening in April 1985.

Howard's pre-match routines, sometimes involving a glass of champagne, became a symbol of those glory years. That should not disguise the energy and the detail that went into his management. He could not only control some strong characters, a few not much younger than himself, he could coax the very best out of them.

The years from 1981 to 1987 were trophy-laden for a tremendous football club. The players as you are about to read left all their effort out on the field for a man they all admired and many adored.

Those were the halcyon days of Howard Kendall.

This is the inside story.

Martin Tyler
Spring 2025

FOREWORD BY JENNY SEAGROVE

I LIVED with and loved Bill Kenwright CBE for 30 years; 30 years of sharing my life with a man with a deep, loyal passion for his football club – Everton, the Toffees, the Mighty Blues! He chose the blue half of Liverpool at the age of six years old and never wavered. In fact, he used to quote a line from Stephen Sondheim's *Passion*, a musical that he produced – 'loving you is not a choice, it's who I am'. It was, it truly was.

When I first met Bill, I admit I liked football, but I had grown up abroad and didn't have any particular club loyalty. But that was about to change … when you fall in love with someone whose every waking moment is in some way infused with his love of his club, then you either join the party or live half of the life that you might have had. Luckily for me, I joined the party and was welcomed into the Everton family. What a roller coaster it has been!

Bill should have been writing this foreword. I know that he would have delighted in doing so. His stories about watching his team play during those glory years were infectious … how the League Cup game against Oxford United, when they were in a terrible place at the beginning of that 1983/84 season, changed everything. (Adrian Heath scored the winner.) How Bracewell and Reidy alongside Trevor Steven ruled the midfield, Big Nev in goal, Andy Gray up front. Winning trophies, the league twice, the European Cup and then getting banned from playing in

Europe and how that hurt us so much. He would have talked about the friends that he made along the way, the train journeys, the plane journeys ... people with a shared love. Everton. The team. The fans – the best in the world.

The success of those years may have slipped away for now, but his love for the club never did. It is a privilege to stand in for him to ask you to read on. Immerse yourself in Howard Kendall's glory years and the players who lit up the lives of so many Evertonians including 'my' Bill.

And dream ... that those times will come back, because I truly believe that they will!!!

COYB!!!!

MIKE LYONS

Debut: Saturday, 20 March 1971, Nottingham Forest 3 Everton 2

Nottingham Forest: Barron, Hindley, Winfield, Chapman, O'Kane, Fraser, Lyons, Richardson, Martin, Cormack, Storey-Moore (Rees 54)

Everton: Davies, Wright, Newton, Kendall, Labone, Lyons, Kenyon, Kenny (Brown 82), Royle, Hurst, Morrissey

MIKE LYONS was a boyhood Evertonian, and like many, he dreamed one day that he would pull on the royal blue shirt. For Mike, his dream came true. He joined the club as a young boy, serving his apprenticeship before signing professional forms in 1970. His debut came at Nottingham Forest four days before Everton were to play their second leg of the quarter-final in the European Cup at Panathinaikos. He appeared that day in the same line-up as a certain Howard Kendall.

Lyons was an appropriate name for Mike as he had the heart of a lion – a player who could play anywhere if asked, giving nothing less than 100 per cent. In later years, Mike had the honour of wearing the captain's armband, something he did with pride because Everton were his life.

A cruel twist for Mike was that in all his years serving Everton, he was unfortunate to carry the burden of never being on a winning side in a Merseyside derby. On 28 October 1978, a game remembered for an Andy King winner, Mike suffered the agony of not being involved due to an injury.

Mike was awarded a testimonial in 1980/81 for his loyal service to the club.

In the first season of Howard's appointment, Mike continued to captain the team, appearing on 26 occasions and scoring three goals – at home against West Brom, Aston Villa and Manchester United respectively.

The last time Mike donned a blue shirt was when replacing Alan Irvine for the last ten minutes in a miserable 3-1 defeat at Sunderland in mid-April 1982.

In the summer of 1982, Mike left his spiritual home, where he'd been as a professional since 1970, signing for Jack Charlton's Sheffield Wednesday for £80,000.

He returned for the first time in two years to lead out the newly promoted Owls on the first day of December 1984, receiving rapturous applause from his beloved Evertonians. It was a game overshadowed by a despicable foul on Adrian Heath from Brian Marwood which kept Heath sidelined as the club went on a successful search for glory.

After his time at Hillsborough, Mike went into management as player-manager at Grimsby Town. He was appointed on 1 January 1986 and remained in his post until 30 June 1987. He was in good company at Blundell Park, appointing Terry Darracott, his former Everton team-mate, as his assistant. In his side was former Everton defender Neil Robinson, who sadly passed away in 2022.

Talking about Howard Kendall, Mike says, 'He was always like one of the lads. When we were playing five-a-side in training, he was probably the best player even though he was the manager. He was a person that was always very approachable. He was a top guy.

'He was always enthusiastic and got on well with everyone. It wasn't just the first-teamers; it was everybody associated with the club. He was a character who loved the wins he produced as manager for the club who thoroughly loved being involved in the five-a-sides in training where again, he loved to win. He was enthusiastic in everything he did. You would also know when he was angry, but it would take a lot to upset him.

'He took on the role as manager with an option to play. His knowledge and enthusiasm to act as a great role model on the pitch rubbed off on players around him, especially the youngsters that were trying to find their way. In the dressing room he was always the same. He was never a moody sort of person but was strict. Everybody knew where you stood with Howard. If he ordered you to do something and you failed to comply, he would just get rid of you. He was fair but ruthless when he had to be.

'He really taught us all a lot about football as he was a role model to anyone learning the game.

'Off the pitch, he encouraged everyone, players and staff, to socialise. All of the lads used to have a night out in town with Howard and they were always enjoyable nights. He was very good company. I went to Benidorm with him at the end of the season where we had a great time.

'I enjoyed the relationship I had with him and had nothing but total respect for him as he was the boss. He knew his players inside out. Anytime he was concerned about you, identifying something that was bothering you, he would call you in his office and talk with you.

'Howard made a fantastic appointment in promoting Colin Harvey from the reserves to assist him in the running of the first team. I think Colin was a big influence with Howard and the success they achieved. It wasn't long when Colin came in and the tide turned and results and performances became more encouraging. Who would have thought months later, Howard would be stood below the

Wembley steps watching and applauding his captain Kevin Ratcliffe raise the FA Cup?

'He and Colin got on so well. They, as you know, played in the middle of the park together and were very good friends off it.

'I later played under another Howard, Howard Wilkinson at Sheffield Wednesday who was also a good manager. They were both similar in some respects because I think they really enjoyed what they did as managers.'

In what turned out to be Mike's last season at the club and Howard's first, he found the net three times. He opened his account in late September at a rain-soaked Goodison, against West Brom. The home side were awarded a free kick in front of the main stand with Asa Hartford sending a left-footed ball into the box where Lyons connected with precision, sending in a beautiful diving header after fending off opposing defender John Wile and leaving the keeper Tony Godden no chance. The Gwladys Street End and its supporters embraced the winner.

Also that afternoon, Andy King returned to Goodison and made his debut for the Albion.

MARK HIGGINS

Debut: Tuesday, 5 October 1976, Everton 2 Manchester City 2

Everton: Davies, Jones, Higgins, Lyons, McNaught, Hamilton, King, Dobson, Latchford, Goodlass, Telfer

Manchester City: Corrigan, Clements, Donachie, Doyle, Watson, Owen, Power, Kidd, Royle, Hartford, Tueart

MARK HIGGINS regarded himself as an adopted Scouser and was honoured to be made club captain by Howard, who felt he was more than qualified for that leadership role.

Mark was another product of Ray Minshull's youth policy. He joined Everton ahead of interest from both Manchester and north London clubs, having been England Schoolboys captain and played at Wembley for his country before the age of 15. He held the record number of caps (19) at that level. Some achievement. Mark was also part of the Everton youth team that lost to Crystal Palace in the 1977/78 FA Youth Cup Final. Crystal Palace had in their ranks Kenny Sansom, who later went on to play for Everton.

Everton manager Billy Bingham had no hesitation in introducing Mark to the defence at the age of 18 where he made his debut. He was a key member of Gordon Lee's era too.

When Howard Kendall was appointed, Mark didn't feature until the October at West Ham as the Blues scraped a 1-1 draw in a highly competitive contest.

Two days after Boxing Day, Higgins got on the scoresheet for the first time under his new manager, scoring two goals in a nine-minute spell and helping Everton beat the Sky Blues of Coventry City 3-2.

Sadly for Mark, injuries were to play a cruel part in his Everton career and he missed out on all of the success in this great period in the club's history.

At the age of 42, Mark suffered two heart attacks, but thankfully he pulled through and to this day he remains in good health.

Mark still has a role to play at the club these days as he takes the general public on tours of the stadium. It's nice to know the club still values one of their great players.

When asked for some of his memories of Howard, Mark said, 'Howard was a great player. He was a part of the Holy Trinity. For me to be at the club when he became manager, I count myself lucky to have played in the same team as him when he took on the role as player-manager. As a person, a great guy, as a footballer absolutely superb.

'He was a great man-manager. He was superb with the players, he knew what to do, also with the media. He knew how to handle the press well. Some managers can do it, some can't. Howard had it all. Compared to other managers, Billy Bingham was at the helm when I first joined. Billy gave me the opportunity, and I think I was at the time the youngest player to represent Everton in the 70s era.

'Gordon Lee was the next manager, who I got on very well with. The season of 1977/78 we lost our first two games before going on an amazing run which spanned 23 games before losing to Coventry City away in the December.

'Howard came in next, and as I've said, he turned it around. I also have to mention the respect I have for Colin [Harvey]. The best thing Howard did was to promote Colin to the first team.

'At the training ground, you always wanted to be on his side. When Colin got called up to assist Howard, Colin and Howard in the five-a-side would keep playing until they won. You could tell what great players they were with some great touches. They were both winners. We had games on a Monday and Tuesday, and they were proper games.

'In the dressing room? Superb. Howard just knew how to handle different players. He knew who required a kick up the backside, and the ones who needed an arm around. If players weren't doing too well and he thought they needed a break he would take you to one side and tell you. The good thing about him was that instead of dropping someone, he'd have a word with you and give you the reason. The best advice he gave me and others was to play for as long as you can. Howard was a manager that was never afraid to try things.

'When he first arrived, everybody knew things weren't going that well. He brought in what he called the "Magnificent Seven" including Neville Southall, who became the legend that he was. Some players didn't come up to scratch, but that's how it goes.

'It was a sad time for him when the team endured a torrid time with the fans becoming impatient. I remember the times when cushions were being thrown from the stand as performances were below par and the fans would let you know.

'We, at that time, would stand together as a family. He was never one for putting the blame on any of the lads. Whatever problems he had, he always kept in house which I think is right.

'Howard liked to socialise with his players. I went out with him quite a bit as when he made me captain, we went together to different things. When we used to go to away games we stayed in a hotel. My father was a player with Bolton Wanderers and won the FA Cup in 1958. Howard would sit with my dad in the hotel the night before and have a chat and a drink. He was interested to hear my dad's thoughts on his career which goes to show the respect he had for him. Howard would always ask my dad for his opinion on certain things too and listen to advice.

'We, as a group of players, would enter Chinatown in Liverpool which is what Howard liked. He liked everybody to feel part of his squad. Howard was a great believer in team bonding and that was his way of doing it with a meal and a few drinks. He loved his football, and I think Howard was at his happiest when his team were doing well. He and Colin just loved being with the lads.'

The dark nights came in the winter of 1983, as did results which caused a decline in attendances. Fans will remember the New Year's Eve game at home to Coventry as they showed their displeasure. When they were not getting value for money, they wouldn't be shy in letting you know. The supporters became united, protesting vocally and also distributing leaflets asking manager and chairman to step down.

Who would have believed that the club would turn a massive corner a month later as success started to appear?

Sadly for Mark, he missed the celebrations through injury, and recalled, 'The first one was the Milk [League] Cup Final against Liverpool. I knew I wasn't going to be fit for that so you just have to accept it. Then [there was] the 1984 FA Cup Final against Watford, wanting us to win and made up for the lads and of course the fans.

'Ratters [Kevin Ratcliffe] said to me later that he regretted me not going up for the cup as I was the club captain. When the final whistle went against Watford I walked straight down the tunnel.

'I tried to get myself fit for the next season and missed out again the season after when we lost to Manchester United in the FA Cup Final, and the 1985 Charity Shield when we won. I sat on the bench at Wembley six or seven times!

'It was hard for me in 1984, missing out on all the success; sitting on the bench at Rotterdam [in 1985] as a spectator hurt.

'So, I kept my head up and trained but I just kept breaking down. I saw the then physio, John Clinkard, and a specialist in London who told me I was finished. I was only 26 years of age at the time.

'It was a tough time for me and I was gutted for the fans to lose that 1985 FA Cup Final.

'My relationship with the Gaffer? We were going on to win everything and missing out on the success because of the times that I played when I shouldn't have.

'He of course gave me the captaincy. It was strange in the way that it happened because the season before he chose Billy Wright. I played with Billy at the back, a top guy and player.

'I recall a game at Ipswich and Kevin Ratcliffe that day occupied the left-back role. We were both left-footed players and eventually we got paired together. I got an injury and played when I shouldn't have played and Howard kept saying, "Come on, I need you, you're my captain."

'I'll never forget the time when he dropped me. It was when we played Liverpool at home and lost 5-0 [in November 1982]. Glenn Keeley deputised that afternoon as I sat in the stands with Kevin Ratcliffe. I was absolutely gutted for the club, the fans. I looked at Rats during the game with an expression that said it all. I saw Howard on the Monday where he pulled me to one side and said, "Don't say a word, you're back in next week." Howard had this way with players that could be difficult. He was very clever where he would listen to players over certain things, and he would give them a chance.

'If you stepped out of line, he would come down on you like a ton of bricks. He had this way of handling players. He didn't really lose it a lot except for the odd time.

'If you were late for training, you'd be fined. Being late for the team bus was another. The great thing was when players got fined, Howard would put the money into a kitty. I recall Inchy [Adrian Heath] and Reidy [Peter Reid] being fined and we were taken into Chinatown where they had to foot the bill.

'He could also compliment his players. I recall the game when we played Bayern at home in the Cup Winners' Cup semi-final. I was sat in the dugout as a spectator, and I remember Howard saying to me that the game was one I would have enjoyed playing in as it would have suited me.

'Later as years passed, I would often meet up with Howard when I came back to do the lounges at Everton, and we would always be pleased to be in each other's company. He would call me over and ask for a big hug, we were mates.

'Like many, I was devastated to hear of his passing, it was unbelievably sad. I went to his funeral out of respect. I sat with Ron Atkinson. I thought Reidy did a superb job reading the eulogy, a very brave thing to do. We returned back to Goodison with Howard's widow and his sons and had a few drinks which is what Howard would have wanted us to do. A few of the lads got on to the stage and had a sing-song.

'All of the lads went then to the Hilton hotel in town. As I booked a room, and I don't even think I went to bed. It was a proper send-off where Howard would have been proud of us all.'

TREVOR ROSS

Debut: Saturday, 5 November 1977, Derby County 0 Everton 1
Derby County: Boulton, Langan, Nish, Daly, Daniel, Rioch, Powell, Hector, Hughes, Masson, Ryan
Everton: Wood, Jones (Seargeant 74), Ross, Lyons, Higgins, Buckley, King, Dobson, Latchford, Pearson, Thomas

TREVOR ROSS signed for Gordon Lee from Arsenal for a fee of £170,000, where he'd had the pleasure of playing with Everton legend Alan Ball.

Trevor was a very good midfielder who took no nonsense from any opposing player. He hit the net on five occasions in his first season back in 1977, in 20 games. In fact, on his debut, it was Trevor's free kick that found the head of Mick Lyons, whose header secured a victory at the Baseball Ground on Bonfire Night despite a floodlight failure in the second half which was thankfully rectified.

Under the management of Howard, Trevor was a regular first-teamer, who appeared in all competitions 30 times behind Steve McMahon (35), Mark Higgins (32) and Mick Lyons (31) respectively in 1981/82. He registered his only goal early in the season in what was Everton's fourth home game of the campaign, against Notts County.

In the new year, Everton's quest for a Wembley final in the FA Cup came to an end at the first hurdle. Ross took a 78th-minute penalty which was saved by keeper Phil

Parkes. Peter Eastoe scored a consolation as the Blues went down 2-1.

Sadly, his second season faded and he made two first-team appearances, one as a substitute at home to Norwich, then starting the next game at Coventry. He was later loaned out to Portsmouth and Sheffield United before making Bramall Lane his home on a permanent basis.

'Howard was a nice honest guy, and an extremely good coach,' says Trevor. 'Most of all, a very friendly guy and very much one of the boys despite being a manager. You couldn't say a bad word about him unless you had an argument with him.

'I played alongside him in the first team and reserves albeit he didn't play too many games, but when he did play, you could tell his experience and his knowledge of the game. His style of play reminded me a lot of Paul Bracewell when he came to fruition. When he was on the pitch and how he used to talk to you. He would help every single player around, not certain individuals.

'At Bellefield, Howard used to enjoy the five-a-side and train with the lads, and whatever they set out for that session was enjoyable, and he was always delighted after a game when he'd been on the winning side. That showed his hunger to be competitive and be a winner. He did have an angry side to him but not in a way that you would fear him. If we played not at our best and the effort was minimal, he wasn't happy. If you gave your best and lost, he still gave you a piece of his mind but not as much if you tried. If you stepped out of line you would get fined which applies in all football clubs, I guess.

'As manager, he was to the point, a good manager who knew what he was doing, also in pre-season. He had a good coach in Mick Heaton alongside him. Mick was another who could be one of the lads when he needed to be, and a coach when he needed to be. Those two gelled well together. Howard would analyse a lot as a manager then set things out. Was I surprised when he reaped success? No. You could see he wanted success, as did Mick Heaton. Provided they had the backing, you could see he would get the success. He bought a couple of players when he first came that weren't "Everton" players. Eventually, when he signed Andy Gray who was paired with Graeme Sharp, things started to take off for the club.

'He was also successful because he was likeable; he treated players right. Respect was a two-way thing.

'His signings were also effective. Trevor Steven was a good signing that would hug that wing and was always an outlet. John Bailey was an excellent addition. For me, Neville Southall was without a doubt his best signing.

'On the social side, Howard was class company. When we went on tour to Japan, Howard asked me and John Bailey if we were doing anything one afternoon which we weren't, so we went out together and had a fabulous time. We went to a restaurant that Howard had discovered the day before where we ate a beautiful meal and had a few drinks too. He was great to be out with. He was kind, funny, loads of conversation which was in his nature. Everything came natural with him, he never tried to impress.

'My relationship with him was very good until my last term there. I was in and out of the side and we exchanged words then was sent out on loan and would be brought back and go back into his first team. Whenever he put me back in the side, I always gave 100 per cent for him. I was never one of his blue-eyed boys but a player he always wanted in the side. If he left you out of his selection for the game, sometimes he would call you to his office and tell you, and other times he would put the team up on the noticeboard where you find out that way. On a Friday, if you were training with the first team or reserves, you would have an idea of which team you'd be in the following day. One thing I remember him telling me, never to change the way that I play.

'Nobody could deny what a great manager he was. I played under some great managers, but Bertie Mee [Arsenal] was the best. He gave me my opportunity as a youngster which I will always be grateful for. Like Howard, Bertie was a gentleman. Again, he could lose his temper. His assistant Bobby Campbell was an extremely good coach, he was amazing, as was Don Howe.'

BILLY WRIGHT

Debut: Saturday, 4 February 1978, Everton 2 Leicester City 0
Everton: Wood, Jones, Pejic, Lyons, Higgins, Ross, King, Dobson, Latchford, McKenzie, Telfer (Wright 57)
Leicester City: Wallington, Williams, Rofe, Kember, Sims, Webb, Weller, Kelly, Davies, Salmons, Hughes

BILLY WAS snatched from under the noses of neighbours Liverpool by signing for Ray Minshull, the youth development officer. He was sent by Everton to train as a mechanic should his career in football flop, serving his apprenticeship in the trade for two years. During that time, he was turning out for the A and B teams of Everton, progressing into the reserves.

His performances warranted an invitation to train with the first 11 which led to his debut, albeit from the bench.

Under Gordon Lee, Billy was only a step from an FA Cup Final in 1980, suffering the agony of a semi-final defeat against West Ham United after a replay at Elland Road, which was the biggest disappointment in his time at Everton.

A proud moment for him was to receive the captain's armband from the legendary stalwart Mick Lyons, which was a tremendous honour. Billy belonged to a big Everton family, so being a local lad made it more special for him.

Billy started the season under his new manager, scoring in their second home game of the campaign, a 1-1 draw against Brighton & Hove Albion.

He was even made club captain under Howard. Was this a proud moment for him?

'Oh yes, without a doubt. With my uncle Tommy having played for the club too and also having played for the England under-21s and their B team, to get the captaincy off Mick Lyons of all people who was a good mate, was a tremendous honour.'

Billy started 24 times in the league that season. The following season there were another 21 outings for him then the relationship between himself and Howard Kendall over his weight turned sour, leading to him being left out in the cold which resulted in a free transfer to Birmingham City.

Billy's last game in the Everton blue was on 4 December 1982. Did he think that would be his last game under Kendall, and did he think the club would go on to reach the success they did?

'No, not really. Even after I had left and gone to Birmingham City, Everton were still in a transitional stage. I think it was an FA Cup tie at Stoke City if I remember rightly that would have been a make or break for Howard and the team. It was from that day forward that it all transpired and things started clicking into place.'

About leaving the club, Billy said, 'I think I had done my time and Howard had been at me a few times about my weight and one thing and another. We shared a difference of opinion on my weight as I thought I was fine and he didn't. I thought my playing form was as good as it had been prior to this.

'In the end Howard told me that he thought it was best for me to leave the club. It was an amicable departure with a handshake and away I went.'

ASA HARTFORD

Debut: Saturday, 1 September 1979, Everton 1 Aston Villa 1

Everton: Wood, Wright, Bailey, Lyons, Higgins, Ross, Hartford, Stanley, King, Kidd, Eastoe

Aston Villa: Rimmer, Linton, Gibson, Evans, McNaught, Mortimer, Morley, Shaw, Deehan, Cowans, Swain

ASA HARTFORD signed for Gordon Lee at the end of August 1979 after a miserable stay at Nottingham Forest where he only appeared three times. Everton captured the Scotsman for £400,000 after he had originally signed for Brian Clough at the start of August for £500,000. Not bad business.

Fast forward to the appointment of Howard Kendall and Hartford was named in the new manager's first match, against Birmingham City. Although Everton were victorious, Kendall with a win, it was an unpleasant afternoon for Asa. Everton recovered from an early goal by the blues of Birmingham and drew level when debutant Alan Ainscow equalised on 13 minutes at Goodison. The home side were awarded a penalty which Hartford stepped up to take on the half-hour mark after Phil Hawker was adjudged to have made contact with his hand on to the ball. Referee George Courtney didn't hesitate in pointing to the spot. Hartford's penalty was sweetly struck with his right foot only for Jeff Wealands to save. Courtney spotted that the visiting keeper had moved too early, ordering a retake, which produced the same outcome as Wealands repeated his heroics, diving the same way to keep the scoreline level.

Hartford only appeared seven times in Kendall's first season in management, without finding the target. He made his last appearance at home against West Bromwich Albion on 26 September 1981 before returning to Manchester City in October 1981. Howard later explained his reasons for Hartford's departure to Maine Road, 'I was very disappointed that Asa wanted to leave Everton, but the pattern of events should be related to the supporters. When I came to the club, I wanted Asa to be my midfield general and the man who could pass my information on to the other players. He was a very important member of the side and of my plans, and I wanted him to stay. Asa wanted security and wanted it now.'

PETER EASTOE

Debut: Saturday, 7 April 1979, West Bromwich Albion 1 Everton 0

West Bromwich Albion: Godden, Bennett, Statham, Trewick, Wile, Robertson, Robson, Brown, Regis, Mills, Cunningham

Everton: Wood, Barton, Jones, Lyons, Ross, Todd, King, Dobson, Latchford, Kidd, Thomas (Eastoe 39)

GORDON LEE brought Peter to Merseyside from Queens Park Rangers in March 1979 with striker Mickey Walsh going in the opposite direction.

Peter played his last game under Lee's management at Wolverhampton Wanderers on a May bank holiday Monday in 1981, a goalless draw, before Howard Kendall succeeded Lee.

Kendall's 'Magnificent Seven' were brought into the club to stiffen up competition in the ranks. Included in the signings were two forwards, Alan Biley and Mick Ferguson. For the opening game of the Kendall era, against Birmingham City, Peter Eastoe was named in the starting line-up and rewarded his new manager with a goal three minutes after the restart as Everton triumphed 3-1. Peter featured for the next five games, scoring against Notts County three and a bit weeks later. He had a troubling groin strain which led to a visit to a specialist in Stoke who Howard recommended. His absence lasted until his return on 21 November 1980 in a 2-1 defeat at home to Sunderland, when Eastoe was on the scoresheet once again.

In 1981/82, Eastoe made 18 appearances in all competitions, with two as a substitute, with a disappointing six goals to his name. Peter's last game for Howard was at Aston Villa in a 2-1 win, the final match of that campaign.

When asked for some memories of his time under Howard Kendall, Peter said, 'When I think about Howard, I think about what he did for me. He signed seven new players as you know including two new strikers. At the beginning of the season, he played me which says it all really which was a big thing knowing that Howard had faith in me even though he bought forwards. When a manager signs a new player, it does have an effect on you. You think that you will go down the pecking order. In fact, Howard asked me who I wanted to partner me up front giving me a choice, but at the end of the day it was his decision, not mine. He wanted my opinion, but whether he seriously considered it, I don't know.

'Howard was always upfront with you. He knew what he was talking about. If he had something to say to your face, he would say it, and would take the time to explain things to you.

'In the dressing room on a matchday, he was really good. A very good communicator. At Bellefield he also enjoyed the five-a-sides which he took part in along with his coach Colin Harvey.

'Howard also loved the social side with his players. He enjoyed company as we all did. He liked everybody to be part of his company and liked a drink as we did too.

'Howard was very happy combining the role of player-manager in his early days. He had a very good temperament, and not once can I ever recall him showing signs of being angry because he was very gentlemanly.

'Even after he sold me to West Brom [in 1982], he told me that if I ever wanted to come back, I'd always be welcome, which was a nice gesture, again showing what sort of a person he was. He was definitely in the top two or three managers that I played for. I suppose it all depended on whether you were in the team or not. I think Howard was one of these people that knew what he wanted at Everton. Eventually he got it.

'Howard was the boss, and his way of letting you know if you were not wanted, he would get rid of you. Alan Biley, I recall, scored two in one game but Howard knocked him down a peg or two. I think that affected Alan if I have to be honest, and he was never the same player after that which was a shame really.

'If ever you were left out of the side, players knew they would be. You always have an idea especially when you know you haven't performed to the best of your ability.

'Out of respect and courtesy I attended his funeral. I was amazed at the amount of people there. It was an enormous gathering which summed up how loved he was.'

These days Peter is a delivery driver for a supermarket chain based in the Midlands.

JOHN BAILEY

Debut: Saturday, 18 August 1979, Everton 2 Norwich City 4

Everton: Wood, Barton, Bailey, Lyons, Wright, Ross, Nulty, Todd, King, Heard (Eastoe 71), Kidd

Norwich City: Keelan, Bond, McDowell, McGuire, Hoadley, Powell, Neighbour, Reeves, Fashanu, (Taylor 79) Paddon, Peters

JOHN BAILEY was Liverpool born and bred. His birthday is on April Fool's Day which is appropriate for this character. Signed from Blackburn Rovers by Gordon Lee, John had already played with his future Everton manager Howard Kendall at Ewood Park. He was at Goodison for seven seasons and was part of the success that Howard brought to the club in those glory days. Under Howard's reign, John only found the net once – his only goal for the club which came on the last Saturday before Christmas in 1982 as Everton trounced Luton Town 5-0. John opened the scoring in the most bizarre circumstances on 14 minutes. From a free kick for a foul by David Geddis, Kevin Ratcliffe tapped the ball to Bailey who was inside his own half. He drove the ball which bounced in front of the advancing keeper Jake Findlay, who was deceived by its bounce as it eluded him and went into the net.

When Howard signed Pat Van Den Hauwe in October 1984, John's appearances became few and far between, seeing his career away from Goodison which resulted in a move to Newcastle United.

An interesting fact: John was once asked what his personal ambition was back in September 1983. His reply was to win a trophy with Everton. What did he know that we didn't?

John says, 'He [Howard] was a personal friend of mine as well as my manager. I lived with him for two years in Sheffield when he took me as a coach. We were very close, and even now, I still miss him.

'He was the best ever. He was a great manager who you couldn't fool as he'd been there as a player himself. He used to take all the lads out with all of the money he collected from fining players for whatever reason. He knew how to keep the mood in the camp happy as he made the players feel that way.

'When I signed for Gordon Lee at Everton, the training was all running along beaches and up hills. Howard was different, everything entailed working with a ball.

'At the Bellefield training ground, he was there all of the time, spending time on the pitch at every opportunity. He favoured his time on the pitch rather than in the office. Colin did most of the sessions, but Howard was always keeping an eye on what was going on.

'He enjoyed the role of player-manager. I think he found it very difficult to give up the playing side of it.

'He had an appetite to win, no different to any manager; he loved winning games, and after a good win he would sit in the boot room with a glass of wine and smoke a cigar.

'He was a very easy-going man to get on with, but as any human being he could get angry. I have seen Howard angry loads of times, especially when he left me out of the team. If we ever had a fall-out, it was forgotten immediately, no grudges held.

'If any players gave him problems, he would take them in hand. If ever a player had a hard time with him due to being left out of the team, everything would be put right on the Monday after the game where he would take whoever into his office, have a bottle of lager, where things went back to normal.

'That sadly happened to me on the arrival of Pat Van Den Hauwe where I knew Howard was never going to leave Pat out of the side as he'd signed him. I remember one trip to Leeds United where Howard approached me on the bus which was unusual to tell me that I wasn't going to be involved. I was gutted hearing the news. I sat in the dressing room while the match was on, I was that upset.

'Advice was always welcome from him. The best advice he ever gave me [laughing] was, "Don't drink!" He told me to sign for Everton when they came in for me when we were together at Blackburn Rovers. He told me that I couldn't sign for a better club.

'In the dressing room, he could do unusual things. He once brought a silly comedian in the dressing room before a match 20 minutes before the game. This comic came in carrying a suitcase when Howard introduced him. He was brought in to relax the lads. I wouldn't mind, but he was the worst comedian I have ever seen and heard. You had to laugh because he was that bad.

'Comparing him to other managers? Howard was a top manager, his man-management, the players loved him. I worked with Gordon Lee, Jim Smith [Blackburn] who was very strong and fierce. Even though Howard was more relaxed, we knew he was the boss and you knew the boundaries.'

John looks back on the turning point for Everton's fortunes, 'Colin Harvey's promotion to the first team in 1983 ignited a spark, elevating the club as things started to fall into place. Don't forget, Howard and Colin had a friendship which lasted a long time. They were very much on the same wavelength and were a very good pair. Mick Heaton and John Clinkard were also influential in the success of the club.

'Adding to the rise of Everton, Howard brought into the club two fantastic and experienced players who lit up the dressing room. I think the double signing of Peter Reid and Andy Gray was another masterstroke. I couldn't say which one was more of an influence than the other, I can't split them. Andy hardly trained due to his knees being bad, but was an unbelievable professional. Reidy, he had injuries too, but he proved to be different class.

'From January 1983, a winning streak started, having progressed in both FA and League Cup competitions. Confidence kicks in and the league form becomes part of that momentum. To grab a piece of silverware at Wembley in 1984, the first since 1970, gave the Gaffer so much pleasure, but for me, I think what gave Howard the most pleasure as far as silverware goes was when we won the league for the first time, which would go alongside the European Cup Winners' Cup. To win those honours and to be the first Everton manager to achieve them was special.

'I was absolutely heartbroken when I heard Howard had passed away. He was so young and it wasn't his time to go. I went to the cathedral to attend his funeral. It was great to see so many people want to pay their respects. I met people for the first time – Johnny Morrissey. To look around at the packed cathedral and even outside was unbelievable. They brought the coffin in to the tune of "I Guess That's Why They Call It the Blues". I still get choked now thinking about it.'

These days, John can still be seen attending matches at Goodison.

JOE McBRIDE

Debut: Wednesday, 3 October 1979, Everton 0 Feyenoord 1 – UEFA Cup first round, second leg
Everton: Wood, Barton, Bailey, Lyons, Higgins, Nulty, McBride (Varadi 67), Wright, King, Kidd, Eastoe (Latchford 67)
Feyenoord: Van Engelen, Nielsen, Stafleu, Van De Korput, Wijnstekers, Van Der Lem, Jansen, Petursson (Van Til 75), Notten, Peters, Van Diensen (Budding 68)

JOE WAS a member of Ray Minshull's Everton FA Youth Cup side that lost 1-0 on aggregate to Crystal Palace in the final in the 1976/77 season.

He took a while to get his first outing under Howard Kendall. He came on from the bench on 64 minutes to replace Steve McMahon in a 1-0 win over West Bromwich Albion on 26 September 1981. Two minutes later, the Blues opened up their account as Mick Lyons met an Asa Hartford free kick heading past keeper Tony Godden. McBride may have had no part in the goal, but was able to celebrate with his team-mates.

The following week, Joe started on the left wing at Stoke City, bagging an equaliser on 73 minutes to cancel out Lee Chapman's fourth-minute opener. A point looked secure until a lapse in the last ten minutes saw Everton concede twice to end up losing 3-1 and remain slightly below the halfway mark in the table.

Joe's last appearance for the Toffees was at home to Sunderland, a miserable 2-1 defeat in November 1981, before joining Rotherham United in August 1982. Joe gives his thoughts on his time at Everton under Howard Kendall: 'Success is the first thing that comes to mind when I think back to Howard. On a personal level, disappointment, because I missed out on all of that through no one's fault but my own. I made a decision to leave Everton when I didn't have to. It's the worst decision I've ever made in my life. Howard was young when he came to Everton, so was very close to the players in terms of age, as he got to know his players on a personal level.

'His style of management was quite relaxed. You have to remember that I was only there for maybe a season under Howard. He was very organised, meticulous but was always laughing. He always had a smile on his face during training which rubbed off on the players as well. Howard was probably ahead of his time. He made a huge difference when he came to Everton with new ideas, also being a young manager at that time.

'He was very close to the players in terms of their age where I was only a very young lad. He would be closer to the senior players. In the dressing room whatever the players were relating to he knew.

'He took over at the end of the season and we had already planned to go on a tour. His first kind of time with us all was three weeks away in Japan and America. He was great company, loving the company of his players and staff around him. He was never one to throw it in your face about his playing career and what he'd achieved including bragging or boasting, nothing like that. Not everybody was aware of what he'd achieved as a player. He and Colin [Harvey] used to talk about George Best all of the time, and some other opposing players from their era.

'I remember when the tournament in Japan had finished, we went to Los Angeles for a week's holiday. He got us all in the bar and said, if you think brown ale, you'll be brown ale, if you think you'll be champagne, you'll be champagne. He produced I don't know how many bottles of champagne. He poured every one of us a drink and wished everyone well for the season ahead. He did think different, and the players certainly did drink champagne over the next four or five years.

'My time at the club wasn't as long as I'd have liked as I was only there for a year. He had a lot of highs after I'd left which would have made him ecstatic. When his team had just won, I can just picture him sitting in the changing room after the game or in his office after a victory. There's normally a half hour of elation when your game plan went well, the team selection was right, then you realise that you have to do it all again the following week.

'You would never overstep the mark with him as he would let you know about it [chuckles]. He never went totally mental; he didn't have to. He had that kind of presence where you were in awe of him. He had that way of clearing his throat, shall we say. He led by example. He was on the training pitch every day. He'd done it all as a player. He would tell players how to run back in a game and chase players. He was a marvellous inspiration to everyone. If you were fined for anything that you should not have done, late for any meeting or a meal, anything like that, you would have to put a bottle of wine on every table. If it was a big gathering you were in trouble.

'If I didn't have a good relationship with him, it was down to me. He had 20 to 30 players to look after. I was young and foolish if you like, but yes, I did. If I ever met him after I'd left or finished playing, we'd be absolutely fine. The best lesson I learned from him was probably his work ethic on and off the pitch. In training he would run past players and try and retrieve the ball back.

'He was different from other managers that I'd later played for because he was so young. Howard was on the pitch all of the time joining in with training and probably the best player every day. His playing style was that he had a bit of everything. Peter Reid is the first one that comes to mind if I think of a similar player. Determined, technically good, a leader. Peter did have a bit of everything.

'If your confidence was suffering, he would grab you or talk to you on the training ground. I grew up with Colin in the reserves, and I don't know if it's what Colin told Howard to do.

'If you were not selected to play at the weekend or midweek, in those days if your name wasn't on the sheet it wasn't. I once went to see him and he told me basically what I needed to do to get back in the side. He told me that he hadn't left myself out, it was me. At that age it's something I didn't agree with. When you get older and wiser you realise that he was right.

'Listen, overall, my memories of him are good, but a funny memory, it was probably when we were on tour in Israel. There was a 24-hour bar in the hotel. Myself and a couple of the younger ones stayed up until around 2am. Howard was still there with a couple of the lads. We came down for breakfast, and they were still there [laughing]!'

As of the time of writing, Joe was the dedicated coach for the Scottish Football Association's Performance Schools project based at Holyrood secondary school in south Glasgow.

EAMONN O'KEEFE

Debut: Tuesday, 30 October 1979, Grimsby Town 2 Everton 1 – League Cup fourth round

Grimsby Town: Batch, Stone, Moore, Waters, Wiggington, Crombie, Brolly, Ford, Drinkell, Mitchell, Cumming

Everton: Wood, Wright, Bailey, Lyons, Higgins, Ross, Nulty (O'Keefe HT), Stanley, Latchford, Kidd, Eastoe

EAMONN O'KEEFE, a van driver for the *Manchester Evening News*, captured the eye of Gordon Lee, who didn't hesitate to part with £25,000 for his signature from non-league Mossley. In what proved to be Lee's last season in charge, Eamonn featured quite a bit, and he was also given a chance by Howard Kendall in his first season in charge by making 12 starts before leaving to pastures new when Wigan Athletic manager Larry Lloyd welcomed him to Springfield Park.

During Eamonn's time at Everton, he scored an extra-time winner in an FA Cup replay against Southampton to earn an FA Cup quarter-final place. Fans may remember his dismissal in a Merseyside derby for a fight with Liverpool's Ronnie Whelan in a November 1981 defeat at Anfield.

Eamonn spoke of his first memory and introduction to Howard, 'The first day he arrived at Bellefield, addressing the group of players by standing on the staircase saying, "Anybody that wants to leave this football club, this magnificent football club, if you're under contract and you wish to leave, you'll go in my time, when we're ready."

'Secondly, as a player, he's one of the three that Everton are famous for – the Holy Trinity. He is one of them which is magical in itself. The managing side of his career, you can't argue with that either.

'Howard, if you remember, had achieved things as a player, and knew what he was talking about in management. Everton have always been renowned for getting the ball forward, and when you have a creative midfield, you have a creative manager. I think that's how he saw play which he proved with the success that he brought to the club.

'At the training ground he was great, because he liked to join in with everybody. He would always whistle through his teeth in training, telling you how and where he wanted the ball. His style was very similar to Peter Reid, both of them lacked pace but were blessed with wonderful vision.

'As manager, to speak to someone about the game, I had massive respect for him for his achievements as a player. Howard had done it as a player, so, you knew whatever he was telling you, you had to listen because he knew what he was talking about. He certainly did his homework on the opposition when it came to a game. He was aware of certain opposition players, and who to watch out for and get that message across to each and every one of us.

'Gordon Lee who signed me would walk around the training pitch not shouting out instructions. He and Howard were like chalk and cheese.

'He certainly did his homework on the opposition when it came to a game. He was aware of certain opposing players, and who to watch out for and get that message across to each and every one of us.

'My relationship with Howard was so good. I expressed my disappointment at not being a regular starter at Everton, spending many games on the bench. He was very simple when he had to tell you something after making a decision. He would say to you, "Come in here, I want to tell you something." Once he had selected his starting line-up and you were not involved, he would take you in the office and show you a video clip of you, then say, "That's why you're on the bench tomorrow." Then he would pin the sheet up on the board naming the squad. If you failed to learn from the mistake he was showing you on video, he would tell you that if you didn't do what was asked of you, he would bring in someone that would. That was the biggest lesson I learned from him.

'He always knew when there wasn't something quite right with individuals, he knew his players so well; it was easy for him to spot something that wasn't right. Howard would walk around the pitch at Bellefield with whoever it may be to discuss whatever.

'I will never forget the way he supported me after I got sent off at Anfield in the derby in a 3-1 defeat in November 1981. I went in for a tackle with Ronnie Whelan which the Liverpool fans disapproved of. Can you imagine 50,000 fans baying for your blood! They had to unlock the dressing room door to allow me in as there was still more than 20 minutes of play remaining. I sat there a lonely figure thinking about the rollicking that lay ahead when the team returned, thinking what Howard would say. When they came in after the defeat, as you can imagine, each and every one of them dejected, Howard says, "See him [pointing to Eamonn], he was the only one who had a go out there, and not one of you backed him. I'm disgusted with the lot of you!" That was the measure of the man.

'When I wasn't a regular for him, Howard assured me that if any interest came in, he would tell me, which he did. He got me transferred to Wigan Athletic when they showed an interest.

'Later in my career I played for Blackpool and was given a testimonial. I phoned Howard asking would he bring a team to Bloomfield Road which he agreed to. Everton had won the league and Howard brought his first team.

'I can't deny that I played under some great managers in my career. As well as Howard Kendall, there was also Howard Wilkinson. They were both different characters but very enthusiastic about the game.'

Eamonn also spoke about Kendall's partnership with Colin Harvey, 'Howard couldn't have chosen a better assistant than Colin. Colin's contribution in bringing the lads through the reserves into the first team was unbelievable. Colin nurtured those young lads and his knowledge of them all, he knew them so well. Everybody respected Colin. Even when we played five-a-side, he was the first choice. His first touch was incredible.

'He was a born winner. There is nothing better than when you're successful, is there? You can't beat that feeling when you're winning games. I felt so sorry for him when the English clubs felt the force of the ban from Europe due to the Heysel disaster.

'He was a man with a steady temperament, and would occasionally throw a bit of sarcasm into the fray. He said to me once, "Is it right you play for the Republic of Ireland? Is it because you bought a packet of Kerrigold butter which made you qualify?"

'He could also be very disciplined, he had to be, who isn't in management? If you were late, Howard wouldn't tolerate it, and you would be fined. If there were any players that posed a problem or two, who I don't wish to name names out of respect, Howard weeded them out and got rid of them, it was that simple.

'I recall one time we were out on a pre-season tour in Germany, and we [Eamonn, Andy King and George

Wood] arrived back at the hotel ten minutes late after the curfew. Nothing was easy sailing thinking we'd got away with it.

'When we arrived back in England days later, we were called into his office. He started to question the time we arrived back at the hotel. I spoke up by being honest that we were back five or ten minutes late.

'"Kingy and Woody swear blind that they didn't go out," Howard said.

'What Howard did, he gave a piece of paper to the nightwatchman and told him to make a note of the players arriving back and what rooms they were in so he could identify them. Because I'd been honest, Howard made a point of fining those two where they ended up paying for a meal for all of the lads as their punishment.

'He loved the social side of the game too and he would love to be in the company of his players and staff. He was fabulous company when we were all out together, he insisted he wasn't the manager. The first time I went out with him socially was when we went to Japan not long after his arrival. Howard never liked lads going out in groups, he insisted we all go out together.

'Whilst in Japan, we were going to Henry Africa's bar. Howard and Mick Heaton were in the reception of the hotel with their trousers folded over their arms so they didn't crease them. They were stood there in their club blazers, underwear and shoes on. All of the players for a laugh removed their trousers and the guy behind the bar didn't have a clue what was going on. It was a bit of harmless fun. That is my funniest memory of Howard.'

KEVIN RATCLIFFE

Debut: Wednesday, 12 March 1980, Manchester United 0 Everton 0

Manchester United: Bailey, Nicholl, Albiston, McIlroy, McQueen, Buchan, Coppell, Wilkins, Jordan, Macari (J. Greenhoff 64), Grimes

Everton: Hodge, Wright, Bailey, Ratcliffe, Lyons, Eastoe, Megson, King, Latchford, Kidd, McBride

KEVIN RATCLIFFE was a Blue from birth. He represented his county Flintshire at schoolboy level, as a versatile defender who could play at left-back but somehow seemed more effective as a centre-half.

He was discovered by a scout from St Asaph who took him to Everton. Besides that, he was going locally to Chester and Wrexham, who were also interested in taking him. He also went along to Manchester City and Tottenham, but once entering the gates of Bellefield, there was only one club he wished to devote himself to.

Making his debut in March 1980 on the big stage at Old Trafford as a 19-year-old, Ratcliffe only played because regular defender John Gidman was ill. By the end of that campaign, Ratcliffe had made a total of three appearances – two in the First Division and one in the FA Cup.

The following season under Gordon Lee, Ratcliffe became a more prominent feature in the team with a total of 27 appearances in all competitions.

After the sacking of Lee, Howard Kendall also showed faith in the Welsh youngster.

Not everything between Kendall and Ratcliffe ran smoothly. The youngster handed in a transfer request which was refused, but he was later given the captain's armband and took over from the unfortunate Mark Higgins who was sorely missed through injuries. On his appointment as captain at the age of 23, Kevin's presence was noticeable on the pitch through his leadership skills and being vocal.

A goalscorer he was not, but his first goal for the club came at Norwich in January 1983. A run from the right-hand side by Adrian Heath resulted in a ball to the onrushing Ratcliffe, who appeared inside the box to strike it first time – albeit not cleanly – and beat Chris Woods in the Canaries' goal, winning the game. Jim Arnold also deserved credit for saving a last-minute penalty from John Deehan, sending the Merseysiders home with maximum points. Incidentally, Kevin's only other club goal came against the 'enemy' at Anfield – in front of the Kop, I must add – with a tame shot from 35 yards with his left foot. Bruce Grobbelaar in the Liverpool goal fumbled as the ball squirmed under his body and over the line to put Everton one up. Gary Lineker put the game beyond doubt five minutes later to seal victory.

Failing to claim the league title that season, Everton snatched the trophy back the following term, lifting the trophy at Goodison on 9 May after brushing aside Luton Town. Kevin was ever-present that season with a maximum of 42 league games.

'Ratters', as he was known, showed his qualities not only at club level as the captain, but also for Wales too. He was capped 59 times.

Who would have thought that he would have gone on to have such a wonderful and successful career for club and country?

He once expressed his desire to be a lorry driver if he hadn't gone into football. His leadership certainly directed the club on a road to success more than once.

Kevin spoke about the arrival of Kendall, and what he thought was the turning point for the club under him, 'On his arrival, what was noticeable from the off happened at Bellefield. He was way ahead of his time with ideas which brought a fresh approach, making the sessions more enjoyable.

'He participated in the sessions, showing all of the qualities he had from when he was in his pomp. He even stood out from the players that were there as squad players!

'He kept the ball well, a sign of a good player. Just watching him was influential in itself. A very good learning process for players young and old.'

The winter of 1983 brought much discontentment from the terraces as fans were unanimous that Kendall and chairman Philip Carter should stand down. Thankfully that didn't happen with the tide starting to turn, but what made the difference?

Ratcliffe recalled, 'I thought the turning point was Coventry City. I think that was significant because we had to win because Howard would have been sacked. It was for me the start of Peter Reid's career as he came on as a sub. The Thursday after that game he signed Andy Gray. We went on to win our next game at home to Nottingham Forest 1-0, playing ever so well, and I think it clicked then in the midfield area.

'The back four changed a little bit. At one time it was Billy Wright then Higgy [Mark Higgins] then it was me. At right-back was Gary Stevens who found his place with John Bailey cementing the left-back berth. It was the midfield that we were unsure about. Peter Reid came in and maybe Adrian Heath dropping from a striker into midfield helped.

The right-hand side was ding dong with Alan Irvine and Trevor Steven battling it out that season. One got the nod in the League Cup and the other in the FA Cup. It was just getting the right balance in midfield. I don't think that Howard knew what his best midfield was. Sometimes it's by chance, isn't it? One game you get that little bit of luck and Peter Reid coming on with 20 minutes to go perhaps changed it.'

On the experiences of playing for Howard and Colin Harvey, Kevin added, 'They were totally different. Howard was always relaxed; Colin was too tense. Colin was a better coach than he was a manager. People don't realise the transition from a coach to a manager. All of a sudden, it's all YOU. It's all about who comes into the football club, it's not what your coach says about whether a player is good enough, or he isn't, the final decision is down to the manager.

'I think Howard had a good knack of getting a player to fit the bill. As it turned out there was one or two that didn't work out but his man-management was good as well.

'Colin with all respect wasn't the greatest conversationalist and he would even admit that.'

GRAEME SHARP

Debut: Saturday, 3 May 1980, Brighton & Hove Albion 0 Everton 0

Brighton & Hove Albion: Moseley, Gregory, Williams, Horton (Sayer), Foster, Suddaby, McNab, Ward, Clarke, Lawrenson, Ryan

Everton: Wood, Gidman, Bailey, Wright, Lyons, Ross, Eastoe, Stanley, Latchford (Sharp 64), Hartford, McBride

GRAEME SHARP was bought by Gordon Lee from Dumbarton. He was given the opportunity when Howard Kendall took over, maturing into a great centre-forward and inheriting the tag of legend. He will always be up there with all of the Everton giants who wore that famous number nine shirt.

Graeme forged some great partnerships with whoever he was thrown in with, being no stranger to where the goal was and scoring 160 times in 447 appearances for the Toffees to become the club's post-war record scorer, and second on the all-time list behind the legendary Dixie Dean. That is something special.

Graeme once said that he would have liked to have been a journalist had he not made a career in football. He certainly wrote the headlines more than once in the daily papers.

Graeme says, 'Howard was a top manager, a top bloke who I probably got to know better in the latter stages of his life. Once he'd retired, he would attend the games, and I would often see him at after-dinner events.

'When I was younger, I didn't really have much dealings with him. He was a manager, a successful one at that, enjoyed the good times, but socially, he kept himself to his own group of friends, as we did as players. When Howard first came in, he decided to go his own way. He made the famous seven signings paving the way to how he was going to build his team.

'I think through lack of form and injuries, he started to introduce myself and some of the younger lads. It was always going to take time, which was difficult. If I'm honest, I was a young lad in the reserves with Colin Harvey. When Howard signed these players, you felt your chances were going to be limited further of getting into the first team. My early recollections of him were not great as I had no dealings with him and his priorities lay with the first team.

'Once I broke into the side, I think he [Kendall] had a rethink that there were some good young kids kicking around in the reserves that deserved a chance. The established players that he bought were not performing. Making that breakthrough, you got to know him better being involved with the training sessions. I have to say that his training sessions were fantastic. They were like a breath of fresh air. That also applies when it came to pre-season training too.

'Howard had played at the top level, not long finished playing when he joined Everton, and knew what players he wanted. That is what endeared him to the players he got together. The players loved going into Bellefield to train every morning.

'Once he got his feet under the table, assembling the team together, that's when everybody flourished.

'He was brilliant the way he combined the player-manager role. I used to watch him in training, see something and think, WOW! Kendall, Harvey and Ball. We'd heard all of these stories about the Holy Trinity and what a great combination they were. Colin too was a fabulous player. We used to train with him also and play five-a-side. Even though he had dodgy hips, he was brilliant. His awareness and touch. Then I would think, what a player Colin must have been in his pomp.

'Howard also in training would be pinging balls from right to left which made me think, this guy can still play. When the opportunity arose to play, I think Colin coaxed him into pulling the shirt on again. When he played as a player-manager, he was still a fabulous player. He may not have had the legs he had when he was younger, but he had the know-how and the knowledge and the passing ability. He never lost his talent.

'Howard built a young team which was trying to find its way. Colin thought that Howard could help on the pitch, and he certainly did do.'

Colin was establishing a good side who were showing promise in the Central League. His team's performances were drawing attention from Howard, who had no hesitation in appointing his fellow midfield colleague to the first team as his assistant.

What effect did that have on the first team, I asked Graeme?

'Colin's influence on the success and with Howard was MASSIVE. I would say that Colin Harvey was instrumental to everything that happened because a lot of the young players, Gary Stevens, myself, Kevin Ratcliffe, Kevin Richardson had all grown up with Colin in the reserves. Colin was a really hard taskmaster. He could be frightening at times and would lose his temper. He would still play in training sessions and would be annoyed if his team lost, and would top players in tackles, he was so passionate.

'The players that had grown up with him had nothing but respect for the man. When he was promoted to the first team, he never changed an iota, driving the boys on. He always expected 100 per cent, nothing less. He HATED losing at anything. John Clinkard the physio, and Terry Darracott later on played their part. As a partnership, Howard and Colin hit it off from the word go. I don't think that we would have achieved the success if Colin hadn't been alongside Howard.

'Colin earned respect from the word go. If he said "jump" you'd jump. Mick [Heaton] was more of a jovial character.

'Colin was miles ahead of his time. At the time of 1982/83, he was doing video analysis. We would go into Bellefield on a Monday, and he would show us clips of the game on the previous Saturday as to what we could and should have done better. Colin would have been studying that video recording at the weekend. Colin was really instrumental and I don't think the success at the club would have come if he hadn't been involved.

'My relationship with Howard in the beginning wasn't great. I didn't have many dealings with him until I broke into the side. He selected his own team which was fine, and it was a case of me knuckling down by working hard under Colin hoping to get the chance. I think that when the opportunity arose away to Notts County, was down to every other striker being injured. Peter Eastoe, Alan Biley, Mick Ferguson weren't available and Howard had no other option. Colin was pushing my name all of the time. I scored at Meadow Lane in a 2-2 draw, and that was it for me, as I got into the side. I was involved from then up until the end of the season where I missed one game in all that time – incredible really, adding a further 14 goals to my tally.

'I can honestly say that I had a good, but not great, relationship with Howard. I was very headstrong in my opinions, and he had his. Nine or ten times out of ten, the manager wins.

'We had our ups and downs, the downs being when I was left out of the side, or I didn't agree with him. He realised how difficult it was to keep 11 players happy. Everybody wanted to play. I felt sorry for Alan Harper and Kev Richardson who had enough quality to walk into another side in the First Division.

'I remember a time he left me out with some crazy excuses. I'd played against Coventry City in the League Cup third round at home and scored. It was an awful game. The next game I was dropped. I went to see him, as I wanted to know why I was left out.

'He explained and said, "You're not really scoring." I reminded him that I scored in a previous game when we drew 1-1. "Yeah, it didn't count as it was from a corner," he replied. I laughed and said, "So, it doesn't count from a corner and we lost 1-0?"

'I was dropped from the FA Cup semi-final against Southampton in 1984 which was extremely disappointing, but again, I got my head on and worked hard at getting into the side for the final. There were disappointments along the way between Howard and myself.

'He was a man that handled his players very well. He was great for picking his signings as well. Howard was great on and off the pitch and was a great believer in that everybody had camaraderie and had to be together. He instilled that in every single one of us. That was a key ingredient of Howard. He wanted to know the background of the players he was bringing in.

'When he first brought in the Magnificent Seven I don't think he did his homework on that, but after that he did. There was nothing worse than having a split dressing room, and that was never going to be the case with Howard. Very rarely did Howard make a mistake, and if he did, it wouldn't be long before the player was out of the door.

'Howard did his homework with Paul Wilkinson who he bought from Grimsby after scoring against us in the League Cup. Howard had a fantastic knowledge of the game and the players involved.

'My memories of Howard being happy? The image of him after the 1984 FA Cup Final when we went up to collect the trophy, the cameras panned in on Howard to show that big happy smile. That was the start of it. That, and the success he had of winning the league, that was his happiest time.

'He also showed an angry side to him too. If the ball would have been played up to Andy or myself and we hadn't got hold of it, Howard would be moaning like anything. We had our run-ins at half-time, everything was always the strikers' fault. If we were a goal down it would be our fault. Howard just wanted to win; he was a winner. He wanted perfection and wanted his team to do well.

'He made it clear what he wanted, and as players, you knew what he wanted when you crossed that line. Howard made his instructions very simple.

'Everton was always a club about standards. I remember the day that I walked through the door, and me seeing a commissionaire. I'm thinking, what's all that about? When you walked through the doors, you immediately knew about the history of the club. The directors would come down to the changing rooms, and the players had massive respect for the people upstairs.

'Howard had a fantastic relationship with the club secretary Jim Greenwood and the chairman Sir Philip Carter. If you have that sort of backing, you have every chance, and fair play to those two who had faith in him.

'Howard always wanted perfection, no different to anybody else. Fortunately, Howard had a team that wanted the same thing and to challenge Liverpool. Once we got the bit between our teeth, the introduction of Andy [Gray] and Peter [Reid] gave us that belief that we could go places and that's what we did.

'Howard always liked attacking football. The only time I would say we were cautious was when we played Bayern Munich away. We had a lot of injuries and I played up top alone.

'To think of any players that resembled Howard as a player? Howard had his favourites. He loved Trevor [Steven]. Trevor was bought from Burnley for a massive fee, he also bought Inchy [Adrian Heath] from Stoke years before. Howard knew Inchy from his time at Stoke City, so wasn't scared to splash out a big fee for him. Those two players didn't start their Everton careers too well, but Howard had faith in them.

'Kevin Sheedy as well was another of his type of players. Reidy and Brace [Paul Bracewell] gave you something else. Sheeds [Kevin Sheedy], Inchy and [Trevor] Steven were high on his list. I think those three were players he identified to himself, who were good passers of the ball. I would say, Trev and Sheeds with Inchy just behind.'

Howard signed many players before he got the chemistry right, so I asked Graeme who his best signing was.

'If I had to choose his best signing, I would say it's between two – Andy Gray and Peter Reid. I would have to say Andy. Andy was the louder of the two which says a lot because there are not too many louder than Reidy!

'I grew up watching Andy Gray at Dundee United, moving on then to Aston Villa who were my English team when I was up in Scotland. Andy dragged us up when he arrived at Goodison. The dressing room was down as results weren't going too well, and he instilled belief in the team.

'Andy couldn't believe that he came to Everton with a history of injury problems. His arrival came with, "I'm here, and going to enjoy myself at this massive club." Andy would tell you that the team were going nowhere, and he will take all the credit for it [laughing]. Him and Reidy came in and made us cross that final hurdle which made us believe that WE could challenge Liverpool.

'Howard was always happy to give advice. He was always on to the strikers about getting on to that back post. I was a player that scored goals from outside the box, never afraid to shoot from distance. I was never one for scoring enough scrappy goals if I'm honest. He would always want you to be involved in the build-up, get in the box, get to the back post if you can, and you will score more goals. That was the thing that he would hack on about all of the time.

'He came back to Goodison after he'd gone to Bilbao. That particular day I'd scored two or three, Howard was interviewed by the press and he said, "It was nice to see Sharpy getting on the back post." When you are young you need guidance, and he certainly gave me that.

'The Gaffer's passing was a traumatic shock. I attended his funeral which was incredibly sad. I remember getting the news that Howard had passed away. Everton were playing Manchester United that afternoon, I was driving in when I received a phone call. "Have you heard about Howard?"

'"What about him?" I replied. I was told the news and I said that it wasn't true, as it was difficult to digest. It turned out to be a really sad day.

'I arrived at the ground and TV people want to speak to you with your thoughts etc. I had tears in my eyes because Howard was a massive part of my life. For me, growing up in the city, playing for Everton where he was involved. Everybody who was associated with Everton FC was affected, and I don't think anybody had cared if the Manchester United game would have been called off. That game doesn't go down in the history books as it was such a sad, sad occasion and a massive shock to everybody.

'The funeral itself, I thought it was incredible. To have the ceremony where they had it was incredible as was the turnout. The speeches that were made, full credit to everybody who spoke up that day. It was a very tough day.

'Howard was a remarkable man who went too soon.'

Graeme, until recently, was very much still involved with Everton. He was an ambassador and later got invited on to the board as a director. He left his role in June 2023.

STEVE McMAHON

Debut: Saturday, 16 August 1980, Sunderland 3 Everton 1
Sunderland: Turner, Whitworth, Bolton, Allardyce, Elliott, Hindmarch, Arnott, Buckley, Hawley, Brown, Cummins
Everton: McDonagh, Gidman, Ratcliffe, Wright, Lyons, Megson (Eastoe 60), McMahon, Sharp, Latchford, Hartford, McBride

STEVE McMAHON originated from a family of Evertonians in nearby Halewood. In his younger days he served as a ball boy at Goodison Park on matchdays before joining the club as a schoolboy.

He made the most appearances for Everton under Howard Kendall in his first year in charge although, on the disappointment of failing to be selected for the opening game at Goodison Park, Steve later reflected, 'When I was left out on the opening day, I was disappointed. I had worked hard to regain full fitness after my injury and I felt convinced that I was ready. However, the boss told me that he wanted me to get a couple of games in to get real match fitness and put that extra edge on my play. I fully accept that, but I intend to be in there pushing all of the time to get a regular place.'

He was called up for the second game of Kendall's reign, a 1-1 draw at Leeds United. He contributed with two league goals that season, the first being at West Ham on 10 October after just 59 seconds. Alvin Martin equalised for the Hammers five minutes before half-time as Everton took a good away point, keeping them 14th in the league at the close of the day. Kendall saw McMahon as a very valuable asset and decided to sell him to Aston Villa, who were very keen on the youngster and paid £175,000 for him.

Sadly, Steve declined to contribute to this book.

PAUL LODGE

Debut: Saturday, 7 February 1981, Everton 1 Aston Villa 3
Everton: Hodge, Ratcliffe, Bailey, Wright, Lyons, Ross, Megson, Eastoe, Varadi, Hartford, O'Keefe (Lodge 72)
Aston Villa: Rimmer, Swain, Williams, Evans, McNaught, Mortimer, Bremner, Shaw, Withe, Cowans, Morley

PAUL LODGE grew up in a house with the majority of the family members being Reds. He attracted numerous clubs, having a choice of Everton and Liverpool, deciding to put the ink on a contract at Goodison. Leeds United were a third party waiting in the wings.

Paul played for Liverpool Schoolboys with former Everton player Alan Harper, who wore the captain's armband.

He says, 'I ended up going to Everton, which is a long story in itself and gave me the opportunity to go to Everton and my brother to Liverpool. He was fortunate to captain Liverpool's youth team; I was fortunate to play against him at Anfield. I think it could be some kind of a statistic but I think it was the first time that two brothers faced each other on opposing sides in an FA Youth Cup match. That I suppose was my little claim to fame.'

Paul was a pupil of Colin Harvey and Ray Minshull's schooling before fulfilling his dream by making his Everton debut as a substitute a week before his 20th birthday against Aston Villa, who went on to inherit the league championship three months later.

Under Howard Kendall's reign, Lodge's first outing was away at Middlesbrough in late October

1981. A Mick Ferguson double secured the points in a 2-0 win.

Paul failed to hold down a first-team place, and with 24 appearances under his belt he was loaned to Wigan Athletic and Rotherham United respectively before a permanent move to Preston was confirmed in the late season of 1983.

Paul gave his thoughts on working with Howard, 'There are a couple of things. I've got to be honest that we never saw eye to eye in a few respects. The big thing for me, with Howard, he was always as straight as a die, whether you agreed or disagreed. He was a straightforward guy that told you the truth, he never messed about.

'He once sat me down and gave me an ultimatum. "Do better, or I'm bringing Kevin Sheedy in." They were his exact words which have stayed with me all of this time and will do for ever. I have no regrets with Howard Kendall at all.

'The other thing is, I'm proud to say that when Howard was in the role of player-manager, I played three or four games alongside him in midfield. It was such a fantastic experience for me to have done that.

'What is happening today in the modern game, Howard was doing that 30 years ago. He let the players make a lot of decisions; it wasn't uncommon that he would listen to players. In the dressing room he was like one of the boys. He really loved mixing with the lads, bearing in mind that he was only 35 when he first arrived at the club. Although he'd had managerial experience at Blackburn Rovers prior to his appointment at Everton, he was still one of the boys which was probably difficult for him.

'I played under other managers in my career and Howard was as good as anyone, if not better. Everybody knows Howard wasn't going to bring success to the club overnight. He went through a lot of turmoil before the glory, which happens in football all of the time. When he struggled in the first two years, it wasn't because he was a bad manager; he was inserting his stamp and authority on it.

'If you think of the players that he ended up with, to make the club great again – the likes of Peter Reid and Andy Gray as two examples – I'm almost certain that most clubs would never have taken a chance on those two players. Howard saw something in Peter and Andy that no one else did.

'I played against Andy the season he left Wolves to move to Everton, and he looked washed out – finished. I knew about Reidy, where he'd suffered sadly with injuries before Everton. Reidy would admit, the day he walked through the doors at Bellefield, he wasn't anywhere near as fit as he ended up. Graeme Sharp matured as a player under Howard's management. Howard was fanatical on getting the ball up to the number nine. Sharpy was a good player but improved immensely under Howard's management. He would tell Graeme to hold the ball up until he received some support. He hated centre-forwards flicking the ball on.

'Howard's strength was his man-management. He was always around the lads, and had a knack of making players feel better. If any of the lads wanted criticising, he would do it. If he ever left you out of the side, he would name the team and wait for a reaction from yourself if you were left out. I remember being left out of a game at home and he never said a dickie bird. He was obviously waiting for a reaction from myself. I didn't think it was good approaching him on matchday. He would rather you wait until the Monday before going to see him in his office.

'If your confidence suffered for whatever reason, he would pull you to one side, not collectively, and tell you to keep your head up, your chance will come. Work hard in training, you're still in my plans. You had to take whatever he said on the chin like a man. Any weakness you had, stood out a mile. He was very encouraging with the young lads, but would also test you out without you realising it. He always wanted to see if you had mettle.

'He loved the social side too and being around his players. Socially, I had a good inkling of the way Howard was in that environment. He no sooner walked into the club in 1981 than we jumped on a plane for three weeks away in Japan and Los Angeles. For me, the way he socialised with the lads, he was really good. He could sit with the lads, have a few drinks, also in the company of the directors, even [former club chairman] Sir John Moores was on that trip. So, in all fairness, he was comfortable with everyone around him.

'Everyone of a certain age remembers him as a great player, but you know what, he never spoke about his playing career, he wasn't flash in that regard. His playing career had gone, so he wanted to concentrate on his managerial career.

'Never did I see him acting unprofessionally, he could handle himself so well in social circles.

'He was a very happy man on the training ground, definitely. He was compared to Glenn Hoddle when he became the national coach of England. He would ask the lads to do things, as Howard could actually demonstrate what he wanted because he still had the legs to do it, including the capabilities.

'He was also good to give advice. The best advice he ever gave me was, get yourself as fit as possible. I will give you a chance, but you have to be a man and grown up to take it. If you don't take the chance given, there are not many left. I didn't take my opportunity which has led to a regret that I have had to live with.

'I think he admired a lot of players. He was never shy in telling someone what a good player he was, or he would be interested in signing so and so. He was forthcoming in that respect, and didn't shy away from mentioning players he rated.

'There was also an angry side to him as there is with anybody. During games, half-time, after games. He would let you know if he wasn't happy, like all great managers. Once he'd said his piece it was finished, there was a line drawn under it, no grudges, and let's start again.

'He came down on players really hard, he never messed about. He was never one to hold grudges because that player was still important to him. I've worked with managers after I'd played for Howard, and they did hold a grudge and the player would be out of the door.

'Howard loved a fine process for anyone that stepped out of line. There used to be a list in those days with the reasons for a fine which was lateness, untidiness, dirty boots. He always liked the players to train with their socks pulled up to their knees. Howard would fine anybody if he could, just to get money in a kitty. The money would always end up back in the players' pockets as they would be treated to a meal out, a trip or whatever.'

Paul smiles while reminiscing,

'The story I tell the most is that we used to train in the gym at Bellefield before the AstroTurf was put down. We had a young apprentice called Jimmy Coyle who smashed Howard into the wall. This game was a real physical affair too. Howard got up with players gathering round to break up what may happen.

'We all walked into the dressing room, and I was the one with a pot of tea. I asked Howard if he wanted a cup to which he replied "yes". He continued to ask, "Who was that young lad?" "Jimmy Coyle," I replied. "He'll do for me," said Howard.'

Sadly, Paul left the club and missed out on the glory days that lay ahead. He wore the royal blue shirt for the last time in April 1982, being introduced in the 90th minute for Neville Southall, who was forced off with an injury. Mick Lyons took the gloves and the green shirt for the remainder of the game. That afternoon, Everton and Manchester United shared he points in an enthralling 3-3 draw.

Paul was somewhat surprised Howard brought success to the club, but very much pleased for his former manager, 'I've got to say I didn't see what was coming in 84, I really couldn't. I mean this with the utmost respect. I think sometimes you need a certain amount of luck for things to click in place which I think Howard got and I do think that he deserved it too.'

Later in his career, Paul tried his hand at management in non-league football. He became caretaker manager at Southport in 1999, then worked in the North West Counties League with St Helens Town and later as an assistant at Accrington Stanley under John Coleman. Paul told me that his methods of management were lessons he learned from his reserve team manager at Everton, Colin Harvey. That was because he played more games under the man known as the 'White Pelé' in the Central League than he did for Howard.

'When I signed as an apprentice in 1976, Colin Harvey had stopped playing. He was only 32 but had a few injury problems. Now he became my coach or mentor or whatever you want to call it. Some of the things Colin taught me in those days, I still used them in my coaching life until I finished coaching, simply because he was that big of an influence in my career as are many others as well.

'Colin was the one that made that transition for me, from an amateur footballer to a young professional, which was brilliant.'

Paul is now retired, having also had a spell working for Accrington Stanley with the club's youngsters.

ALAN AINSCOW

Debut: Saturday, 29 August 1981, Everton 3 Birmingham City 1
Everton: Arnold, Wright, Bailey, Walsh, Lyons, Thomas, Ainscow, Eastoe, Biley, Hartford, Ross
Birmingham City: Wealands, Langan, Dennis, Broadhurst, Hawker, Todd, Brocken (Handysides 75), Dillon, Evans, Gemmill, Van Mierlo

A FRIDAY teatime phone call from Birmingham City manager Jim Smith alerted Alan Ainscow of Everton's interest. The tea was thrown into the bin as he made his way to Merseyside for talks with Howard Kendall, who would be his new manager.

Alan was another signing who made up the Magnificent Seven brigade. He was a very experienced player who'd played first-team football with Blackpool and Birmingham City.

Howard showed faith in the Bolton-born Ainscow, who obliged his manager with an equaliser against his former club on 13 minutes, cancelling out Van Mierlo's opener in his debut on the first day of the season. Incidentally, Ainscow's only other goal that season came in the reverse fixture at St Andrew's six months later, completing the double against the Birmingham blues.

His first season was disappointing as he only appeared 16 times in all competitions due to an in injury at Notts County on 2 November courtesy of a tackle by Brian Kilcline, who received a red card. This made his stay on

Merseyside nothing more than a disgruntled one with only 25 appearances in total under Howard, then after a long period of absence through injury, he was loaned out to Barnsley after regaining fitness, eventually joining Eastern AA in Hong Kong.

Alan says, 'Howard was still playing when I joined Everton. He could still play a bit to be fair. His training methods were different to what I was used to. He also made training enjoyable. There were no long runs like what I'd been used to with other clubs.

'His man-management was good, as he let the players get on with it to a certain extent. Mick Heaton would come out and warm us all up every morning then Howard would actually take over the training session. Having been a player and still being a player, I think he appreciated what the players wanted. You never ever found his sessions boring.

'As a player-manager in the dressing room, he liked to be one of the lads, but only so far. He knew how to get in with the bunch of lads, and as manager, he had to keep his distance. He loved training with the lads, and once he hung his boots up and realised he wasn't going to be playing any more I think he missed that. I must add when we trained and Howard got involved, he was still quality. His style was very similar to Peter Reid and Kevin Sheedy. Quality, good passers of the ball. Howard liked players who had different qualities, like John Bailey, a character who was good for the dressing room.

'He was a man that loved the social side with the lads, but not me, not at that time, I was married with four kids with another on the way. When my wife was in hospital being induced with the last one, Howard gave me the day off. Howard actually phoned the hospital requesting me to play in the reserves that night at Huddersfield so I could speak to Norman Hunter who was manager of Barnsley about a proposed month's loan.

'My relationship with him? In all honesty for me, probably not the best. I wasn't one of the lads that used to go out together for a Chinese. Because I had such a large family, I couldn't justify going out all of the time. I think he got more familiar when he was out with the lads.

'When I got injured in a game at Notts County, and because I was out for such a long time, I wasn't part of his plans. I wanted Howard to give me encouragement like "Come on, get yourself fit," that sort of thing. We ended up having a few words because he was the one that bought me from Birmingham to do a job for him on that right-hand side. He never ever sat me down and told me exactly what he wanted from me. I think that hindered my time at Everton in some ways.

'We did have words once in a pub toilet not far from the training ground after a game on the Saturday. After a few pints I guess tongues loosen, you then become a little bravado and sometimes it does good to get things into the open as the truth was spoken.

'I was called into Howard's office at Bellefield on the Monday, and Howard told me that he'd been thinking about what I'd said, telling me he'd given it some thought. I was in the squad for the following weekend's game against Arsenal. He was giving me notice to get myself mentally prepared for the game five days later.

'I've known him to get angry after a performance that didn't go well, I can't pick things out individually, but I'm sure he would have been angry about the way the team performed, things of that nature.

'With his players, to be fair, he was one of those people that would pull people to one side then get them in the office. He was never one for chastising people in public.

'He would fine you for the basic things like being late for training or breaking a curfew if we were away. He would have a word with [captain] Mick Lyons where they would come up with a system of fines. The money would be pooled which would pay for a night out for all the players, staff etc.

'Comparing him to previous managers that I'd played for, he was more cool, calm and collected. As he'd not long finished playing, I think he tried to do things as if he were still playing. He was never one for ranting and raving like some I've worked under.

'The biggest lesson I learned from him was, I guess, when you get knocked down you get up and try again. What happened to me in the end, Ipswich Town was my last game for Everton. I'll never forget this: he pulled me in on the Monday before telling me I was playing. Then in the next breath, he tells me I'm getting a free transfer. I've been gutted to leave all of my clubs, but Everton was the one I felt more. It's not very often a club like Everton comes knocking. These are the teams you dream of playing for when you're a kid.

'Like many, I attended his funeral at the cathedral in Liverpool. I was amazed at the amount of people that attended. People of different ages from different eras. A lot of ex-football people, the whole event was massive. He was massive for the club so it was expected really.'

MIKE WALSH

Debut: Saturday, 29 August 1981, Everton 3 Birmingham City 1
Everton: Arnold, Wright, Bailey, Walsh, Lyons, Thomas, Ainscow, Eastoe, Biley, Hartford, Ross
Birmingham City: Wealands, Langan, Dennis, Broadhurst, Hawker, Todd, Brocken (Handysides 75), Dillon, Evans, Gemmill, Van Mierlo

MIKE WAS another who made up the numbers in the Magnificent Seven gang, having been a member of the Bolton Wanderers side that suffered the heartache of the League Cup semi-final defeat in 1977 as Bob Latchford's headed goal sealed the Blues' trip to Wembley the following month.

When his contract was coming to an end at Burnden Park in 1981, Bolton were then in the Second Division. Mike had a burning desire to get back into the top flight having been relegated the season before.

Eager as he was, he wrote to 22 First Division managers making them aware he was about to be a free agent. To his surprise, Everton took notice of his availability and he couldn't wait to put pen to paper.

He featured in Howard's first game in charge, appearing then for the next nine consecutive matches before serving a suspension for three yellow cards. He came back two weeks later then suffered an injury, allowing Mark Higgins to replace him. Sadly, Mike never got back to his favoured position with his Everton career. A further eight appearances that season and two more the next term proved to be the end for Mike, who then had loan spells with Norwich City and Burnley respectively before joining Fort Lauderdale Strikers in 1983.

'Howard gave me an opportunity and luckily, I did get into the team straight away,' says Mike. 'I picked up a hamstring injury after about 11 games and I didn't get a chance to play again at centre-half which was my preferred position. Once you lose your position through whatever reason, there is always competition which can jeopardise your place which you are not guaranteed to get back.

'I think I played the first ten games or something like that. I remember playing at home and I pulled a hamstring. Mickey Thomas left the field after five minutes with a hamstring too. In those days it was one substitute wasn't it which left me having to carry on for the duration of the game. I made it a lot worse. When I came off, my leg was black and blue, which made it longer for it to get right. By that time, Mark Higgins and Billy Wright had got in with Lyonsy [Mick Lyons] playing regularly.

'Howard told me that he wanted me to challenge for the left-back role, but I had always considered myself to be a centre-back which disappointed me because I never considered myself good enough to play at full-back as I didn't have the pace, whereas at centre-back, I was comfortable. I did have a couple of games at left-back but never got in again.

'Howard was very good at man-management. I remember us once getting a poor run of results which led to us being taken out for a Chinese meal. He was great with stuff like that. I enjoyed his coaching as well, the way he set the teams up after that first initial spell when I got in. I went out on loan a couple of times, and when I came back, I never felt part of it then. I later understood things clearer as I became a manager later on in my career. Players are still in your plans but you always strive to get better.

'He was very encouraging for the lads to socialise together. The social side of it was important to him as it always seemed to be good for team spirit.

'He never ever spoke about his playing career to anybody in conversation, but people often ask who he was similar to in his playing style. Well, I think there are a few players that have similar strengths who were there at that time. Asa Hartford was a fabulous player. Peter Reid had a lot of Howard's attributes too as did Steve McMahon.

'My relationship with him was good at first, we got on really well when I was in and around the team. When I lost my place through injury, obviously you want your place back, but it doesn't work like that. My second year wasn't a happy one for me and it would have suited both of us if I'd gone elsewhere. As I say, socially he was OK, but he could let you know if he wasn't happy with anything, he could have a sharp word with someone if he needed to if things weren't the way he wanted.

'He was different to my previous manager at Bolton Wanderers, Ian Greaves, who was very strict but was loved by everybody, and players would do anything for him. Howard was more laid-back, but everybody has a different style in management.

'Howard always tried to be honest with his playing staff. Some players needed a rocket, some needed an arm around. The only player I can recall who stepped out of line was Mickey Thomas for refusing to travel with the reserves to Newcastle. The result was an exit to another club.

'He never left me out of the side, and only for the injury I lost my place; he never had any reason to leave me out, so I understood he has a job to do with players, and having been a manager myself, I fully understand that there are parts of the job which are unpleasant, and leaving players out of a team is not a nice decision to make, but it's part and parcel of the job.

'The biggest lesson I learned from him was, Howard had an attitude where you never gave up. The team he was assembling worked fantastic in his early managerial career. He was a man that stuck to his beliefs and had certain ways where he liked team spirit to be important, which he was very good at.

'When the club reached the heights I was not surprised that he became the club's most successful manager. It took him a while to get it right, but when he got it right, the team that he had were absolutely flying. I could never see anybody ever beating them. In those days, they were playing two games a week. The players then never cried off about the number of games they were playing, needing to rest and rotate.

'Howard had a great 15 players that were winning leagues and cups and would have ruled Europe but for the ban on English teams due to Heysel.

'It was such a sad day when I learned of his passing, he was far too young. Meeting so many of the ex-players on the day of the funeral in Liverpool was nice, but it was a very sad day. Everyone that attended seemed to be celebrating his life rather than mourning him. Howard enjoyed his life, and that's the way those who paid their respects portrayed it.'

ALAN BILEY

Debut: Saturday, 29 August 1981, Everton 3 Birmingham City 1

Everton: Arnold, Wright, Bailey, Walsh, Lyons, Thomas, Ainscow, Eastoe, Biley, Hartford, Ross

Birmingham City: Wealands, Langan, Dennis, Broadhurst, Hawker, Todd, Brocken (Handysides 75), Dillon, Evans, Gemmill, Van Mierlo

ALAN WAS the first of the Magnificent Seven signings. The forward, who resembled the looks of Rod Stewart, was a very good friend of former Everton favourite Andy King as their relationship went back to their apprentice days together at Luton Town. He spoke about his love for the club which convinced him at the time of Howard's interest to join. Alan was playing for Colin Addison's Derby County before being transferred to Goodison Park. He'd scored ten goals in 29 outings for the Rams before signing for Howard Kendall.

He says, 'When I first joined, it was a dream come true to sign for one of the biggest clubs not just in England, but in Europe. To make your debut at home in front of a large crowd and a packed Gwladys Street End and score in front of them too was a dream come true. The game was televised by what was known then as *Kick Off Match* in the Granada region, showing the highlights the day after the game. My hero Denis Law was also present at the game which was another added bonus. The goal I scored came as late as the 88th minute, a ball played through to me by Asa Hartford, giving me an opportunity to lob the Birmingham keeper Jeff Wealands, sealing victory.

'I scored the opener at Elland Road [Leeds United] on the Tuesday after my debut where we got a valuable point [1-1] away from home. My only other Everton goal was away at Notts County towards the end of November.

'I was a regular starter until mid-October when I was named as substitute against Ipswich Town, replacing Mickey Thomas on a quarter of an hour. My appearances were very limited as I was to become the 12th man. Results for the club were not great, in fact very mixed. I played my last game in the Football League Cup fourth round in December 1981 at home to Ipswich. I started but came off with 12 minutes remaining.

'I felt I was no worse than anybody else, giving nothing but 100 per cent, which applied to training too. Howard made the sessions at Bellefield very enjoyable as he participated himself, as would Colin Harvey. Howard, like any manager, tried various formations and line-ups, looking for the right formula. If you remember, he even played himself for a spell when he first took over.

'Even in games when I didn't find the net, I would be contributing to making goals as well. I just couldn't understand why he lacked faith in me. I don't hold any grudges against Howard and have nothing but total respect for him because he achieved what he set out to do and became the most successful manager at the club.

'Reserve team manager Colin Harvey was always giving me advice and encouragement. I'm so disappointed that it didn't work out for me and Howard and that I didn't have the longevity of a career at Everton. I, of course, was then loaned to Stoke City on New Year's Day 1982 which then paved the way for Adrian Heath to join the Toffees in what was a record signing [£750,000]. It's a funny cliche but another door opened for me at the Potteries where I enjoyed my spell, and for Adrian, his career blossomed despite struggling in his early stages. Everton too struggled, but eventually things changed for the club a while later with inclusions to the dressing room of Peter Reid and Andy Gray, who by the way, were big characters. Results and performances improved with trips to Wembley, league championships and European success added.

'Howard got what he worked for as things clicked into place. I'm sorry that I wasn't part of the success that he brought to the club. I don't have any regrets about what happened at Everton, other than the fact I didn't have a chance to enjoy the fans who took me to their hearts. They even christened me "Spike" [because of his hairstyle], God bless 'em.

'I loved my career and I was very fortunate to live what youngsters dream, to play at a professional level, something I'm very fortunate to have done.'

MICKEY THOMAS

Debut: Saturday, 29 August 1981, Everton 3 Birmingham City 1
Everton: Arnold, Wright, Bailey, Walsh, Lyons, Thomas, Ainscow, Eastoe, Biley, Hartford, Ross
Birmingham City: Wealands, Langan, Dennis, Broadhurst, Hawker, Todd, Brocken (Handysides 75), Dillon, Evans, Gemmill, Van Mierlo

MICKEY WAS part of Howard Kendall's new batch of signings, a great player who was known for his exciting ability. His Toffees career was short-lived, however, appearing ten times in the league and only once in the League Cup without finding the net. Sadly, a refusal to accompany the reserves in a Central League game at Newcastle ended up with Mickey heading for the exit door.

He was capped 51 times for Wales between 1976 and 1986.

Mickey reminisces about his time at Everton under Howard, 'I think about how good he was. He had a strong personality. Not only did he have good knowledge of the game, also about players. It's not easy because you have to get the right players in, don't you? He was very unique and clever.

'He brought into the club the best goalkeeper in the world in Neville Southall, what an incredible find that was. He also brought in players like Trevor Steven, Kevin Sheedy, Andy Gray, Peter Reid. Those players were great signings that fitted in well, bringing success to the club. It's like a jigsaw, you have to have the right pieces to complete the puzzle.

'To select his best signing, there are so many, aren't there? Neville Southall wasn't just the best goalkeeper in the country but the best in the world. It's cruel to select one man as there were so many talented players at the club who were full internationals. So, I would have to select Nev.

'Howard was prepared to dig in on the field too, and would have been proud of himself to undertake such a massive responsibility, by combining the two roles as player-manager at such a young age, at a massive football club which Everton was and still is. It was a demanding job, no two ways about it, and the fans want success. It took time for Howard to get the right ingredients, but when he did, he produced a successful side which has still to be bettered.

'His style of management was very straightforward. He told you what he wanted, and if you failed to deliver you were gone. I was a prime example.

'He was in his element on the training ground where he loved taking part. He was still a player of high standard. He got things right on the training ground which paid off on matchdays. I remember him in his playing days at Everton, a style very similar to Peter Reid who was very tenacious.

'Howard earned his respect in the dressing room from the lads which is very important, but also had the respect as from his own playing days which was a big plus for him. He knew how to get the best out of his players, and I don't think he ever had problems with the players.

'I broke the rules by doing the wrong thing. I had a silly argument with him which I realised later, never regretting it if I'm being honest. But there is only going to be one winner, and that will always be the manager. He had to have a very strong personality as a manager to show his authority. I was the first one in line to receive that treatment. If Howard was faced with a problem, he would nip it in the bud immediately.

'His team talks in the dressing room, especially at half-time, Howard would identify the problem very quickly as he was a great tactician. If something needed changing, he wouldn't hesitate in doing so. From that touchline he couldn't take control on it, but knew what to do when it was required.

'He never shied away from giving you advice. The best advice he gave me? Jokingly, shut the door on your way out. Seriously, no, that would have to be when he conducted his team talk. He would tell you what he wanted and you would have to deliver. He did things his way by getting results which led to success, and the trophies speak for themselves.

'He was one of the best managers I'd ever played under, there's no question. You can't knock what he did at Everton because it's there for all to see. He had done it all as a player, but to replicate that as a manager and be more successful than Harry Catterick, no disrespect, he is the most successful manager of all time at Everton.

'Let's not forget a man that never got the recognition he deserved, Colin Harvey. His contribution speared the club to success, who, in his own right was a quality player like Howard, and fellow Holy Trinity member who awon the 1969/70 league championship. He was also a man that would light up the dressing room when he appeared. Most importantly, he was an Evertonian through and through, who the fans loved. He would have been an integral part of the success along with Howard for sure.

'Howard's departure from this world came too early. At his funeral, I could just imagine him having a big smile on his face. The turnout was what was expected, such a favourite of former players, managers and supporters. He deserved the send-off he received.'

JIM ARNOLD

Debut: Saturday, 29 August 1981, Everton 3 Birmingham City 1

Everton: Arnold, Wright, Bailey, Walsh, Lyons, Thomas, Ainscow, Eastoe, Biley, Hartford, Ross

Birmingham City: Wealands, Langan, Dennis, Broadhurst, Hawker, Todd, Brocken (Handysides 75), Dillon, Evans, Gemmill, Van Mierlo

JIM WAS a very late starter in his Football League career. Non-league football was where it all began, keeping goal for Stafford Rangers as well as working for Staffordshire County Council as an accountant until Howard Kendall, then manager at Blackburn, offered Jim an opportunity to play at a higher level.

Jim's honours in the non-league game consist of two FA Trophy winners' medals, in 1979 with Stafford and 1987 with Kidderminster Harriers. He also played for the England non-league side at international level, so what a dream it was for him to play in the First Division, to win honours and to be on the bench for a European final, which Jim did just six years after his first medal with the part-timers in Staffordshire.

They say that to be a goalkeeper you have to be mad. I wouldn't argue with that as he enjoyed painting and decorating around the house as well as other bits of DIY when he was on his rest days.

The hours he worked with the council were nine to five, so football was a different way of life, but he was determined to grasp the opportunity to achieve a once-in-a-lifetime dream. Who says you're never too old?

As well as football, Jim played cricket in the summer to maintain his fitness levels.

Howard's partnership with Jim at Ewood Park convinced the manager that his goalkeeper was a trustworthy addition. When Howard's appointment at Goodison was confirmed, Jim became part of the Magnificent Seven, never failing to let his boss, the team and the fans down when he pulled on the green shirt.

Jim was the first-choice goalkeeper on Kendall's first team sheet, on the opening day of the 1981/82 season. He played the first ten successive games before Neville Southall replaced him for the 11th.

Kendall was prepared to find his best solution, but over the course of the season Jim appeared 16 times, which Southall bettered by ten.

The following season, Jim was preferred to Southall until Nev finally claimed the shirt on a regular basis.

Jim offered his thoughts on Howard, 'I had nothing but respect for Howard to be quite honest with you. As you know I went into football very late. I was a semi-pro until the age of 29. I was an accountant. It was Howard that persuaded me to go into full-time football when he went to Blackburn Rovers as I was at Stafford Rangers.

'I was in awe of him all the way through. He was such a character, such a man. I had a great relationship with him. He was quite a family man in the early days. I was very similar where my family was very important to me.

'He brought me into football which I will never ever forget. I think when Neville was playing more and I was unlikely to get in, there were a couple of occasions when we [Jim and Howard] would have a chat about things. He made it quite clear where my role was and expected to play at the highest possible level, but his attitude was we've got 11 players out on the field and should anyone get injured, I want somebody equally as good, or as good as possible to step in. He made it quite clear to me that if anything happened to Neville, Howard wanted you at that level to fill Neville's boots so to speak.'

I asked Jim about Howard's team bonding sessions. He said, 'I didn't bother. Nev and I didn't really drink. We were like two peas in a pod in that respect. We both came through non-league together and didn't know much about the professional game. I think both of us found it very difficult to start in the morning and finish at lunchtime. We were both used to being working men. We turned to each other at lunchtime and said, "What do we do now?"

'Some of the lads would say that they were going to the pub for a drink whatever the case may be, but that wasn't for me and Nev, and then we developed post-lunch training for goalkeepers and started our own specialist goalkeeping school, which I think Howard quite liked the idea of. He never asked us about what we did, and why we felt the need to do it, and how he could assist us in developing our skills.

'Howard was in his element when he was on the field which made him very happy indeed. When he was player-coach at Blackburn, he looked so involved, and there was no pressure on him in terms of off-field pressure. I suspect when he went home overnight, he was so comprehensive about matters, he'd be thinking about tactics, players and God knows what. I don't think he enjoyed that side of it initially. After the games at Blackburn, he'd have a drink and was one of the lads. He taught you that there was a fine dividing line, you called him "Boss" all the way through, when he was on the ground. When he left for Everton, I still referred to him as "Boss", and would do even if he was around today.

'About his man-management, some people might disagree about his style of management, but I thought he was the best manager that never managed England. He was excellent in all areas when he was player-manager, the way he communicated on the field. He was a leader by example even at Everton when he played a few games. I think even at the age he was, he was arguably our best player on a couple of occasions.

'His PR was excellent, the way he dealt with the players was excellent. Whether you were in or out of the team, in my case when Neville was in the team for a long period, Howard would keep you involved. You were as important to him when you weren't playing as when you were playing. He recognised the fact in time that you were as good as your replacement.

'In the dressing room and at Bellefield, he was very succinct. I saw an interview recently with Adrian Heath and Howard, who was so far ahead in terms of his training. When you went into training, most of the pros that had been in the game for some years were expecting run, run, run. I didn't know anything different as I'd never experienced anything different. From day one, out came the ball. Yes, you did the running, but you thoroughly enjoyed training. Howard made everything so simple.

'He was a very easy-going bloke who was a very mild character. Looking back, I don't recall any time he was angry. He was very sharp-witted and could be sarcastic especially when we went away on tour. Strangely enough, Neville and I never wanted to go on tour post- and pre-season. We both tried to get away, but he wasn't having any of that. He developed a strong squad and expected us to go out and enjoy ourselves and at the same time play hard.

'I get asked occasionally what he was like compared to other managers that I'd played under. I didn't have as many as you'd expect. I was 29 years of age when I went into full-time football, and the only manager that I'd had prior to that was Roy Chapman at Stafford Rangers.

'I can remember filling in one of those questionnaires for the matchday programme as to who'd had the greatest impact on me in football and I wrote Roy Chapman. Howard sent for me when seeing it and said, "Hey, what's all this? I'm the manager who's had the greatest impact on you, and don't you forget that." He was quick to put me in my place.

'He never spoke about his playing career. He kept his cards close to his chest. Never did he once mention it. We all knew about his playing career and were aware of him. I admired him that much I kept a Panini card of him. I was so in awe of the man for what he achieved and what I'd heard about him.

'He would treat his players firmly. When there was a problem – which wasn't very often – I think my first time I came across Howard in that capacity was the Mickey Thomas situation. Mickey refused to go to a reserve team game at Newcastle United. Howard would have talked to Mick Heaton and Colin Harvey about the situation, firm hand, he wanted to set the scene for everybody else where players knew that there was a line in the sand where you dare not cross. If you dared to cross that line you would be shipped out.

'He would enforce discipline if and when he had to which he did as [chuckling] he fined me. My fine was when we went on tour to Switzerland. There was an upstairs area to the hotel where we were staying. There was a glass door, and I remember Sharpy [Graeme Sharp] being up there messing about, so I locked him out for the night. When I came down next morning Howard sent for me and Sharpy. Howard explained his reasons for calling us together as

Sharpy had to break the glass door to get in and he fined us £200 which was for the damage caused and Sharpy £100 for messing about.

'I had never been dropped in my life, even at Stafford Rangers. I did well at Blackburn, and when I was fit, I was always playing. The first season at Everton I remember getting injured at Birmingham City in a collision with one of their players which was towards the end of the season. The following season, I got dropped after a performance at home to Birmingham, being replaced by Neville Southall. Neville then went on a good run, hitting some form. I do recall Neville having a bad game at bottom of the table Wolves on a Boxing Day where we were beaten 3-0. I went to see Howard in his office and tell him of my disappointment of not being given another chance. Before I could say anything, Howard said, "I know what you are going to say." I told Howard that I got dropped for having a poor game as did Nev but yet he was still prepared to stick with him, so tell me the difference?

'Howard explained to me that Nev was in for the next game and he had to play well. "If not, he'll be out and you will be in for the rest of the season, I promise you that."

'If your confidence was suffering, he had this knack. Howard built the confidence up in the early days of my time there when he felt you needed it to make you feel good about yourself. I remember distinctly that I had a couple of good games against Liverpool and Manchester United.

'Howard was once watching a video, unaware I was in the room, of a Manchester United game with Mick Heaton. Bryan Robson had a shot which skipped in front of me which I somehow smothered and held on to the ball. Howard said to Mick, "Bloody good save, that was." I spoke out, "He just hit the ball in front of me, Boss." Howard replied, "If I'd have known you were there, I wouldn't have said anything about it at all. Keep your feet on the ground, don't get too big for your boots." That was Howard's way of keeping your feet firmly on the ground.

'If there was one lesson I learned from the great man, that was respect for my colleagues. Try and be confident in everything I did, and try to work on my game. You never ever stop learning. Nev and I only started learning when we joined Everton.

'If there was one regret I hold to this day, that was not going to his funeral. I received a phone call from my daughter when the story broke that Howard had passed away. I never rated myself as a high-profile player and guess I didn't want to get in the way of the big-name Everton players. I didn't want to go to Liverpool just to stand outside the cathedral.

'I saw on TV at the funeral how much people respected the man, which I thought was brilliant, but told myself I should have been there, bearing in mind I was his first signing for Blackburn and his second signing for Everton.'

One game in particular stands out involving Jim Arnold – the goalless draw at Anfield in March 1983. Ian Rush, who had been denied on two occasions, tried for a third time by playing a dangerous low ball into the path of the goal with the onrushing Craig Johnston intending to make an impact. Jim's heroics caused concern by inflicting injury upon himself. Play was stopped with Howard Kendall racing from the dugout to the aid of his keeper. The St John Ambulance team were preparing a stretcher to remove Jim from the field but he was defiant and rose his feet, earning applause from the Liverpool fans in the Kop behind his goal. That tells its own story.

MICK FERGUSON

**Debut: Saturday, 5 September 1981,
Southampton 1 Everton 0**

Southampton: Wells, Golac, Holmes, Baker, Waldron, Nicholl, Keegan, Channon, Moran, Armstrong, Ball

Everton: Arnold, Wright, Ratcliffe, Walsh, Lyons, Thomas, McMahon (Ferguson 75), Eastoe, Biley, Hartford, Ainscow

MICK BECAME another part of the Magnificent Seven signings by Howard Kendall. He joined from Coventry City but seemed to be cursed by injuries. When he was mobile, he was a natural at finding the back of the net.

When Ipswich Town were a force in the late 1970s, manager Bobby Robson said on the day his side were playing Coventry, 'If he [Ferguson] would score that afternoon, I would sign him.'

He was often linked with a move to Ipswich Town when they were a force under Bobby Robson in the late 1970s, once soaring four against them for Coventry, but the call from Robson never materialised.

He then had the misfortune of two proposed moves that broke down, to Nottingham Forest and then Aston Villa. When a move to Notts County looked certain, Everton came in for him and the rest is history as they say.

At that time, he was suffering with an ankle injury but appeared as a substitute in the third game of the 1981/82 campaign. He never made his full debut until 6 October, coincidentally against Coventry, at Goodison in a League Cup tie in which he scored.

Of his move to Goodison, Mick said, 'I liked Howard. I got a call and he asked me to come over.

'[Coventry manager] Gordon Milne had mentioned to me that Everton were interested in me, as my time at Highfield Road was coming to an end, sadly. He said that Howard would like to speak with me, so I took my wife over and met Howard at the ground.

'I liked Howard and still do. He was such a nice bloke and I knew that I could do a good job there. He told me of his plans for the club and said it was a fantastic big club and you couldn't get any bigger than Everton, which at the time was right for me.

'The reasons I signed were, one: it was a big club, and two: I had to like the manager, and I took to Howard straight away.

'He was very good with my wife, sorting me a place to live, selling my house for me back home. Not every club back then was like that, but nowadays they are.

'I lived on the Wirral and Kevin Ratcliffe became one of my best mates. He used to pick me up for training and sometimes he would car share with Ian Rush who lived nearby. Rushie was a good guy as well.

'Football is about people, so it was Howard and Mick Heaton, God bless his soul, who was also a great motivator and great fun to be around.'

GARY STEVENS

Debut: Tuesday, 6 October 1981, Everton 1 Coventry City 1 – League Cup second round, first leg
Everton: Arnold, Stevens, Bailey, Walsh, Lyons, Thomas, McMahon, O'Keefe, Ferguson, Ross, McBride
Coventry City: Blyth, Thomas, Roberts, Jacobs, Dyson, Gillespie, Kaiser, Whitton, Thompson, Gooding, Hateley

GARY STEVENS served his apprenticeship playing regularly for the reserves in the Central League. His career could have gone down a different road as he was prepared to become a draughtsman and work for his stepfather's firm.

His performances were catching the eye of the manager, and when Howard was trying to find the right blend with different team selections, Gary was called to the front line determined to make the right-back position his own.

Gary's combination with Trevor Steven down that right-hand side excelled, causing many a problem for the opposition.

His club performances earned him international recognition and he played for England in the World Cup in Mexico in 1986.

Gary was never renowned for his goalscoring – his first career goal came at Birmingham, opening his and the club's account for the new year on 2 January 1984. Everton went on to win 2-0. He eventually scored ten career goals including a memorable strike at Anfield in the League Cup third round in October 1987.

Gary says, 'Howard's man-management was second to none. Some of the players would require a kick up the arse, others would need an arm around them. He knew each and every member of his squad. When we were away on a trip, some of the lads could get up to a bit of mischief because they were bored, but Howard filled the gap to make sure they were otherwise occupied. He gave us an inch, but as a group of players, we had too much respect to take the mile.

'He adopted the player-manager role when he arrived. At that time, he was coming to the end of his playing career, but still had enough quality, by all rights, to select himself to fill a place in the team. Everton were a rudderless ship at that time, going nowhere fast. Establishing himself on the park, drawing a line in the sand, he more or less said, we don't want to be fighting relegation, we want to be safe, and then we can stand in this league. He, of course, took us through those modes, and he was big enough to realise that when it was his time to step down, he wasn't going to think of the glory days, and not a question of, well, I've done my bit.

'When he took over in the summer of 1981, he had to look around for new blood as the squad wasn't producing, which I think was to my benefit, because he came in with a very fresh pair of eyes. There were no points for the number of games you played, or how old you were, or where you'd been. He picked what was his best squad, which eventually proved right.

'Howard always had a smile on his face in the dressing room. It was just a question of how to entertain. He could get serious after a game if we hadn't performed well, but he always had that ability to say, "You know what?"

'Some managers shout and curse, potentially burn bridges or put barriers up between themselves and some of the players just by being a little exuberant on the day. Howard was a bit smarter than that. He would know to wait, have a look at the footage, and afterwards, that was the time that he could do the post-mortem, once he had established all of the facts.

'If you go off on one as a manager, you've got to be aware sometimes that you're wrong, at that time, or, it's a bit questionable. In football, half of an inch can make a hell of a difference. Both of you could be right, but he was smart enough to know, you know what? I can maybe wait to have a chat tomorrow when everything has calmed down, or even when the lads were out having an Italian, maybe that was the time for Howard to have a word.

'He was an easy-going guy who would let you know if he was upset. He would show signs of being angry when we hadn't performed. He had every right to show his anger. He would be angry about the performance on the pitch. He wouldn't pick on individuals, but en masse, he would have a go.

'Howard was at his happiest when we were playing, and happy when we were a group of players, whether that was in the dressing room, on the pitch, or somewhere else.

'He could be funny too. I remember during one of our Chinese afternoons out. We couldn't leave while there was still a bottle of wine left on the table. The problem was, Howard would order another bottle of wine as the last one was finishing.

'His discipline? In our day, the game wasn't as professional as it is nowadays. These days, you wouldn't be able to take the boys out for a win or lose booze, that kind of scenario. Drinking was a bit of a culture at that point. We were that way that we could look at ourselves in the mirror, the old adage, if we worked hard on the pitch, he would let you enjoy yourself off it. Sometimes, some of the players would have a bad day at the office, but Howard wanted the whole team to pull together.'

Pull together they did. After going through a very bad patch the club turned a corner which led to the start of a period of success and silverware.

Gary continued, 'Who would have thought what we were about to achieve after that winter of 1983 which was grim to say the least. The fans made their voices heard, wanting the manager and chairman to stand down. Howard was very confident that he had the squad there that he had trust in. We buckled away by working hard on the training ground.

'The club was at a very low ebb when we lost that game against Liverpool in November 1983 at Anfield, and the season from then on could not have got any worse, could it? At that time, we were at our deepest depths which changed from then on, I would say.

'We knew what was going on at the club with all the calls for Sir Philip Carter and Howard to go. You just cannot keep that away from the players, it's impossible. We as a group of players knew that things were about to turn, knowing that was only around the corner. There are a lot of cliches out there but we just needed that little slice of luck with another 10 or 15 per cent confidence from a couple of wins.

'We talk about several games that turned things around, and I will give you my definition as to which game that was. The Oxford United League Cup game away, we edged a replay through a late equaliser from Inchy, keeping us in the cup. Then later, a win in the replay which was the first win, or one of the first wins which kept us on course which proved to be important, which fans saw when we went on a good run.

'I remember when Howard took over, we went through a spell where we were losing all of the time. It was a bit of a task turning the team around. I suppose from my perspective, I was only very young which didn't necessarily grind into me as it did with some of the older players. Don't forget, I had only started my career. I was happy to be involved in the first team.

'You are probably aware that myself and [Brian] Bugsy Borrows were in and out of the team. I would have four or five games then was dropped, and he would also go through the same. The both of us were a similar age with similar experience. Some of it was above my head if I have to be honest. I was just happy to be playing.

'The club stuck by Howard. I can't understand it about Philip Carter being wanted out. He was awesome for Everton Football Club right through his entire association with them. He was always there in the background but wasn't one to get too involved, but he was always there to back you up. He did have a soft side to him. I had a lot of time for him.

'As for Howard's number two Colin Harvey, what an appointment he was. Personally, I wouldn't have done anything, if it hadn't been for Colin Harvey. I think he was an unbelievable coach. He turned me into a right-back from a winger, but he certainly made my career. Again, you have the respect of your players. On the coaching staff, you have a manager and his assistant who had done it themselves for the club as players.

'Winning a trophy was important; the first one came about in May 1984, triumphing at Wembley in the end-of-season finale, the FA Cup Final. I was very fortunate to have played in every game including the final itself. In retrospect, I've always said that the league is a marathon. The league medal, as much as the European Cup Winners' Cup medal – you might think that might be the most important trophy, but it was all about getting the identification of Everton etched on to a trophy. Howard was successful with a lot of silverware, but the first one has to be the most special.

'Most of the decent managers and coaching staff are there because they have gone and walked the walk. Colin was the bad cop to Howard's good cop image. Colin was a little bit redder-blooded, shall we say. There might have been a bit more finesse, and having spoken to some of the players and some of the fans that watched the "Golden Vision" [prolific Everton striker Alex Young] in the 60s, Colin was the one that would run around and put his foot in. Alan Ball could do a bit of both. Howard was more of the finesse, but what a complement to each other on the park.

'Whatever Colin threw at you verbally, you had nothing but respect for the man, and that was because he was right 99 per cent of the time.

'Howard's signings and who was his best? Taking Kevin Sheedy from Liverpool was a masterstroke as far as signings go. I don't think anybody else could have played in Sheeds's position as Kevin in the entire First Division as it was then.

'Reidy was another where Howard took a chance. He cost £60,000 which is nothing in the football world. People thought Reidy's career was finished three or four years before Everton signed him. Reidy was the glue, the final piece of the jigsaw.

'Howard of course had to change a few things which he did radically.

'The news of Howard's passing was a complete shock, devastating news. Unfortunately, I didn't go to the funeral, but I watched it online. Peter Reid's eulogy was outstanding. The words Peter expressed that day, he said on behalf of everybody.'

At the time of writing, Gary was working as a physiotherapist in Perth, Western Australia.

NEVILLE SOUTHALL MBE

Debut: Saturday, 17 October 1981, Everton 2
Ipswich Town 1
Everton: Southall, Stevens, Bailey, Walsh, Lyons, Thomas (Biley 15), McMahon, O'Keefe, Ferguson, Ross, McBride
Ipswich Town: Cooper, Mills, McCall, Thijssen, Osman, Butcher, Wark, Muhren, Mariner, O'Callaghan, Gates

WHOEVER THOUGHT that a former bin man, hod carrier and non-league player would have reached the heights of becoming what many people believe to be the best goalkeeper in the world. Neville Southall was another of Howard's first signings and, as I'm told, a workaholic. That explains his attitude of being a perfectionist which gave him the reputation as the world's number one. He was actually spotted by Howard while playing for Winsford United; at the time Howard was managing Blackburn Rovers, who were well equipped with goalkeepers. Southall had moved to Bury by the time Howard decided to sign him for Everton.

He said about joining the Toffees, 'The transfer came as a complete surprise in the summer. The first I knew of it was when I was back home in Wales. I picked up a paper on a Sunday morning and read that Everton were interested. I reported to Bury the following day and signed for Everton on the Tuesday.'

It's amazing to think that he had unsuccessful trials at Crewe Alexandra and Bolton Wanderers.

When asked many years ago what he wanted to do after his playing career was over, he said that he would like to have his own farm.

On his memories of Kendall, Southall said, 'Howard is what a gentleman should be, not necessarily associated with football or anything else, just a figure. What I did like about him is that he did everything properly. If somebody phoned him and left a message, he would call them back. He was a man of his word. Everything was about doing the right things all of the time. I learned a lot of his ways from him.

'If he saw something in a player and he trusted them, he would back them all the way. The trust and respect you got from him was based on that, no egos, or anything elaborate, it was based on good old-fashioned trust and respect for each other. You could have your say as he did, and if he was right, I would hold my hand up, if I was right, he would hold his hand up.

'I received a massive rollicking from him when I refused to go up for my medal at Wembley in the Zenith Data Systems Cup Final in April 1991. He taught me a lot about respect for other people and other things.

'He was a very mild-mannered man and never one to lose it in the dressing room. His team talks were simple. In all fairness, of all the managers I've met in my life, I very rarely took any notice of anything that was said in his team talks. I didn't need anyone to tell me what I had to do. From 1.30pm onwards I was switched on and focused on the game.

'If I have to select one dressing room memory, that would be where he opened the window of the dressing room at Stoke City in the FA Cup third round in January 1984. He told us to listen to the noise of the fans.'

That tie at the Victoria Ground was the start of the run which ended up at Wembley with Everton comfortably beating Watford in the FA Cup Final and achieving their first piece of silverware since the league championship success in 1970.

Southall continued, 'The Bayern Munich game at home was the other where he told us all that the fans behind the Gwladys Street goal would suck the ball in the net as we trailed by the one goal at the break. He told us to go out and let the opposition know what British football is all about.

'His knowledge of the game was second to none. When he first arrived, he was trying to build a team until he found the recipe. Who else would have looked at two reserve players at Liverpool with Kevin Sheedy and Alan Harper who became great players? I think out of all the signings Howard made, I would have to go for Peter Reid as his best. When we were struggling in that infamous Coventry City game and Reidy came on. When you struggle as a team and lose the ball, players drop off, inviting the opposition to get on top of you. What Reidy did, he was having none of that, and decided to close the ball down. By doing that, he took Brace, Sheeds and Trevor with him, and before you knew it, the team was pressing with the ball again. Reidy then became the leader with players following suit. For me, Reidy was the catalyst.

'Howard loved the social side and the company of his group of players. Everybody is entitled to enjoy their life the way they want to. It never bothered me really. I think the bonding sessions that Howard introduced were more psychological than just a booze-up. He wanted his players to realise that if they worked really, really hard, you are entitled to play hard and bring in a team spirit where you live and die together. It was an opportunity where the lads could tell the truth in a circle of trusted people.

'My relationship with him was great to be fair. I never ever had a problem with any manager that I played under.

There were times he would tell me that I was at fault with conceding a goal and I would disagree. I would see the incident on *Match of the Day* later and think, yeah, he was right. There were times when the roles were reversed and he would say "I was at fault", realising that I was right.

'I never enjoyed the social side of what we had to do, and if I wanted to do my own thing Howard was always all right about it. As long as I did what I had to do out on the pitch, he never bothered about anything that I did off it.

'Howard loved nothing more than a journey home from an away game when we'd won. There was no media, no pressure, we could have our fish and chips washed down with a beer. Howard would play cards and smoke his cigar and be what he wanted to be which was one of the lads, nothing more. He was around people that he liked and respected.'

As the winter of 1983 appeared, the dark nights did too, matching the performances on the pitch. Everton's reserves were managed by former player Colin Harvey. At the start of the 1983/84 season, the second string won their first ten games. Howard never hesitated in recognising his attributes appointing him as his assistant.

The introduction of Colin Harvey to the first team was massive, said Southall, 'Howard set the parameters building the team, but Colin drove the team. Colin at the time had a hip which was in need of repair. He demanded so much from you, and had this winning mentality. He wanted to win at everything. Colin's personality was the driving force of the team. Colin was the stone-cold assassin.

'Colin was a person that wore his heart on his sleeve more than Howard. Joe [Royle] and Willie [Donachie] were of the same ilk to Howard and Colin. They worked really well as a pair. Don't forget, they were similar generations, and they had a habit of doing the right things at the right time.

'In those days where the team were not performing Howard really came under pressure from the fans and the media during the mid-80s before he got the right ingredients. Howard rode the pressure of the fans wanting him and Sir Philip Carter to stand down. His professionalism showed as he never brought whatever was going through his mind into the dressing room.

'If you watch a *Carry On* film, and the characters in the film are sat there having their dinner, with somebody attacking the building, bullets flying everywhere, I think that's what Howard would have been like during that period. He never showed us any emotion whatsoever. I think that was because he was an old-fashioned guy with morals. He came across where whatever he was responsible for, he was never letting the players take the blame for it.

'Sir Philip Carter must also take a great deal of credit for showing faith in Howard. I think Sir Philip showed the respect and patience in Howard that Howard saw in us. I think that Sir Philip's decisions had a knock-on effect right throughout the club.

'I think the way Sir Philip's patience paid off was something that Manchester United replicated with Sir Alex Ferguson. He was one game away from the sack and look what happened years later.'

Out of all of the trophies Howard brought to the club during his reign, which one did Southall think gave him the most pleasure?

'The first league championship in 1984/85. The FA Cup has an element of luck depending on who you draw and who has the home advantage. The real test for him was to win the league that would prove beyond doubt that he and

Colin were the best management team. To win the league over 42 matches as it was back then, and once he had that instilled in him, at that level, you want it again.

'Even after winning the league and collecting more trophies after that, Howard and Colin demanded consistency and never tired of that success.'

Of that first championship success in 1984/85, 42 matches were played with a further 21 in other competitions – Neville was present in every one of them. Fans from that era talk about the acrobatic save, turning a goalbound header from Mark Falco at Tottenham Hotspur which his opposite number Ray Clemence applauded from the Park Lane End of White Hart Lane, in the April of that season. From the first day of February 1985 until the first day of March, Southall had kept five consecutive clean sheets.

It was in that same season that he made his first penalty save, the first of seven of his club career, on his 125th club appearance, in March 1985 at Manchester United.

Referee Norman Wilson had no hesitation pointing to the spot as early as the third minute when United's tricky winger Jesper Olsen was brought down by Gary Stevens inside the box, but as Gordon Strachan ran up to take the penalty, Southall guessed right and made what was nothing more than a comfortable save. Kevin Sheedy also missed one on 78 minutes, seeing his spot kick saved by United's Gary Bailey. The game ended in a 1-1 draw.

Southall's performances were recognised by the Football Writers' Association, receiving their Footballer of the Year award in 1985. He was also included in the PFA Team of the Year selections for the 1986/87, 1987/88, 1988/89 and 1989/90 seasons.

Southall sadly didn't attend the funeral of the club's most successful manager.

'I didn't go,' he said. 'This is ironic. We took a lot of young kids over to Bayern Munich and that happened to be on the day of the funeral. It brought back memories of when we played there in 1985.'

ALAN IRVINE

Debut: Saturday, 19 December 1981, Everton 2 Aston Villa 0

Everton: Southall, Stevens, Ratcliffe, Higgins, Lyons, Kendall, Irvine, Ross, Sharp, Eastoe, Lodge

Aston Villa: Rimmer, Swain, Gibson, Evans, Blake, Bullivant, Bremner, Donovan, Geddis, Cowans, Morley

ALAN WAS signed from Scottish part-timers Queen's Park, known as the Spiders. When fans talk about Howard's homecoming and the introduction of the Magnificent Seven, Alan was actually the first. That came about because the previous manager Gordon Lee brought him to the club, but was unfortunately sacked before Alan could put pen to paper.

Alan's debut came in December 1981 and he went on to make 25 appearances that season. It could have all gone a different way for Alan as he was at Manchester City at the age of 15 but was told after his time there that he was too small.

The rejection from the Maine Road club gave him an idea to look for something out of football to fall back on should his dream never come true, so he decided to go into the business of insurance broking, encouraged by his father.

Alan was a key figure in the 1983/84 season, where he played in the historic League Cup Final at Wembley, a first meeting between both Merseyside teams in a major final. He also played a major part in the FA Cup run at the end of which the trophy was lifted, playing in every round until the semi-final and the final itself.

In his later career he was back at Everton, taking over at the academy from Ray Hall, and eventually assisting David Moyes with first-team duties.

Alan says, 'First of all, Howard was the man that gave me my league debut in England. I signed on the day that Howard joined which is an interesting one. When he arrived, he signed a group called the Magnificent Seven. Howard actually signed eight players, I was the other one.

'Everton had been monitoring me when they tried to sign me the previous October when Gordon Lee was in charge. Gordon was the one that set everything up. I had 23 clubs to choose from. It came down to two clubs – Manchester City, who were FA Cup finalists that year, and Everton. I met Gordon Lee the day he was sacked and the day that Howard joined. Gordon told me that he wasn't going to be there, but I should sign for this club. I actually signed for Howard without Howard knowing anything about me. My last game in Scotland was for Queen's Park at Central Park against Cowdenbeath, and my next game was for Everton in Japan against Inter Milan. That was the step that I was taking. I never expected ever to play for Everton's first team.

'He was very good. In my first season I made my debut against Aston Villa in December 1981, staying in the team right through until the end of the season, featuring in 25 consecutive games. And to be perfectly honest, they should have left me out with about a month of the season remaining. I was done.

'I remember Howard protecting me, coming out in the press about the physical abuse I was getting when full-backs could kick the shit out of you in those days, and not get booked. Howard was good from that point of view; he kept me in the team. I remember once coming back from an away game and my head was on the floor, simply because I knew I wasn't playing well. He said, "Come on son, we're going for a pint." We went for a drink and he said, "Relax, you've done really well, way above your own expectations and way above our expectations." That was Howard's way of managing my situation.

'I didn't think that I would play one game for Everton in my first season. I didn't think that I would play one game for Everton in the three years of my contract. So, to play from December until the end of the season was way beyond my wildest dreams. He got me back to that by saying, "What's your problem? You're playing every week and have done brilliantly." I just felt after that I had nothing left. I was knackered, I had no spark. I needed that spark for the type of player that I was. Being in my position on the field you had to have that explosive change of pace which I didn't have any more.'

Alan registered his first goals for the club with a brace in a 3-0 away win at Wolverhampton Wanderers on 23 January 1982.

He said, 'I expected to be in the reserves under Colin Harvey, which I was at the time. That included Mark Higgins, John Bailey, Graeme Sharp, Kevin Ratcliffe, Kevin Richardson and Brian Borrows, Steve McMahon, Joe McBride. We had a very strong young team developing under Colin.

'The next step, Colin joined Howard with the first team, then after a while we all started to make our way into the first team.

'Colin's influence towards assisting Howard was very big. I don't think anyone would underestimate the part that Colin played. I think if you look back at the results, I think they upped the results which coincided with Colin's promotion to the first team. The younger players actually breaking through was also a plus. Colin would have told

Howard how good the young lads had been doing, hence they were given a first-team opportunity.

'Things weren't working out for Howard as he had hoped at that time, so bringing Colin in was a great move. Funnily enough, as the first team results went up, the reserves had won 11 out of 11 until Colin left – a good number from the reserves went into the first team then the form of the reserves dropped.

'The role Howard played when he first arrived as player-manager, I think I got more coaching with Howard when he played in the reserves alongside us than I got when he was the manager. What he did was, he talked us through the game, in real time which was brilliant. I played on the right wing; he played as a central midfield player. He instructed me when to go, when not to go, told me when to get tucked in, when to go wide. I learned loads at that time with him playing. His knowledge of the game was fantastic, he was obviously a very good player as well. In my point of view, he could be more organisational on the pitch, than he was off the pitch.

'Howard was a technical player with a good range of passing. He had a good understanding of the position he was in; he was an intelligent midfielder who would make a tackle and a challenge. He was the type of player that could take the ball and make good passes.

'The problem trying to compare midfield players from those days to the modern day, you're either a defensive midfield player, or an attacking midfield player. At that time, you were a midfield player, and when the opposition had the ball, you were expected to defend, and when you had the ball, you were expected to create. So, as a midfielder, Howard had to be able to pass it, create chances for the team to score goals, also had to be able to defend when the opposition had the ball. Howard was the complete package.

'As we all know, Howard endured a sticky period in the mid-80s which brought pressure from the terraces and also the media. I think he would have been under a lot more pressure at a lot of other clubs. Sir Philip Carter, he was a really good chairman to have. He was terrific for the club, and like a lot of owners and chairmen nowadays, they react very quickly with things. I don't think that Sir Philip put Howard under any pressure, and I didn't think that Howard believed he was under pressure. As a player, I didn't see it.

'I remember the Coventry City game. I remember the leaflets getting handed out and stuff like that. I remember at the time, there's a team coming here, don't break this up, there's a team in the making. I was desperately hoping that Howard would stay and was desperately hoping that he was given time for a team that he was building to come through.

'I'm pleased for Howard and his staff that things improved. I thought it was coming. I felt that wasn't something that happened quickly; I felt that was something that had started in 1981. I could see that the team was maturing. Howard had made a couple of extra good signings.

'Howard as a boss was fair. He had a couple of situations with a couple of players that he dealt with well. There was an issue with both Billy Wright and Mickey Thomas which I thought Howard handled very well. He didn't make a massive noise about it, he dealt with it in his own way. Howard's man-management was very good. The players liked playing for him. You knew where you stood as did Howard, but you knew there was a line that you wouldn't cross, and he would deal with players that stepped over that line.

'I remember one time when we were playing against Norwich City. I scored our only goal in a 1-1 draw with a strike from outside the box. We hadn't been playing particularly well, and Howard decided to take me off. I was over on the far side of the pitch, and as the number went up for me to come off, all of the fans started booing. I responded to that neatly. I made it known by coming off, storming past Howard and heading toward the tunnel. I got a right rollicking after that. "Don't you ever do that again." I never ever did that again. I have also told players the same when I've been a manager which is a lesson learned.

'I have been in management and as an individual, I think about things that I have learned. I look at Howard who was a manager. You look at some managers, and they're a coach. Howard's strengths when I look back at that time, and as I've said, I learned a lot from him playing alongside him. I didn't learn so much when he WASN'T playing alongside me.

'I learned more from Colin in the training sessions from a coaching point of view. I like a lot of Howard's man-management. He was one of the first ones that I became aware of, right from day one, the ball was out, where we trained with the ball in the main.

'A lot of managers and coaches never used that method, they just made the players run and run. I've always had the ball out from day one, that has been an influential thing for sure.

'In terms of my coaching, there may be other managers that were influential with their coaching, probably because the more I got involved with the game, after doing my badges in 2006, and at that time, I started to observe what managers and coaches were doing, and how they were dealing with things.'

I asked Alan who he thought Howard's most influential signing was. 'There has been a lot said about it being Reidy, or it being Andy [Gray]. What they brought to a young team was older heads, experience. Those two coming in coincided with the change of winning ways. Those two were very influential and we were very fortunate to have some very good young players coming through as well. Howard knew that he needed some experience to mix with the younger lads.'

How were Howard's team talks? 'Like a lot of other managers, it was varied. I think one of the things those good managers do is they never react the same way week in, week out to situations, whether winning, losing or drawing. He never ranted or raved or threw cups around, but he was perfectly capable of making his point.'

What about comparisons with Howard and other managers? 'He was different. He was a very good manager of people. I've worked with some managers who were unbelievably aggressive, who were not good to play under, to some who were very gentle and very soft, and probably not great to play under because of their manner. Howard had both sides.

'Howard was always happy on a Saturday night after we'd won, it's as simple as that. I was a young player that didn't know him that well. Some of the older players probably knew him better than me. I was more in awe of the club than the manager.

'The bonding sessions were massively important to him. That was the thing about that group and don't forget, a lot of us had come through together. We were a bunch of youngsters that grew up together and we were really close, remaining close.

'He was always ready and willing to offer advice and there was one occasion when he invited me for dinner. He spoke about the importance of self-confidence, instilling my confidence by telling me of the better things about my game. He tried his best to make me more confident and positive. Those things were a big help.

'I had to attend his funeral out of respect. I was astounded by the amount of people being really sad about the fact that he had gone. A lot of people remembering good times. A lot of people remembering funny times. The feeling that day showed there was a lot of respect and admiration for Howard.'

ADRIAN HEATH

Debut: Tuesday, 19 January 1982, Everton 1 Southampton 1

Everton: Southall, Stevens, Ratcliffe, Higgins, Lyons, Richardson, Irvine, Heath, Sharp, Eastoe, Lodge

Southampton: Katalinic, Golac, Holmes, Williams, Nicholl, Waldron, Baker, Channon, Moran, Armstrong, Ball

ADRIAN HEATH, 'Inchy', as he became known to his team-mates, was signed in January 1982 for what was a record fee of £750,000. The fee broke the previous record set by the transfer of John Gidman in October 1979.

It was Howard Kendall who persuaded Heath to sign, being well aware of his ability having played alongside him in the team at Stoke City.

Howard said when buying Heath from Stoke, 'I see great things in him with the amount of ground he covers, the way he breaks things up and starts us moving. He is just what is needed in midfield.'

On signing his contract, Adrian showed his appreciation, 'I shall be eternally grateful to Mr Kendall for paying such a large sum of money for me at a time when big fees in the market were disappearing. And I intend to repay his faith in me all the way. I would never like to think there would be a time when he would regret the move.'

He also went on to say in 1982, 'The club is hungry for success and the manager is planning to give it to the fans. There's also the same feeling amongst the players.'

Whether Adrian had a crystal ball is anyone's guess, but no one could have forecast that success wasn't too far away.

Finding it difficult to settle at first, he eventually came into his own, playing a very big part in Everton's glory years. Many Evertonians class his interception from Kevin Brock at Oxford in a January 1984 knife-edge League Cup tie as a turning point in the club's fortunes. Then there was the wonderfully executed header at Highbury which sent Everton through the FA Cup semi-final three months later, setting up a Wembley visit in May to bring the first piece of silverware back to Goodison after 14 barren years. It was the furthest Heath had gone in the FA Cup in his career: while at Stoke he had never gone beyond the third round.

Inchy sadly missed out on the league championship triumph of 1984/85 after a cruel tackle by Sheffield Wednesday's Brian Marwood sidelined him from December, missing out on the glory of Rotterdam too.

For 1985/86 he was back, scoring in the Charity Shield showpiece at Wembley in August as Manchester United were beaten 2-0. Heath scored 15 goals that season from 32 starts in all competitions.

Everton won the title once more in 1986/87, when he started 41 league games out of a maximum 42, netting 11 times.

The banning of English clubs from Europe due to Heysel led Inchy to seek out pastures new and he joined Espanyol in 1988. Twelve months later he was back on home soil, joining Aston Villa, then teamed up with Howard Kendall at Manchester City before heading home to Stoke where he first made his bow in league football. He then had two spells at Burnley from 1992 to 1995 and in the 1996/97 season, with Sheffield United sandwiched in between. I don't think anyone can argue with a career which produced 120 goals in 559 league appearances.

After deciding to hang up his boots, he went into management and Burnley were his first club. Bramall Lane was his next destination, before accepting a caretaker role at Coventry City. The opportunity then arose to manage in the USA where he joined Austin Aztecs, followed by two spells with Orlando City before settling down at Minnesota United where he remained until 2023.

'Howard was a player-manager,' says Heath. 'He always used to tell us that he would give us enough rope to hang ourselves, and to be fair to him, he did. We felt like we owed him something and we would do whatever we could to make sure that we succeeded for the club and for him.

'He was a mild-mannered man. A total gentleman but if he needed to get straight to the point then he could be cutting.

'He left us as players under no illusions as to what he expected from us, and if you did not deliver, then you knew that you would not play under him. His motto was play well, and keep your place in the team, but know the consequences if you do not.

'To Howard, the badge on the front of the shirt meant more to him than any name on the back, so it was always a collective effort to succeed for Everton Football Club, and that is the way that football should be.'

BRIAN BORROWS

Debut: Saturday, 13 February 1982, Everton 0 Stoke City 0
Everton: Southall, Borrows, Ratcliffe, Higgins, Wright, Richardson, Irvine, Heath, Sharp, Ferguson, Ross
Stoke City: Fox, Kirk, Hampton, Dodd, Watson, McAughtrie, McIlroy, O'Callaghan, Chapman, Bracewell, Maguire

BRIAN BORROWS was another product who had been nurtured by reserve coach Colin Harvey. He and fellow reserve graduate Gary Stevens competed for the number two shirt.

He was blessed with speed and was known to cross a ball too. Unfortunately, his Everton career was one of frustration for him, not being able to hold down a first-team place. Brian was probably in the right place at the wrong time with Everton struggling to find any kind of form, which made things more difficult for him. Making 15 appearances in his first season with another 12 the following campaign, his last game happened to be in one of the worst days in Everton's history, as their neighbours Liverpool ran riot, punching their blue rivals to a pulp with a five-goal thrashing.

Brian departed Merseyside to join Bolton Wanderers and later Coventry, where he seemed to have more of a settled career.

He recalls, 'Howard was the guy that gave me my debut, also the manager that got rid of me in the end as well. He was progressive in his style of management. Certainly, at

Everton, there is only one way to play, but it was that you played out from the back, that was the spine of Everton. You had to be able to handle the ball.

'He was quite demanding I guess which you would expect being at a club as big as Everton. The club are expected to win games, aren't they?

'He was fairly forward in how he spoke to you in the dressing room on a matchday, demanding hard work which developed good habits. He was still reasonably young when he was at Everton, and when you saw him and Colin Harvey in training, they were still outstanding individuals. In fact, when fans make comparisons to players similar to Howard from his playing days, Peter Reid and Paul Bracewell are two that are similar, who obviously played in a similar role to Howard.

'Howard loved to socialise with his players. They would often go out for Chinese banquets, etc. I'd been away on certain trips when Howard was involved, he liked a drink and always encouraged the players to socialise, but I don't think I was ever in his company socially. You have to take into consideration that I was a lot younger than some of the lads.

'Howard was a good character and was happy, [laughing] probably when I'd left! He started to have a bit of success, and seeing his team flourish obviously gave him an awful lot of pleasure.

'He was never one to show any anger. Again, I'm trying to remember what that looked like. My last game was when we got beat by Liverpool in November 1982, the 5-0 one. That game for those who witnessed it will be engrained in everyone's memory.'

That humiliating derby defeat had a knock-on effect as the Blues failed to record any victory until 11 December, seven games on including First Division and League Cup.

Brian recalls, 'I know at that time we were struggling. I even remember a week before that game whether I was going to play or not. In hindsight, it might have been a good thing if I hadn't. After that game, he made four changes for the League Cup game three days later for the visit of Arsenal, so he must have been angry after the derby defeat, but I can't be certain. It was so long ago.

'My relationship with him back in the day, admittedly, I was quite shy, withdrawn. I probably needed to leave Everton to mature as a person and as a player. I would say that I didn't particularly have a great relationship with Howard. That wasn't because he got rid of me, you probably think as time goes by it may have been the right decision at the time. I needed to develop too. I was in and out of the team which was struggling, and all of a sudden it clicked.

'Howard was a very good manager, but at that time I was what, 19, 20? I think Howard and the team got better after I'd left if the truth's known, only having him for a short period of time. I played 29 games in total.

'In hindsight, I turned out to be a half-decent player. I would have loved to have been the player that I was when they had the success.'

How did Howard deal with players? 'Howard was fair as to how he handled the players. I remember the situation with Mickey Thomas. Mickey was down to play in the reserves at Newcastle United but refused to travel. He was sold not long after which may answer your question. Howard was one that would never suffer fools.

'When he selected his team for a match and you were left out, he basically told you that you weren't playing. I do recollect us having a conversation leading up to my last game. He more or less said, "I'm not sure whether I'm going to play you." He told me he wasn't sure if it was me or Mark Higgins and playing Billy Wright at right-back. As I've said, because it's so long ago, he may have given reasons for leaving you out of the team.'

On Howard's signings, Brian said, 'He spent a lot of money on Adrian Heath. He pushed the boat out to get Inchy who he knew from his days at Stoke City. He thought a lot of Adrian, and quite rightly so.

'Even then, Neville wasn't in the team but turned out to be one of the best goalkeepers in the world. Kevin Ratcliffe was at the club before Howard came, again wasn't a regular then either. Kev was a left-back but was transformed into a centre-back by Howard. I think Howard would have appreciated all of the players that brought success to the club.'

Brian's career blossomed when he left Merseyside, staying local with Bolton before finding his feet in the West Midlands and Coventry. In the Sky Blues' greatest hour, their first FA Cup triumph in 1987, Brian featured in every league game plus the run to the semi-final at Hillsborough. In the last league game of the season at home to Southampton, a week before the trip to Wembley, he asked his manager at half-time if he could play in midfield for the second half. That proved disastrous as he injured his knee which forced him to miss the big occasion; he attended on crutches.

His only consolation was that he appeared in the Charity Shield at Wembley in August, albeit for four minutes after coming off the bench to replace Micky Gynn against Everton; the Toffees were victorious.

At the time of writing, Brian worked for the PFA as a regional coach educator.

STUART RIMMER

Debut: Saturday, 1 May 1982, Swansea City 1 Everton 3
Swansea City: Davies, Marustik, Hadziabdic, Irwin, Kennedy (L. James 21), Rajkovic, Curtis, R. James, Stanley, Stevenson, Latchford
Everton: Southall, Stevens, Walsh, Higgins, Wright, McMahon, Irvine, Heath, Sharp, Rimmer (Richardson 75), Ross

STUART RIMMER always had an eye for goal at an early age. In Howard Kendall's first season, he was prepared to take a chance on the 17-year-old, giving him his debut at Swansea City. In the summer of 1982 Stuart played three games for England Youth in a tournament in Norway. Let's not forget that he was also a member of the Everton side that reached the FA Youth Cup Final against Norwich City, only to be the bridesmaid as they were defeated in a third game as the two-legged affair ended even at 5-5. Everton won the toss for home advantage in the decisive fixture but it ended 1-0. On reaching the final, he netted seven goals in ten matches.

He also topped the scoring charts in the Central League with 14 goals in 24 outings in 1983/84.

Stuart thought his career would be more successful away from Merseyside, and he signed for Fourth Division side Chester, becoming the club's all-time record scorer.

'Howard was a good man who gave me my league debut, and for that alone, I owe him everything,' says Stuart. 'He sent me out on loan to Chester which was one of the best things that happened to me too. After I left Everton, when we met, he was always pleased to see me.

'He was ahead of his time with his management. His training was short and sharp which is what they do now 30 years on. There was none of this long running, even in pre-season. Everything Howard applied in training involved a ball which is why he was probably so successful. He was different with the younger kids. It was mostly Colin Harvey that was in charge of me.

'Howard would participate in the training with Colin, and even though Colin's knees had gone, he could still play, both of them could. As I was only a youngster, there wasn't any added pressure. He never let anything like that get in the way. Everything as far as we were concerned was a normal everyday routine. I trained with the reserves mostly and trained on the other side of Bellefield. I think one of the reasons he was successful was because he believed in his methods and persevered, and as everyone knows, the proof was in the pudding.

'Compared to other managers that I'd played under, he's the best one overall by far. The only other one that was good for me was Chester manager Harry McNally, he was the biggest motivator. He was more meticulous than Howard when it came to going over the opposition. Howard would let the players get on with what they had to do. As a player going down the leagues, I had to concentrate more on the opposition.

'If Howard left me out of the side, he would pull me to one side. Some managers I've played under didn't even tell you. I only played three senior games and each time he left me out he gave me his reasons as to why.

'He was also a disciplinarian. That was the biggest lesson I learned from him. It was a good grounding. He detested players arriving late for training, team meetings, catching the team bus. He hated players getting booked for dissent as well.

I think you had 25 per cent of your wages deducted if you got booked for dissent. I think getting sent off implemented a 50 per cent deduction. The players got it all back in the end with a night out in Southport as the fines paid for the event. If any players caused him concern, from what I can remember, I think he used to put them in the reserves then sell them. That is what most managers do I suppose.

'Howard was a winner and showed the emotion after a win. He could also show his anger when required. When I played in the reserves and lost, he would come into the dressing room and rollicked the young lads, but not the senior lads who were coming back from injury. I once returned from an England youth game injured and Howard was fuming.

'He encouraged the lads to get together socially. I was a young lad, too young I guess to be in that circle, but on one occasion I did go out for a meal with all of the lads.'

Stuart made his debut on the first day in May 1982 at Swansea, playing his part in a 3-1 success and was replaced by Kevin Richardson on 75 minutes.

'Howard told me to go out and play my normal game as I did in the reserves which was the best advice he ever gave me,' he said.

Stuart departed the top flight, finding comfort in the fourth tier of English football with Chester City under ex-Southampton defender John McGrath, and later played for several other clubs including Walsall, Notts County and Barnsley.

'Once I left Everton and went to Chester, I would go back to Goodison to watch games and Howard would always take the time to come over and ask how I was getting on. Sometimes I would see him around Southport too, and again he would chat with me.'

At the time of writing Stuart was a milkman in Southport, and still enjoyed a game of cricket.

KEVIN RICHARDSON

Debut: Saturday, 28 August 1982, Watford 2 Everton 0
Watford: Sherwood, Rice, Rostron, Blissett, Bolton, Jackett, Callaghan (Taylor 83), Armstrong, Jenkins, Lohman, Barnes
Everton: Southall, Borrows, Bailey, Higgins, Wright, Heath, McMahon (Richardson 72), Johnson, Sharp, King, Sheedy

KEVIN RICHARDSON originated from Newcastle, and like most young boys he idolised the black and white stripes of his hometown team and worshipped his hero SuperMac – Malcolm Macdonald. His association with football was with Montagu and North Fenham Boys Club as a youngster where he would walk a mile and a half to get there and kick balls against boards. That technique stood Kevin in good stead.

His future might have turned out differently as he'd spent time with Burnley as a youngster. He was advised to go to Everton which was a good move as he stayed for six weeks. When the decision had to be made between the Clarets and the Toffees, he chose Everton and joined as a schoolboy in 1978, turning pro in 1980.

Kevin came through the ranks to reach the first team. He was similar to Alan Harper, who could fall into any position comfortably. He never disappointed, showing his versatility playing at right-back, but preferred a midfield slot. It was only the quality of his fellow players that prevented him from starting on a weekly basis. Twenty-four starts in his first season summed up his ability. He was given the chance to prove himself, which he did with flying colours.

At the age of 19, Kevin played 13 successive matches in the first 11 after deputising for Steve McMahon. Howard Kendall felt that he was near to proving his readiness for first-team football.

His superstition on a matchday was always to touch the Everton badge as the players edged out of the tunnel on to the pitch; he always wanted to excel and delight the fans.

Kevin's impact on the club's success was massive with some very important goals. A late strike in the first leg of the 1984 League Cup semi-final while sporting a lightweight plaster cast on his right arm at Goodison gave Everton a comfortable two-goal margin to take to Aston Villa for the second leg.

He set the Blues on their way in the FA Cup quarter-final at Notts County a few weeks later by heading home into a gaping net.

Last but not least, his cross from the left contributed to the opening goal at Wembley in 1984.

As the next season progressed, a three-minute brace followed at Southampton at the end of March which set up the next game at White Hart Lane four days later, which more or less decided the championship as the Toffees stretched their lead at the top of the table, distancing themselves from the threat of Tottenham.

Looking back at that FA Cup Final victory over Watford, Richardson said, 'I filled in that day for Sheeds on the left. I cut inside and crossed the ball for Sharpy, who did the damage by scoring the first goal.

'When the whistle went, it was great to see all of the fans so happy. It's a great day out for them too. It was special for them and their families. There are a lot of good memories of all those Blues fans to be so delighted, and I couldn't believe that we had won at Wembley as it had been so long since Everton had won a trophy before that.'

Kevin deservedly won medals for his services before being sold to Watford for £225,000 after Everton's first home fixture of the 1985/86 season. Many times, Kevin would be told he wasn't to be included in the team.

He remembered, 'He [Howard Kendall] would call us into a room on a Friday, and not being a regular, I knew what was coming as it happened to me quite often. He would give you his reasons as to why you were being left out but at the same time praise you for the time that you'd deputised. He would want to play the player that was more suitable for the opposition. He's made his mind up which he's not going to change, and you had to accept it.

'If I made the bench and got the opportunity, it was down to me to show him why I should be in the team.'

Like any young player, Kevin wanted first-team football, but sadly it wasn't to be at Everton.

He says, 'As time went on, I knew I couldn't give any more and realised it was time for me to move on which is why I ended up going to Watford.'

On working with Kendall, Kevin added, 'Howard was a great player in his time, especially the great midfield trio which he was part of. The balance of football they played and created. I was fortunate enough to play for him and what a fantastic moment for a young kid to be playing with this legendary figure in midfield. For me, to have Colin [Harvey] as well on board, things couldn't have got any better. As a young kid, I had the pleasure and the honour to have played alongside Howard in a game away at West Ham.

'I'll never forget the time he said, "Richo, when you get it, just give it to me." "OK Gaffer," I replied, and that's all I did. When I got the ball, I just looked for him.

'Howard never put any pressure on you as a player as he went through a few stages where he bought players that didn't work, and then he had to put the young ones in, which was a massive, massive gamble at the time. The young players like myself, Gary Stevens, Trevor Steven, Mark Ward, Joe McBride, Paul Lodge and Steve McMahon were given a chance.

'That's when he suddenly turned around as when Howard picked you to play, he trusted you, told us to go out and play and do your best.

'That is what I remember about being a young kid when I played with Howard. Also, he still put his boots on now and then and it was a pleasure to have played in midfield with him. As a kid I'm thinking, I'm standing next to Howard Kendall here. I thought of the Holy Trinity, Kendall, Harvey and Ball, as this was just unreal. Even though he was the Gaffer, he was a player on the pitch, you could criticise him, praise him. On the pitch he was just one of the players, and off the pitch he was the manager and you showed a lot of respect for the man.

'It was an honour and a pleasure to have played with Howard on the pitch and a pleasure to have worked with Colin too on the training field where I learned a lot.

'He was caring, thoughtful, he wanted his group of players to express themselves on the pitch just like him. That was the way that he came across. He didn't come across like a big important person that will do what I say, and you will play the way I want. He had been through that himself as a player, but Howard had characters around him who were like him, and he wanted that feel-good factor in the group. He wasn't like a headmaster, he was flexible and wanted you to create and score goals, just like the way he played. Back in the day that was a great thing and all of the players that were lucky to have played under him would give 200 per cent for him.

'Now and then, there would be a rollicking and rightly so, but in the main he was so encouraging and just one of the lads. He gave you enough confidence and belief to go out on the pitch and play attractive football.

'Even when he was training a bit, the things he would come out with where you wouldn't be sure about. Because he could do it, you knew he was the Gaffer, and you needed A, B and C to do certain things which he does in training, you knew you had to get your finger out. It was that nature of him – relaxed, his personality, he was great, which made everybody else relaxed and comfortable. Any problems, pressure, you'd go and see him and would sort it out. He just wanted the lads to play without any distractions, and play for him, the club, to try your best, win games and hopefully be successful.

'He was fair with his squad and as far as I'm aware, the Mickey Thomas situation where he refused to board the bus for a reserve team game was probably the worst situation I remember. Howard as I've mentioned would never deal with other issues with players publicly. It would always be dealt with in private. In situations that are uncomfortable, the manager will realise that it is not a good spirit for the group and will want to deal with it straight away.

'If Howard would have left you out of the team no matter how good you thought you were, you would be expected to treat everybody with the same respect and Howard would not want that bubble to burst. If your confidence had been damaged, you would get taken to one side with a warm arm around the shoulder for a chat. He could probably tell in your body language that you were affected for whatever reason. He knew that I was competing with so many great players for a starting place. He told me that should anyone get injured, he wouldn't think a further second but to select me as I'd proved to him that I could do a job and maintained a standard and pushed myself. Your training had to be the best, even if you were to play in the reserves, it had to be what Howard expected.

'As time went on, I knew I couldn't give any more and realised it was time for me to move on which is why I ended up going to Watford.

'The best lesson he taught me was: you will have a few disappointments in your career, but disappointments will make you better and stronger.

'Best advice? Always know your next pass. Whether you do it in one, or whether it's done in two.

'Howard loved players with character. He loved players that expressed themselves and loved the game. A couple of his signings that he made, Andy Gray and Peter Reid, were two big characters but characters that were critical as well as very supportive towards others.

'I think the positions of them was part of the spine of the team, a striker and a centre-midfield player. Ratters [Kevin Ratcliffe] was a great captain, but any problems on the pitch Reidy and Andy would look after you if any skirmishes occurred. They were also very encouraging as well as critical because they knew that you could do better which is not a bad thing.

'All employers have rules. Howard was no different and could be a strict disciplinarian. If you stepped out of line there would be a fine. I think in the tone of his voice you could sense an anger, but I can't recall one moment where I would see him physically doing something. He would say something verbally but it wasn't very often.

'The fine was always implemented for a football matter such as arriving late for a team meeting, or if you failed to show for training and failed to contact anybody to give a reason for your absence. If anybody had an issue with a team selection or answered back, Howard would have been down on them like a ton of bricks. If you pushed Howard too far you would know about it but that was very rare.

'I always remember one situation where I was a substitute at Southampton away. He said to me, "Richo, get yourself warmed up, you're going on." As I was warming up, a couple of incidents happened on the pitch. The linesman was on my side as I was warming up which prompted me to give him some stick and I went too far. The linesman raised his flag and the referee came over and booked me. I went back to the dugout where Howard asked what had gone on. I told him the story and he insisted that I sat down and shut up.

'My relationship overall with him was decent because I was always knocking on his door. "Gaffer, why am I not in the team?" Managers have got difficult jobs and a group of players from who they have to make a team selection. Players that don't get selected can be a problem, I don't think the group we had back then were anywhere near as big as they are today, but we had a variety of characters and personalities amongst us. Howard introduced this spirit amongst the lads where he shared the same craic. He looked after all of the players including the ones like myself and a few others who were in the wings so to speak. Compared to other managers I'd play for, I think as time went on in my career, there were differences in their behaviour, but I never played under anybody with the character, the personality, his desire to win. Everything he did, he wanted to win which isn't a bad thing to have. Other managers that I'd played under had their own character, their own style. Howard could switch off and on to suit the mood.

'As a good player that he was, I would like to know his success rate in winning. As a manager, his way of winning and to be successful and the occasions in domestic finals and in Europe was for the fans as well as us, it was brilliant. It was fantastic for everybody.'

On the social side of life at Everton, Richardson said, 'I went out with him, but in a group – never just the two of us. With me being such a young kid, it wasn't the right impression to give. As a group, again, he was just one of the lads. With him being one of the lads, you'd run through a brick wall for him. He respected and treated all of us well. That's the way that he was as a person and as a player. At the end of the season, he always took the lads for a little break to Magaluf. It was more or less a thank you for our efforts. He was a likeable, laughable, loveable fella who loved the banter and the craic.

'I drove down from Newcastle with Dave Watson to pay our respects at his funeral. Arriving at the cathedral, it was total sadness. The turnout showed the respect that he had which speaks volumes. I'm sure that there were people far away in different countries who couldn't attend and were thinking of him on that day. There were people there from all walks of life as well as football people.

'I recall Peter Reid and Bill Kenwright getting up to speak about the man who they regarded as a great, great fella.'

Kevin remained involved in football and coached the under-18 team at Newcastle United until retiring in 2023.

KEVIN SHEEDY

Debut: Saturday, 28 August 1982, Watford 2 Everton 0
Watford: Sherwood, Rice, Rostron, Blissett, Bolton, Jackett, Callaghan (L. Taylor 83), Armstrong, Jenkins, Lohman, Barnes
Everton: Southall, Borrows, Bailey, Higgins, Wright, Heath, McMahon (Richardson 72), Johnson, Sharp, King, Sheedy

KEVIN STARTED his career with Hereford United before catching the eye of Liverpool. Due to the Reds' success and competition for places, his first-team appearances were limited to three, spending the majority of his playing days in the Central League.

Howard Kendall saw something in Sheedy, who proved to be an exceptional signing with the fee a mere £100,000 in 1982. The move across the park never really concerned Sheedy who was once quoted as saying, 'The fans will judge on what I do for the team. Not what team I used to play for.'

He was the first player to be transferred between the two Merseyside clubs in 20 years and was certainly true to his word as it didn't take him long to get off the mark, scoring his first goal in the royal blue shirt in Everton's second home game of the season, on 4 September, opening the scoring after seven minutes against Keith Burkinshaw's Tottenham side.

He failed to find the net again until December, at Ipswich Town – his first away goal – and a last-minute goal by Kevin Richardson sealed a 2-0 victory. It took him until the latter part of 1982/83 to find goalscoring a natural habit. His total goal tally was 13, of which 11 were league goals, and two in the FA Cup. His last-minute goal away to Newport County in the third round of the FA Cup spared Everton's blushes, cancelling out Dave Gwyther's opener.

In Sheedy's first season at the club, he was called up for the Republic of Ireland squad by coach Eoin Hand for a game against the Netherlands at Dalymount Park. He appeared as a substitute, replacing Kevin O'Callaghan on 74 minutes. A shock was on the cards as the hosts were cruising by two goals but they were pegged back with the Dutch masters Ruud Gullit (two) and Marco van Basten scoring.

Sheedy was a master of set pieces and had this art of knowing where to put the ball, which was evident in an FA Cup tie with Ipswich in March 1985 with an exquisite free kick which hit the back of the net. He was ordered to retake it by referee Alan Robinson, not a popular figure among Evertonians who remembered him for denying the Blues a penalty after an Alan Hansen handball at Wembley in the League Cup Final 12 months earlier. Kevin once more outwitted goalkeeper Paul Cooper by placing his retaken effort into the opposite side of the goal.

Kevin was a key member of the Everton side that enjoyed the success they thoroughly deserved. In the 1984/85 season, the most successful in the history of the club, Sheedy registered 17 goals in all competitions.

Kevin sadly declined to take part in this publication, but he did say on hearing the news of Howard Kendall's death, 'It was with great sadness that I heard of Howard Kendall's passing. I was privileged to have played under Howard in Everton's most successful team in history. He was the best manager I have ever played for, and personally, he got the best out of me with his fantastic management skills. I had nothing but admiration for him as a player, a manager and a friend.'

ANDY KING

Debut: Saturday, 28 August 1982, Watford 2 Everton 0
Watford: Sherwood, Rice, Rostron, Blissett, Bolton, Jackett, Callaghan (L. Taylor 83), Armstrong, Jenkins, Lohman, Barnes
Everton: Southall, Borrows, Bailey, Higgins, Wright, Heath, McMahon (Richardson 72), Johnson, Sharp, King, Sheedy

ANDY KING 'rejoined' Everton, signing for Howard Kendall in July 1982 in exchange for Peter Eastoe who went to QPR.

King had initially signed for Billy Bingham as a very young and upcoming player back in April 1976 and didn't take long to establish himself as a fan favourite. 'Andy is our King' became the anthem from the terraces.

His first season back during his second spell showed that his knack of scoring goals had never left him. In Everton's first home game of the campaign, against European champions Aston Villa, King added a third goal following a brace from Adrian Heath. Graeme Sharp netted two in the second period as Everton demolished their opponents without reply, moving 15 places up the table to fifth.

He appeared 24 times in 1982/83, hitting the net on nine occasions, with a further eight appearances in cup competitions producing four more goals.

Andy suffered a heartbreak in 1984 when Kendall had to make a decision as to who to have on the bench in the final of the League Cup. Alan Harper was preferred to

King, but a consolation to him was that he was the substitute in the replay after the first match had ended in a 1-1 draw.

Andy missed out on the FA Cup Final in May 1984, making his last appearances five days earlier at West Ham, in what was Hammers legend Trevor Brooking's last game for his team.

He was then released at the end of that term, moving to Sweden where he joined Örebro SK.

Devastating news broke on 27 May 2015 that Andy had passed away at the age of 58 after suffering a heart attack at his home.

His funeral was held on 4 June at St Luke's Church in the shadow of his beloved Goodison Park. It was so appropriate that the 'Z-Cars' theme was played as he was carried into the church. Many ex-players were in attendance, and following the service, a private burial took place at the Anfield cemetery.

DAVID JOHNSON

Debut: Saturday, 28 August 1982, Watford 2 Everton 0
Watford: Sherwood, Rice, Rostron, Blissett, Bolton, Jackett, Callaghan (L. Taylor 83), Armstrong, Jenkins, Lohman, Barnes
Everton: Southall, Borrows, Bailey, Higgins, Wright, Heath, McMahon (Richardson 72), Johnson, Sharp, King, Sheedy

DAVID JOHNSON was born a Red but gave everything to Everton once he pulled the royal blue shirt over his head.

He returned to Everton in August 1982 for what was his second and final spell. He never would have believed that he would be in a tug-of-war triangle with both Manchester clubs as well as the Toffees.

David made the short journey from Anfield to Goodison Park for a fee of £100,000 aged 32, Howard Kendall looking to him to use his wealth of experience to try and steady the ship in his second season. Johnson wore the royal blue shirt on 29 occasions followed by a further seven the next season when he then joined Barnsley on loan.

'You talk about the best formations and in the late 60s, early 70s, Everton had the best midfield three [Alan Ball, Howard Kendall, Colin Harvey] that I have ever seen,' Johnson reminisced. 'Bally had everything, and was the best player I have ever played with. Colin, not only his tackling, but his knowledge of the game. Howard was the glue, the one that gelled them all together. Howard had certain attributes like Colin, they could both tackle.

Howard was ferocious in tackle and could also play. Bally wasn't a tackler, he was heart and his fitness levels, with his contribution from start to finish pulsating. Bally was supported by two great players, Howard and Colin.

'Going straight through from his playing career into management, I would say on my second spell at Everton where he [Kendall] brought me back, it was so evident that he had the ability to spot a good player. He never went out and bought bad players, he bought exceptional players. When he started to build a squad and the number of players he recruited, I don't think he quite knew what to do with them and the way he wanted them to play. So, consequently when I arrived, our midfield was as good as anybody's in the country, but we didn't quite get it right. I recall once, he was trying to find a position for Kevin Ratcliffe. Rats was naturally left-footed so he was tried at left-back. Rats wasn't a left-back. He was then tried as a centre-half, but Mark Higgins was centre-half and was also left-footed. Howard said that he could not play two left-footed centre-halves. In the end Howard got his formula right.

'He could still play a bit too which he did as a player-manager. The players who were at Everton under his leadership could still see at the age he was then [35] what a great player he still was as he was always part of the five-a-side session we used to have in training.

'If I'm honest, my second spell was not the best two years that I ever had, and I don't think Howard realised until he promoted Colin from the reserves to be his number two. Not only did he have the ability to spot a player, he understood how to play them as well. For some reason, Howard wouldn't play Peter Reid. I would approach Colin and ask why he wouldn't play him as I thought that Reidy was the link between the midfield and the forward men. The ball bypassed the midfield to me and Sharpy which wasn't the best way to play. I think in the end, Colin mentioned to Howard what I'd said. Peter then became a regular and Everton took their first step to what they became. Reidy then became the glue just like Howard was when he was playing.

'Howard was a player's manager. He was great. He understood the pressure players could be under. He liked a drink which he encouraged the players to do. When we went away, he always made sure we all had a drink. Wherever we went, Howard always made sure we had a good time. He had a great sense of humour and liked to be in his company. I'd love to have said that my fondest memory was to say we picked this trophy up, and this trophy ... but it didn't happen.

'I have memories too of when I was with Howard in my first spell at Everton in the 60s and early 70s when both teams were a match for each other. Howard was an integral part of that.

'All managers want success, Howard was no different. Once he unlocked that secret door, he would take me into his office and have a beer with him. He asked me, "I've brought you here from Liverpool, so come on, what's the secret?" I told Howard that there was no secret. Bob Paisley bought players who suited the system that Bob wanted to play. The players come in, pick up what they are supposed to do, and if they don't do it, they're gone, simple as that. When I was at Liverpool, all we did was play five-a-side. We didn't work on tactics, set pieces, we just played. I think once Howard realised there was no secret formula and found the players that suited his system, he went on to enjoy success. He was only concerned with his own group of players and making sure he got the best out of them. He bought good players. He had an eye for a player that suited Everton.

'The success he created – some credit has to go to his coaching staff. Howard's right-hand man at the time of his arrival was Mick Heaton. To be fair, Mick wasn't a coach. When Colin was promoted to Howard's number two, if you were pulled to one side you would listen to him because he had done it at the top level where Mick hadn't. I think Howard listened a lot to Colin when he was at his side as his assistant. A lot of praise in my mind should go to Colin for his involvement in the success of the club during the 80s.'

I asked David if he found any similarities to Harry Catterick, who he'd played under during his first Everton spell. 'No, not at all. They were chalk and cheese. Harry Catterick was a tyrant. If ever you were in a corridor and walking towards each other, if there was a door that you could escape through you would do it so you didn't have to speak to him. If you got called up to his office, you knew it wasn't good. Harry wasn't a manager that would give you a cuddle or an arm around the shoulder. If he didn't play you, you were gone. Harry Catterick would get the best out of you through fear. Howard would get the best out of you throwing an arm around you or giving you a cuddle. He was just an all-round nice man; they were that different.

'My relationship with Howard? We bumped into each other an awful lot when we both finished our careers. Once we had a couple of drinks things came out. I think he was annoyed things didn't work in the two years that I was there. He wanted me to be successful which is not a bad thing for a manager. It obviously looks good on him as he's brought a player in that improves the team. If he left me out, he'd call me in his office and tell me straight that I wasn't playing. He would tell me that he had other ideas that he wanted to try out as something wasn't working. That happened a lot. When I was playing, he told me to put the shirt on and go out there and play and score goals. I knew what he expected of me.

'He got angry with me a couple of times. The openness we had when he first came, and not agreeing with his route-one football which developed into arguments as I was beginning to get on his nerves. I enjoyed my time there and there was a great bunch of lads who were good players.

'I would have loved to have played for Howard when the curtains had opened for him when he could see the whole picture. Who knows, things may have worked out for me then. It would have worked better for me and Sharpy, but when Andy Gray came in, his partnership clicked with Sharpy. The forwards got the benefit of the midfield service.

'The press would often put the question to me and Sharpy and ask if we were worried because neither of us were hitting the net. We would answer them by asking them how many chances did we miss, which they replied none. That was because we weren't getting the service. He had a good bunch of players who were all good lads who all wanted to do well. There weren't any big-heads amongst us, there were a lot of good young lads amongst the group that finally managed to get success years later.

'Howard was quite a strict person. All managers in any walk of life would be. They have a responsibility to their seniors too. If he had to fine you, he would. The main culprit would always be John Bailey. John's fines paid for all of the nights out we had with the money Howard raised from the fines. Howard would make a speech at the nights out to propose a toast to Bails for paying for the lads' night out. Bails would always turn up late for a meeting or whatever.'

Sadly, David passed away in November 2022 after suffering from throat cancer.

GLENN KEELEY

Debut: Saturday, 6 November 1982, Everton 0 Liverpool 5
Everton: Southall, Borrows, Bailey, Keeley, Wright, McMahon, Heath, Johnson (Richardson 74), Sharp, King, Sheedy
Liverpool: Grobbelaar, Neal, Kennedy, Thompson, Johnston, Hansen, Dalglish (Hodgson 82), Lee, Rush, Lawrenson, Souness

GLENN KEELEY was signed by Howard Kendall on a loan spell which ended up miserably, the pair having been familiar with each other from when they were team-mates at Blackburn Rovers.

A phone call from Howard persuading Keeley to join on loan warmed his heart as he was having issues at Ewood Park and was made to train alone. Keeley agreed to come as Everton were a big club.

The debutant was brought in for cover, not realising a Merseyside derby was the first fixture on the agenda. The club were short of a centre-half and Glenn had only played one game for the reserve side prior to his full debut. There was a practice game at Bellefield on the Monday prior to the big event which went well. Howard then gave Glenn the nod to start in the derby even though Glenn felt he wasn't ready.

Everton were unbeaten at home, winning four and drawing two of their previous six Goodison games in the league going into this fixture, which means so much to the people of the city.

On the half-hour mark, Keeley was struggling to keep up with the pace of Kenny Dalglish, which ended with the Scottish forward being upended leaving referee Derek Civil no option but to send Keeley off. Those in the crowd of just under 53,000 witnessed one of the worst records in the history of the club as Liverpool romped home with a five-goal margin.

Glenn never appeared again as he had to serve a suspension for the red card offence prior to the end of his loan spell.

'Howard was the best manager that I ever played under,' Glenn says affectionately. 'He was smart, always had a smile and was clever. He was also very astute. He made training fun and enjoyable, very professional. I liked the fact that he had a very good sense of humour.

'He knew how to handle people, a great man-manager I thought. He was just a great person to be around. He was a top-class guy, and a top-class manager who I genuinely believe should have been the England manager.

'Howard knew how to coach the important parts of the game. Organising things was something that he did really, really well. So, he knew how to get you organised as a side, something that he did really, really well, unlike some coaches.

'He was brilliant at involving players individually. He would seek the opinion of every player in the team as to what they thought about the game, and what more could be done. Anything that could make the game better, always constructive, which showed how good he was as a manager.

'I've worked under so many managers who were scared of their jobs, scared of the players, scared of so many different things. Howard was pretty fearless. He was prepared to engage and mould players into his thinking. He wasn't doing that just to please you. He would swallow any input he was given by his playing staff, then come out with a decision. Howard was his own man.

'I have played for a lot of managers who would take the blame. Some managers would blame you because they didn't want to take the blame themselves. A lot of managers would play the blame game which for me is not constructive. It doesn't help anyone.

'When you start pointing fingers, it doesn't get them on your side, it makes them angry. The blame game doesn't work and Howard never played that. When we were at the training ground, all he wanted to do was involve everyone in the training session, and make it enjoyable which he did.

'In the dressing room, he would engage with players before the game, and sometimes, if the opposition presented a problem, he would look at ways of solving that problem. He always wanted the players to speak up, if they knew of ways how to improve things for the side, or stop the opposition playing. If there was something that Howard wanted to bring to your attention, such as doing something that he wasn't happy with, he would pull you to one side and say this, that and the other. This is not what I want, I need you to do this. He would then ask you if you were OK with his comments and had he made himself clear.

'If he ever came across players that caused him upset and problems, he just spoke to them as individuals. I remember whilst at Everton he had an issue with the centre-back Billy Wright. I think it was common knowledge that Billy had problems with his weight and was warned by Howard to lose some. Howard obviously saw no reaction from Billy and therefore sold him.

'Going out socially? Well [laughing], professionally, socially, yes. Personally, socially, never. Howard liked to build a team spirit. The way he built a team spirit was by getting the whole squad together which meant you were going out drinking somewhere. Sometimes he would choose the back room of a pub and play charades. You can't imagine a group of modern-day professional footballers playing charades, but he would split the team up in two. We would all sit there getting drunk together by playing charades.

'Going out on to the football field and winning made him a very happy man. I think when you're a professional and enjoy sport, you will come out being a winner. You are at your happiest when you're winning.

'On a personal note, I had a very good relationship with him. He was ruthless in a very quiet and controlled way. I liked that about him. That for me is the part of being a brilliant manager. He had full control which brought admiration from everyone.

'When I got sent off in the derby game, we played Arsenal away in the League Cup at Highbury three days after. He wanted me to play but obviously I couldn't. I couldn't believe that Howard was prepared to take that chance on me after what had happened on the Saturday.

'He showed me a way tactically, showing me some good ways to play. He could at times be ruthless but at the same time keep it under wraps. You would find it harder to find a bigger fan of Howard than me.

'Compared to other managers? Simple, he was the best. I loved Joe Harvey at Newcastle United. Joe was a very good man-manager. Joe was a manager that would bring in the best players he could get, then send them out to play. Joe's thing was, I've paid a lot of money for you, you don't need me to tell you what to do, go out and play. He was also very good at handling you as an individual. Trust me, he handled some really tough characters at Newcastle, he really did. Joe was a lovely man with two sides to him.

'I also worked with Bobby Robson at Ipswich Town, who I have to say was an excellent coach, but he wasn't always good with individuals. Howard had both. He was technically, tactically, very savvy indeed.

'When I first met him, I was 23 or 24. I thought I knew the game inside out which in many respects I did, but Howard told me new ways to look at things. He gave me new options to the way that I would play. He was brilliant at it. He was one of, if not the bravest manager that I've ever seen and known.

'I know in one game, we were playing a 4-4-2 system. We were getting murdered because we couldn't stop their full-backs. Literally after 15 minutes, you knew it was a matter of time before changes would be made. Howard made changes immediately. He changed the formation to 3-4-3, and we went on to win that game 2-0. There would be very few managers brave enough to see what was happening and to act on it with immediate effect.

'At the end of the season the squad would go away. Howard's favourite holiday destination would have to be Majorca. He liked to have a drink, go on the beach, and genuinely have a good time with EVERYONE. That's another good thing about him, he loved people to be around him, he loved life and what it had to offer.

'He very rarely spoke about his playing career because it spoke for itself. I think he was very unlucky not to get several England caps. Howard was probably one of the best midfielders in the world.

'Howard was excellent in a tackle, would always win the ball fairly. Nobody phased Howard except for one person I played with up at Newcastle, and that was Jimmy Smith.

'I remember going to the funeral with a friend and witnessing masses of people there. I just thought it was a shame that he was never the England manager. A very well-respected gentleman and loved by so many.'

TERRY CURRAN

Debut: Saturday, 4 December 1982, Everton 0
Birmingham City 0
Everton: Arnold, Stevens, Bailey, Higgins, Wright, McMahon, Curran, Heath, Sharp, King, Sheedy
Birmingham City: Coton, Brazier, Van Den Hauwe, Stevenson, Blake, Broadhurst, Dillon, Evans, Ferguson, Curbishley, Handysides

TERRY CURRAN, aka TC, signed for Everton, his ninth club, in December 1982. There is no denying that Terry was a journeyman, but a character who was much needed at Goodison at the time he joined. He was a player who enjoyed entertaining the crowd, possibly the first one to tread the Goodison turf since the days of the magical displays of Duncan McKenzie.

This was of course a loan spell, appearing seven times and scoring one goal in a 5-0 drubbing of Luton Town. The deal eventually became permanent which was greeted with an enthusiastic response from the fans who knew he was just what the doctor ordered. Terry was versatile as to where he could fit in. He could play as an attacking midfielder because he had the skill and flair, and also as an out-and-out striker simply because he had an eye for goal.

He once stated that his personal ambition at Everton was to win a trophy with the club, which sadly failed to reach fruition.

TC says, 'With Howard and my time at the club, it was nothing more than happiness really. I found him to be a lovely man and a gentleman. What he had achieved for Everton as a player and as a manager, he has to go down in history as the greatest of them all, that includes going ahead of the late Harry Catterick. Howard was a level-headed guy who knew how to get his team to play football. Howard ate and slept football; it was his life.

'I loved the way Howard wanted us to play football. When I first went there on loan, things weren't going particularly well which brought a lot of fear inside the dressing room.

'The training was fantastic, it was a friendly club where you were made welcome by everyone. The team at the time was on the fringe of being a good team which they became with the glory they reaped not long after. He had a great characteristic, he was always so jovial after games, especially when results went his way. He always came across happy in training too. You know what? I can honestly say that I never ever saw him lose his temper.

'The backroom staff of Colin Harvey and Mick Heaton were a good blend. I have to add that the introduction to promote Colin Harvey to the first team was a massive appointment, I reiterate, massive.'

Things didn't go as well for Terry as he thought, and he often found himself on the bench.

He continued, 'I had moments where I was frustrated because I wasn't getting games, but I had nothing but admiration for Howard as a player, and also as a manager. I put Howard up there with Cloughie – both wanted you to play football. They both played the game in the right way for me.

'People said that Brian Clough was not the same without his number two Peter Taylor. What happened is, Howard's backroom staff, Colin and Mick, they all gelled. Colin, I imagine as a player wouldn't take any nonsense. Colin was one of those that would take the pressure off Howard and at the same time would dish out rollickings. I think all three together, like the team itself, all played a part together. The success on the field generated from Mick and Colin. To get success, what Everton had, was down to having the right manager and coaches. I would also include the physio John Clinkard for his part too. It was a happy club. I never saw anybody at the club ever fall out.

'Howard never really faltered in the transfer market and made some good signings. There were two signings that stood out. One is obviously the goalkeeper Neville Southall. The other one was me. Even though I never played many games, I was one of those players where I believed that we would never get beat.

'I can't leave out Peter Reid who was a snip at £60,000 and Andy Gray who at the time was completely finished with his legs. What Howard got out of Andy, who also deserves credit too, when Wolves wanted him away because he was injured.

'Compared to other managers I'd played under? I played for Lawrie McMenemy, Tommy Docherty, Jack Charlton, Howard Kendall and Brian Clough. When you're winning trophies, Cloughie would have to be the one. He won trophies with Nottingham Forest and Derby County, that aren't the most popular clubs with respect.

'Howard had everything that Cloughie had. Cloughie as everyone knows never shied away from speaking his mind to the press and the directors of the football clubs he managed. Howard was very much more respectful in that way. They were two different personalities. Funnily enough, they both gave me the best advice, which I took on board. Calm down, stop being impatient, you'll get back into the team.

'Before I arrived at Everton, Howard was under so much pressure as the fans were totally against him. He never let it into the dressing room, keeping it away from his players. When I arrived, I went to his house. On his garage door there was graffiti saying KENDALL OUT with a couple of hangman images.

'Howard to be fair didn't show the hurt. If there was any, he must have kept it inside. It's not nice when managers take abuse from fans. I was aware of what was going on from the players that were there.

'I remember we were going through a bit of a bad time as we were struggling and we had a team meeting. Howard told the lads that we had to turn things around. I told him that we were as good as Liverpool.

'When you have the ball, you have to be tactically aware player-wise and to make sure that the opposition find it hard to come through us. But we have to be more defensive and be able to express ourselves and not to be frightened of these players. Our back five picked itself as did the midfield and the forward line.

'Howard never looked back, he started to believe in himself, a great player in his day, a great ball player and indeed a great manager. A lovely man too. I don't think that any player had a bad word to say about the man.

'The night at Oxford United in the League Cup when Howard could have easily lost his job– I could never see us losing down there that night. People go on about what David Moyes did for Everton. Howard Kendall had won Everton the league, they are a massive club that did win silverware and a club that produces a lot of great players.'

Terry was sidelined as the Toffees were enduring an FA Cup run with Wembley in sight. 'Howard's army' were facing TC's former club Southampton in the semi-final at Highbury.

'I was in and out of the team at times which was frustrating,' says Terry. 'Everton were on a good FA Cup run in 1984. I asked Howard near the time of the semi-final against Southampton if I'd be involved. He told me that he hadn't made his mind up. Only later, I thought, what a stupid thing to do, to ask. Howard pushed me into the semi-final. I'd only played two senior games prior to that game and wasn't fully fit, I needed game time. I played in youth team and reserve team games to get game time to play in that semi-final.

'If you look at my record, it's not been bad as I've always had success. When I first went to Everton, I think they were second-bottom of the league. We had a crowd of about 13,000 against Birmingham City. After my six games and by the time my loan spell was over, there were 27,000 at my last game against Nottingham Forest. Like I have said, the first period was fantastic but despite what people think or say, I don't think my second period was that bad. I know that I wasn't in the team but we won everything throughout the game barring the European Cup but unfortunately, we never got the chance to play in that competition because of what happened at Heysel.

'The injury I got at Everton, eventually I came back, got back in the team again, then got injured with the team going on a run which made it more difficult for me to get back in.'

In April 1985, Terry was released by Everton, mainly because he had suffered from injuries.

He would have loved to have been a jockey if he'd not made it as a footballer due to his small size as a young boy. If that was the case, I don't think he would have failed in that profession as he had the hunger and determination to be the best.

PETER REID

Debut: Tuesday, 28 December 1982, Everton 3 Nottingham Forest 1

Everton: Arnold, Stevens, Bailey, Ratcliffe, Higgins, McMahon, Curran, Sharp, Johnson (Heath 81), Reid, Sheedy

Nottingham Forest: Sutton, Swain, Gunn, Todd (Walsh 60), Young, Bowyer, Proctor, Wallace, Birtles, Hodge, Robertson

THE SIGNING of Peter Reid could have only been sanctioned by Howard Kendall. Taking into account Peter's injury record, no other manager would have given him a second glance. Peter's introduction to the dressing room saw his character infect the younger lads, who were lacking in confidence.

Peter was a winner, like an Everton legend 20 years before him – Alan Ball. Anything less than 100 per cent was unacceptable for him. His presence on the field contributed immensely to the success of that magical era in the 80s. His performances were greatly admired, and he was unanimously voted as the PFA Players' Player of the Year for 1985 – an honour which took pride of place on his mantelpiece accompanying the First Division and Cup Winners' Cup medals for that same year.

After Kendall departed to Bilbao, Reid played one more season for his successor Colin Harvey.

His performances for his club led to playing for his country, catching the eye of Bobby Robson, who included him in the England squad that was cheated out of the World Cup quarter-final in Mexico 1986 by the 'Hand of God' incident as Argentina became the eventual winners.

Peter recalled, 'Howard was a player who I played against and an extremely top-class player. Playing for him at Everton and also at Manchester City, he was very astute, and above all a great guy. I will always remember that smile when he won his first trophy against Watford at Wembley in 1984. That was the happiest I'd ever seen him. He'd been under so much pressure months earlier, so I guess it was a relief which was evident to see.

'He was a really good manager who was tactically aware. They go on about tactics in the modern game, but Howard was way ahead of his time with tactics. The way he trained players as well. Sports scientists came into football, and rightly so, but Howard was way ahead of the game.

'He was a calm person inside the dressing room, but it takes all sorts. Colin [Harvey] had an aggressive way about him, Howard could get out of bed with you, but in a nice way. He fostered a really good team spirit and don't forget, he came through tough times at Everton which he overcame which shows the steel and the mental strength he had as well.

'His team talks. The one that I always come back to and everyone goes on about is Oxford United in the League Cup, Inchy's goal. For me, it was the FA Cup third round away at Stoke City at the old Victoria Ground. Up to that point, we were going through a really bad spell after the Coventry game on New Year's Eve. Howard opened the slats on the window and you could hear the hordes of Evertonians, and he just said, "Go and win it for them." I think sometimes, the least said the better.

'In the mid-80s he came under immense pressure from the fans, the back-page headlines were far from complimentary. They were tough times which will always affect you, he's human. He tried to shield the players away from it. When there's cushions coming down from the stand and only 10,000 inside the stadium, it's not a nice place to be. From that dark period over the next couple of months we gained some momentum. We had a lot of young players in the dressing room, and it's always difficult when you have young players in there. The young players grew up overnight, Howard was very much a big part of that, or helping them grow up on the football pitch.

'With his players he was very disciplined as any manager would be. Amongst the group you would have an awkward player or two, and there's always personalities. Myself, Andy Gray and Neville Southall were big personalities and you have to handle them. Howard handled a team of personalities into a team ethos really well.

'He of course would let you know if he wasn't happy. I think everyone has a bit of anger in them otherwise you wouldn't be human. Certain things he wouldn't be happy with but being a leader of men sometimes, you've got to keep certain things to yourself which he did well.

'Neville was a very young man when he joined Everton and Howard groomed him into the best goalkeeper in the world. I think Neville was his most influential signing too because of his longevity. You look at teams that win things where goalkeepers are big influences. Sticking it in the net as an outfield player is difficult enough, but if you have a great goalkeeper, you have a great chance of winning things in my opinion.

'He of course had the help of a great backroom staff. No man's an island, you need people around you. It's the whole staff including John Clinkard, Doc [club doctor Ian] Irving, it was the whole ethos of the club.'

Peter of course played under some great managers in his time, but how did Howard compare to them?

'Sir Bobby Robson and Ian Greaves [Bolton] were two outstanding figures. You can take a lot out of good managers, and what I call not so good managers. Howard certainly was up there with the best. Time has proved what a fantastic manager he was – he was successful at other clubs he went to after Everton.

'Football teams need a balance about them. You've got the acquired educated left foot of Kevin Sheedy brought into it. Paul Bracewell, Trevor Steven was outstanding. He took a chance on both me and Andy Gray where he rolled the dice. He also looked at characters which is a tribute to Howard for getting the balance, and the mixture of players which was another one of his strengths.

'He was always at hand should you need advice and pick you up if you were suffering with your confidence. He would give you the time and a chance and tell you that he needed you to deliver. Players have got to handle pressure, and the way that he put you under pressure was very good. He had a gift for doing that. It was pressure but a relaxed pressure.

'The best advice he gave me was when I came back from the World Cup in Mexico and he told me to drink about six crates of Guinness as I had lost a lot of weight.'

Peter later moved into management with his first role as a caretaker manager at Manchester City, being installed as player-manager a week later in November 1990 to succeed Howard Kendall, who had decided to return to Everton. Peter had a seven-year spell in the north-east with Sunderland before taking over as England's under-21 coach. He also had spells elsewhere, but what methods of Howard's management did he find useful?

Peter says, 'I would say a fair amount, certainly the structure of pre-season training, especially having a look at certain things. I was always a people person, as was Howard. I used to go into work with a smile on my face and I don't think there's anything wrong with that, and certainly as a manager I tried to adapt that which was what Howard had.

'It was heartbreaking to hear the news of his passing, and there was no way I was going to miss his funeral. I was very honoured to have paid my own tribute on the day by reading a eulogy.

'I remember meeting all of the lads in the bar of the Holiday Inn on the morning of the funeral. Andy Gray came in and ordered four bottles of Laurent-Perrier champagne. The Gaffer would have wanted us to have a glass.

'The warmth from the city, red and blue, tells you how much he was held in high esteem, which for me says it all.'

DEREK MOUNTFIELD

Debut: Saturday, 23 April 1983, Birmingham City 1 Everton 0
Birmingham City: Blyth, Hagan, Van Den Hauwe, Blake, Dennis, Phillips, Handysides, Halsall, Harford, Gayle (Broadhurst 46), Hopkins
Everton: Arnold, Stevens, Bailey, Ratcliffe, Mountfield, McMahon (Ainscow 46), Sheedy, Richardson, Sharp, Johnson, Heath

DEREK MOUNTFIELD was a product of Tranmere Rovers, guided through by ex-Everton midfielder Bryan Hamilton. A fee of £30,000 was money well spent for both parties involved. Derek, a boyhood Evertonian, became a regular first-teamer and forged a relationship with captain Kevin Ratcliffe. It was no surprise that Derek had the appetite to be a defender with Derby County's Roy McFarland being his football hero.

He became established in the first team in 1983/84, making 47 appearances and scoring three times. His first goal came in February 1984 in a 1-1 draw at West Bromwich Albion.

Derek had a keen eye for the net, registering 14 goals in 58 appearances in all competitions in 1984/85. He was a strong and reliable defender who never once let the team or the fans down. When talking about his favourite goal, he said, 'I know which one the fans would say and that would be the one in the [1985 FA Cup] semi-final against Luton Town. I always say the one in the round before that against

Ipswich Town. We were in front with Sheeds's twice-taken free kick before going 2-1 down and with minutes to go I scored from a right-wing cross from Pat Van Den Hauwe. That was my first goal in front of the Gwladys Street End and kept us in the FA Cup. If that goal hadn't gone in, there would have been no semi-final to talk about.'

Derek came from a household of Blues with his father and grandfather both Evertonians. His grandfather was actually a spectator on the Goodison terraces the day Dixie Dean made history when netting his 60th league goal in that memorable 1927/28 season.

On the subject of memorable goals, 14 from Derek in 1984/85 would have been something any striker would have been proud of, let alone a defender. His headed goal despite sporting a black eye in extra time of the FA Cup semi-final against Luton at Villa Park proved to be the winner, paving the way for the club's second successive final.

He recalled, 'As a fan standing on the terraces, I was only a young lad when Howard was in his pomp at Everton. He was a good footballer with a great first touch who was a good passer of a ball. There is nobody else in the modern game I could compare Howard to as a player.

'Howard gave me the opportunity to play for the club I've supported all of my life. I received a phone call one day whilst at Tranmere Rovers and it was Howard telling me that he wanted to sign me. That was my first contact with him. I will be for ever in his debt for that.

'After spending two and a half years at Tranmere, it was totally different to what I expected. There was more team spirit, bonding, ball work, laughs and jokes.

'Pre-season at Tranmere is a prime example. Pre-season was run, run, run for the first ten days then a football came out. We would also run up and down the sand hills at New Brighton, but at Everton from day one, it was with a ball.

Howard would say that you don't run on a football pitch five miles during the game. You do everything in short, sharp sprints, so all pre-season was done with a ball.

'Howard was ahead of his time in that respect. His team spirit and man-management are something that he thrived on. He got the players working for and with each other and that was one of his biggest strengths.

'In the dressing room he didn't shout and scream like any other managers I've played under. He was calm and composed and yes, he could lose it. When I first got into the side after my first season there, he was struggling slightly as the team weren't playing well. I think Howard's demeanour changed a lot when Colin Harvey got promoted to the first team to work alongside him. Colin took a lot of pressure off Howard. Howard was the man-manager; Colin was the coach.

'As for his team talks, Stoke City away in the FA Cup will always spring to mind. Sometimes, a team talk is not necessary because there might be something that has been quoted in a newspaper about what a manager may have said, and put on a noticeboard and players told to read it. Prior to January 1984, we'd been through a real tough spell for three or four months. We went to Stoke on the Saturday lying 17th in the league, and there must have been eight or nine thousand fans in the crowd singing and singing. Howard opened the window and said, "Do it for those people." I thought of that as a remarkable occasion. I would never have thought of that if ever I was a manager. Four months later, all of those fans are at Wembley singing and dancing after we'd won the FA Cup.

'Howard was always good for keeping the team spirit at its best when things weren't going so well. We may have hit a bad run of form which led to the Chinese meals that he used to take us on, the team get-together on a Tuesday afternoon in Southport. That was another one of his strengths.

'He knew his players so well and would identify when any of his players were feeling a bit low, maybe their confidence was affected, or were feeling the fact they were trying to get back into the first team if they had been dropped. He never really had to pick me up as I was delighted to wear the blue shirt all of the time. If you are injured or out of the first team setup, you do become isolated. That is when you need someone to take you to one side and pick you up.

'If he left you out of the side, sometimes he would tell you in the right way, sometimes in the wrong way. He did it to me on a couple of occasions and it wasn't the words I expected him to use.

'The FA Cup Final at Wembley in 1984 against Watford was a day for everyone associated with the club to remember. Everybody talks about winning the first trophy, and if you look back to 1984 at Wembley when we won the FA Cup, the TV cameras panned down to Howard from the sidelines, he was looking up wearing a huge smile on his face watching his lads collecting the trophy and their medals.'

How would Mountfield describe your relationship with him? 'I had my ups and downs, my arguments and disagreements like anybody else. Nobody should be hunky dory with the manager. I'll never not thank him for signing me for Everton Football Club, but I won't forgive him for some of the things that went on between us which I won't go into.

'Howard did put me on the bench in 1987 for the last game of the season against Tottenham to make sure I got my league medal. Whenever I put the shirt on for him, I never gave less than 100 per cent. I always gave my best whenever he selected me.'

Mountfield had a clear opinion on who he felt was Howard Kendall's best 'signing': 'Colin Harvey. I know he didn't sign him but he promoted him. As a player it could have been Andy Gray, [or] Peter Reid. They both came in towards the end of their careers with injury issues but were magnificent for the club.

'Neville Southall was another masterpiece of a signing who was given a chance and became the best in the world. It could have been Trevor Steven, who was magnificent. It could have been Kevin Sheedy who had a wand of a left foot and proved a lot of people wrong at Liverpool. It could also be Alan Harper, who played in so many positions.

'Howard made so many good signings at that time. If I had to select one, I would say that Andy Gray was the one that turned us around because he was a winner. He won trophies early in his career, and he wanted to be there again, he took Everton to a different dimension for 18 months.

'Howard had a good balance amongst the squad. I've known players to come to the club not for large fees but with high hopes and not perform. They would be moved on very quickly. He gave players opportunities, and he wasn't afraid to tell you to your face if you were struggling, you weren't good enough and you'd be getting dropped. Players come and players go, that's football.

'Howard was a good judge of a player and character. Who could I compare him to with fellow managers? I was at Aston Villa for two years where I had Graham Taylor who was very similar to Howard. He had very similar beliefs as Howard, their philosophies were on a par.

'The news of Howard's passing came as a shock to everybody that was associated with him. I was unfortunately away on the day of the funeral; I had already booked a holiday in Spain. I do remember sitting on the beach at Punta Prima in Spain as the sun went down with a bottle of beer in my hand taking a picture which I put on Instagram and a quote of, "One more for the Gaffer."

Derek's dream before football was to be a Formula One driver. He certainly made the right choice as a footballer and steered the Blues to success.

ALAN HARPER

Debut: Saturday, 27 August 1983, Everton 1 Stoke City 0

Everton: Arnold, Harper, Bailey, Mountfield, Higgins, Richardson, Steven, Heath, Sharp, King, Sheedy

Stoke City: Fox, N. Chamberlain, Savage, James, Dyson, Bould, Painter, Griffiths (McIlroy 73), O'Callaghan, Thomas, Maguire

ALAN HARPER was born in Liverpool, growing up in the Netherley area of the city. He belonged to a household of Liverpudlians. He went to Gateacre comprehensive school, joining Liverpool, who were the only club showing an interest after he finished his studies in 1977. He played for Liverpool Schoolboys, winning the English Schools Trophy in 1976.

Howard Kendall plucked Alan from Liverpool's reserves in the summer of 1983 after he had failed to make a first-team appearance for his boyhood club. Alan was disheartened watching some of his team-mates make the breakthrough from the Central League at Anfield where he'd collected four Central League championship medals. A new three-year contract was offered to Alan, which he declined. An increase in salary couldn't whet his appetite, but things changed for him when he received a phone call from Colin Harvey telling him of Everton's interest. He arranged to meet Howard the following day and agreed to sign for less money than he was on at Liverpool.

Alan was a 'jack of all trades' and his versatility to settle into any position in the team, when required, was invaluable. I think he filled in every position apart from standing in between the goalposts.

While at Liverpool his preferred position was midfield, but in his last year with Roy Evans' reserve team he was given the opportunity to play at right-back, which eventually became his regular place.

'Bertie', as he was known to his team-mates, was a very valuable squad member whose contribution played a key part in Everton's 80s success. Alan was constantly in the manager's mind. He was a substitute in both League Cup final matches against Liverpool in 1984, replacing Kevin Sheedy for the last 25 minutes of normal time and extra time at Wembley, and deputising for Sheedy in the replay four days later at Maine Road.

He went into the last month of 1984/85 holding the tag of the 'lucky mascot' as he hadn't featured on the losing side in the first team that season.

An interesting point I'd like to add: Alan was the first player to cross the park with his fee settled by a tribunal.

Alan made the first of his 198 appearances at right-back against Richie Barker's Stoke City side in August 1983. That season saw Alan appear 33 times in all competitions for the Blues. Ironically, his solitary goal in 1983/84 came against his childhood team with an equaliser five minutes from the end against the Reds. At this point, Alan's allegiances were totally committed to the blue corner.

Alan scored a memorable goal at a rain-soaked Stamford Bridge in March 1987. Kerry Dixon had just drawn Chelsea level on 72 minutes when Harper took a pass from Peter Reid, and from 35 yards out on 77 minutes he smashed the ball high into the net, giving Tony Godden in the home goal no hope. That strike and win took Everton to the top of the league, where they remained, and they won the title on the May bank holiday Monday at Norwich City.

Alan says of Kendall, 'Under Howard, they were good times. It was enjoyable to play in the games under him. Everyone enjoyed working with him. Everybody was relaxed, but you had to be on top of your game. We worked hard under him, and had a good time when we were off. That was the way Howard and his assistant Colin worked.

'He was a manager, but a coach on a Saturday with team tactics and things like that, but during the week, he liked to join in with everything. If you remember, he was still a relatively young man. When Howard and Colin joined in with training sessions, they showed you how good they still were.

'Colin did most of the midweek coaching, Howard did more on a Friday and Saturday where he selected his starting 11 and also tactics.

'If we went in after a game at the weekend and hadn't won, he'd question why we hadn't won, where we had the week before. I went in moaning, and the following week I came out as if I'd played for England. He could make you feel that good. That for me is a good man-manager where he could organise the squad, but to be fair, he knew how to handle everyone. That for me was a good thing.

'At the training ground he was good fun. He was cheerful every morning, but could be hard as well if things weren't going right which is what you'd expect. Monday morning sessions were relaxed, but Tuesday, Wednesday and Thursday it was harder work. The day before the game it was more relaxed again.

'He enjoyed being around the lads and I would say that was when Howard was at his happiest. He loved being around his players, enjoying the banter. He and

Colin would both join in the training sessions. If you saw the things they did in training when they were in their 40s, it made you wonder what they were like in their younger days.

'If there was one thing that he detested, that was lateness. If you were late for training or a team meeting you would be fined and the money would go into a pot with fines collected from other squad players which would pay for a Chinese meal when the lads went out.

'In the dressing room on a matchday, Howard was never a person that was ever angry with his players. I've been in dressing rooms with other clubs I've played for where managers have been raging. Howard would have a go, but in a tactful way. He didn't have to rant and rave to make a point.

'The team always had an end-of-season tour which Howard and the players loved. He really enjoyed that. Magaluf was a place he enjoyed. We would always have a drink with him and he would relax around his players.

'On a personal note, I had a very good relationship with him. I thought I did. He bought me three times which says something. He bought me from Liverpool. He then took me from Sheffield United to Manchester City, then from Manchester City to Everton. I think with Howard, he knew what he was getting with the same thing applying to me.

Silverware crossed Alan's palms with two league championship medals, European Cup winners' Cup success and Charity Shield honours completing the set before departing Goodison 12 months after Kendall's decision to join Athletic Bilbao.

Alan played for several managers in his career after leaving, including joining Howard Wilkinson at Sheffield Wednesday. He recalls, 'Compared to other managers, he [Kendall] was different because he was a good man-manager. I worked with Howard Wilkinson at Sheffield Wednesday. I didn't like the way he did things, but he changed things. He also changed things when he went to Leeds United too.

'I also worked with David Pleat at Luton Town who was a good tactician. Howard Kendall was different, he had people around him that did all that for him. He understood the players he worked with, but they all have their own methods, don't they?'

Kendall returned to English soil from northern Spain to take over at Manchester City in December 1989 after two and a half years in the Basque country. Alan once again teamed up with him.

Almost 12 months later, Howard was back at his spiritual home where Harper again linked up with the legend in the summer of 1991. Unfortunately, their previous success at Everton was not to be repeated.

Alan tried to think about players who reminded him of Howard, 'There would be a bit of Reidy certainly for his determination. Trevor Steven was another for the way that he could do things. Brace as well for his good football and being mentally strong.'

Like many, Alan was shocked by the passing of Howard and spoke about the day of the funeral, 'Howard's funeral was a day to remember. I remember all of the lads turning up and thinking, WOW, what a turnout. I knew there would be anyway, the lads worshipped him. I was with Kevin Ratcliffe, and met up with the other lads afterwards. We all agreed that it would be the wrong thing to go home, so we all went for a drink. Howard would have wanted us to do that and not to be sad.'

Alan never lost his love for Everton where he returned to coach the youth team from 2000 to 2005. Two years later, he started to scout with Colin Harvey for Bolton Wanderers. His other scouting roles have been with Liverpool, West Ham and QPR.

TREVOR STEVEN

Debut: Saturday, 27 August 1983, Everton 1 Stoke City 0

Everton: Arnold, Harper, Bailey, Mountfield, Higgins, Richardson, Steven, Heath, Sharp, King, Sheedy

Stoke City: Fox, N. Chamberlain, Savage, James, Dyson, Bould, Painter, Griffiths (McIlroy 73), O'Callaghan Thomas, Maguire

HOWARD KENDALL was adamant that Trevor Steven was going to be a very important piece of a jigsaw that would bring success to Goodison. Before Trevor moved to the Lancashire town of Burnley, he accrued seven England schoolboy caps alongside future Evertonian Paul Rideout. Mark Walters, who also went on to play at the top with several clubs, was in the same team. Trevor joined the Toffees in 1983 from Burnley where he'd learned his apprenticeship, but he found the early stages of his Goodison career unsettling.

In his first season wearing the royal blue shirt he made 23 league appearances, finding the net only once, in mid-April against an already relegated Wolves team.

As time progressed, Trevor's skill and trickery were warming the hearts of the Everton faithful who surrounded the terraces of the stadium where he earned the nickname 'Tricky' which has stuck to this very day. The Everton midfield at that time was drawing comparisons to the Holy Trinity of the late 60s.

Incidentally, Trevor's desire was to be a draughtsman had he not made a career in football. I'm sure I speak for everyone when I say – aren't we glad he did?

Speaking about his debut and early Everton days, Steven said, 'As far as the game was concerned, it was a whole new experience, a whole new pressure. The fans wanted a lot from me, but I think it was a bit too much for me to take on as a 19-year-old. I have to say that I struggled to make any impact in the early stages. Howard then left me out after about ten games, the team weren't doing well, I wasn't doing well, and as people know, it was a difficult period.

'I eventually got back in when Howard decided it was the right time as he was very good to me. He told me that I was going to be a very big part of the squad, and he took very good care of me at that time which Howard was very good at.'

Steven continued to talk about the legendary manager, 'I think of Howard as a confident man, someone who always had a smile on his face. When he wasn't happy you knew it. He was a bubbly character who loved a laugh and a joke with the players, something that you don't see in the modern game.

'He was a great footballer with a fantastic vision in him, wanting his team to have that. When he bought me, he saw me as an Everton-style player. He knew what he was looking for to get the team that he wanted. How he built a team with players from different areas and different clubs who were different ages and different qualities. That was magic for him to do that, and also, he made a lot of errors prior to that, but he learned from that. Eventually, he did get it right in the end and with style.

'He was terrific at man-management and helped me immensely when I arrived at Everton because I joined as Steve McMahon left. I was less experienced than Steve, and was different, but I was going to make a difference for Everton. I was 19 when I joined and came from a club that fought relegation and were relegated. Although we did well in cup competitions at Burnley, we struggled in the league to put any decent runs together.

'Going to Everton was a massive lift for me and my confidence and something I had to adapt to psychologically. Going to Everton from Burnley with the reputation of the club and the players they had there, plus the expectancy of the supporters.

'The first few months at Everton were a real struggle for me. On that basis, Howard took me out of the team as he felt we weren't playing well with a lot of pressure on me, and I had to try and get at being solid and watch which is what I did for a bit. It was only a matter of months where I had to wait my turn which feels longer when you're not playing, but I learned a lot. I learned a lot about myself during that period.

'So Howard gave me that guidance knowing how to help me survive a setback early in my Everton career.

'On the training ground Howard wanted to train every day. He expected 100 per cent commitment from everybody. His sessions, 99 per cent of the time, included a football.

'When I was at Burnley, our preparations in pre-season involved a lot of running, a lot of fitness. We did it in different ways with Howard. A lot of small-sided games, head tennis, full-sided games where it entailed breaking things down. Colin Harvey joined up with the first team and settled very quickly. Howard just demanded performance, nothing more, which is what he got. You are only as good on a Saturday as how you are in training. It's an exercise that you have to repeat.

'As far as the games were concerned, it was first and foremost about atmosphere, spirit, the music on the bus, the joking and the mickey-taking out of one another. Howard loved the lads having a laugh. Howard was there to win football matches and bring back the glory days which is what drove him.

'It wasn't something that overpowered him or got him down. He was always on the front foot and bubbly. He was a great communicator and in the dressing room he would speak to the group clearly. He would also talk to individuals, but would walk from one to another. He was like a bee going from one flower to the next. His organisation was excellent which I think was driven by Colin as he worked on set pieces.

'Howard was the ideal person to play for and I believed in him. If he selected you, you knew that you were doing good. The spell Everton endured where there was a lot of pressure on him and the chairman for changes; Howard grew a moustache which is always a bad sign in a moment of crisis. The players could not avoid what was happening because the fans were vocal. The fans were very much united with wanting Howard and Philip Carter out as they refused to attend games as things were bleak. It was a period of about four to six weeks where the situation got intense and the Evertonians lost faith in him.

'What the fans were seeing was a very disjointed, underperforming team. They needed to settle down and scrape some victories, and get a draw here and there. How we came out of it was full credit to Howard. There was no way that group of players would have survived if they weren't steered properly. Howard managed to keep hold of the reins and kept the bottle to play. All the team had to do was gather some momentum by playing much better to take the pressure off Howard. That is what materialised and things got better and grew as the season went on.

'Howard had to deliver success and eventually did that. What a season, going from that extreme to winning an FA Cup. Things then went to the next level as the confidence grew which became a long distant memory by the following January and February.

'Howard left me out of the side that played in their first major final since 1977. It was a huge disappointment for me to be left out of the team that played in the first Merseyside cup final at Wembley in 1984. I thought I had a chance of playing and didn't, not even on the bench. It was tough. I had to get over it, what else could I do? I had to try harder. Alan Irvine was doing well in the team at that time, so I had to bide my time. Yes, I was disappointed, but that's life.

'Talking of disappointments, not playing in Europe was the biggest disappointment, and not only that, in 1986 we should have won the double. We should have done it but we didn't.

'Colin was a key element in our success. Colin and Howard never trod on each other's territory. They had their own responsibilities and Colin was a stickler for detail, more than what Howard was, but Howard would not want to take that role. Colin would never hesitate to pull anyone up for anything.

'Colin, unlike Howard, wasn't a bubbly character, he was dogged which is what you need, and a mix is something that is required. You cannot have two or three people that do exactly the same thing. The backroom staff were a good team, with Mick Heaton in a supporting role, even down to the likes of Terry Darracott who joined the coaching staff after Howard had left and was replaced by Colin. These guys were the nuts and bolts that were driven by Howard and arranged by Colin.

'Howard was a great player in his day, and had that ability even in training sessions. He had self-belief, and he was challenged in the first few months of the 1983/84 season. He withstood that and was consistent through it. He never said "I'm going to try something completely different". The only change he ever made was bringing Colin in which gave a bit more of an edge to training, but the environment was still the same.

'Howard was likeable. The players wanted to do well for him. When we started, we were all over the place a little bit. Even the likes of Adrian Heath were still settling in and he had been there a while. Players were also coming through at the right age. Kevin Richardson was becoming a serious pro, and the players that we brought in from elsewhere all came to fruition at the right time, then it had to be led.

'Howard had his finger on everything. If players were injured, he wouldn't give you much time. He would check up on you, but that was about it. You were under the command of John Clinkard, but depending on the situation, Howard would have a brief chat with you, but generally, he would be getting on with things he had to do with the first team.

'I remember the day he asked me if I would take penalties. I think everybody was having a go but was missing. We were in the shower one day when he asked me, and this goes to show you what esteem I held him in. No matter what he would have asked me, I would have said yes.

'I had never taken a penalty since I was a schoolboy. Without hesitating I said yes. He would only ask you if he believed it was something you could do. That was part of his knowledge of understanding players' strengths and the kind of team he wants them to play in.

'It was a bonus when success finally rewarded him, his staff, also his players. Winning the FA Cup in May 1984 gave Howard the most pleasure because it was the first of many. I think he knew that if he could get the first one, there would be more to come. We turned such a corner and momentum was gained. The players were coming through who he could rely on and trust. There was no reason for us to be not thinking of ourselves as winners all of a sudden.

'No trophy at the club had been won since he last won one as a player; he joined the dots which was special for him. That doesn't mean to say that winning the league title the following season wasn't an out-of-this-world feeling for all of us, also for him. We had become winners by that point, with a different mentality, and grew again, but the springboard of that was winning the FA Cup in 1984.

'I know Howard had problems prior to his team coming together, and he was the one responsible for putting these players together. His vision of what was needed to be successful, to be a top team, and a top winning team which was a completely different thing, that's the ingredients of what made him a successful manager.'

Trevor was a craftsman when it came to scoring goals. But which was his favourite one? 'The one I scored against Bayern Munich at Goodison is the one that stands out. It was the importance of the goal as well as we were leading 2-1 and if Bayern would have scored, they would have gone through on the away goals rule. So, mine finished off the game, and to score in a game which is remembered by all Evertonians and the players that played that night will tell you that was the biggest game that we played in.'

Speaking about players he could compare to Howard Kendall, Steven said, 'I often think about players in the modern game that reminded me of Howard as a player. What I saw in Howard was a great first touch, good body strength because he wasn't big. He was quick over 10 to 15 metres. He was a great passer of the ball. Howard had a bit of everything including aggression. He had all of the big assets that you would want from a really great midfield player. He had energy, box to box as it was in those days. He had intelligence and was good at reading the game.

'Don't forget, when he was at his peak, England had Bobby Charlton playing, so the competition was tough. Howard was an all-round player. There are great players in great teams.

'Howard was a bit of Roy Keane, a bit of a Paul Scholes, who also played with style. You would have to take a bit of several players to get a Howard, but they would all be top players.

'Howard was shrewd in the transfer market. When I think back, Andy Gray was his best signing. Every one of Howard's signings was a great signing. [Gray was] the one that gave us identity, certainly gave us aggression, or added aggression. Andy had shown his capability at that level previously. He may not have been that influential prior to his Everton move due to injuries, but without a shadow of doubt, Andy Gray was the most influential.'

Steven said his most remembered team talk would have to be at half-time at home to Bayern Munich. 'It was an obvious choice because it was a simple message. When we came into the dressing room at half-time Howard was positive. "We just need something," he said. His last words before we returned on to the pitch were, "The Gwladys Street will suck the ball into the net."

'Giving advice was also reassuring. The best advice he gave me was to be patient. When he wanted to take me out of the team he said, "Don't think I'm taking you out of the team because you can't do this because you can, but what you're surrounded with at the minute is not good for you, and you can't help the team as the team can't help itself at the moment."

'Two days later, I played in the reserves against Bolton Wanderers at Goodison. We won 2-0 and I scored both goals. I put my trust in him that he had a plan for me, and not once did I ever go and knock on his door. I never once questioned him for leaving me out. I could have spoken to him after that reserve game and demanded that he played me on the Saturday in the first team but never did. I trained with the first team at a really high level but never questioned me being left out until he said to me, "You're back." That was his management on a personal level for me.'

Did Howard ever talk about Heysel?

'Not really. We had to accept it; I don't think anyone expected the ban to be for as long as it was. I thought the ban may have been in for one season, if that. When it was announced that it was going to be for an indefinite period, we couldn't believe that we as a team would suffer because of something that went wrong with other supporters in another country thousands of miles away from us. The ban was like a punishment to warn everybody else.'

After Everton had clinched their second league title in three years, Howard was about to announce the news that shocked everybody associated with the club.

Steven said, 'Howard's departure came as a shock when he went to Spain. After the season had ended in 1987, we went on to Hawaii, New Zealand and Australia. I never heard anything myself on that trip about Howard leaving Everton. I never saw Howard again until we went over to play Athletic Bilbao in a friendly.

'Howard's passing was sad and unexpected. I was unable to get to his funeral as I was in the Middle East and was contracted to work for six days. It was the worst feeling knowing I was unable to go.'

At the time of writing, Trevor was still involved in football as a media pundit.

ANDY GRAY

Debut: Saturday, 12 November 1983, Everton 1 Nottingham Forest 0

Everton: Southall, Harper, Bailey, Ratcliffe, Higgins, Reid, Irvine, Heath, Gray, King, Sheedy

Nottingham Forest: Sutton, Anderson, Swain, Todd, Fairclough, Bowyer, Wigley, Davenport, Birtles, Thijssen (Walsh 55), Hodge

NO OTHER manager would have taken a gamble on signing Andy Gray from Wolves with his history of injuries, but Howard Kendall did, and what a signing he proved to be. His experience and knowledge of the game was taken into the dressing room and rubbed off on some of the younger players as confidence grew and performances blossomed.

Andy's injuries were self-inflicted as he was always one to throw himself into every challenge, or dive at the feet of defenders to head a ball. His bravery was second to none and he was often described as a 'warrior'.

He gave his thoughts on Howard, 'When I think of Howard, I think of a terrific footballer first and foremost. I remember him in that famous trio of midfield players – Harvey, Kendall, Ball. I played against Howard when he was at Birmingham City, and I remember him as a terrific footballer. Everybody knows what a great player Howard was during his time at Everton. To find someone similar, it would be like Reidy and Paul Bracewell, those type of players. Those were the type of players Howard would build his team around. If I had to select a player similar to Howard, I would have to say Reidy.

'As a coach and a man, he was a person who, even if I had never worked for him, he's a person that you would want to spend time with. He was lovely company; bubbly, vibrant, he always had a story or two to tell, he loved the company of the players, and loved nothing more than having a couple of beers with the boys, talking and having a laugh. But there was a very serious side to him as a coach which drove him to what he achieved at Goodison. There was a seriousness about him where you knew there was a time and a place for enjoyment, but when we work, we work, and show that we want to be the best we can be, and I think he epitomised all of that.

'His style of management was a man-manager. He was terrific at keeping players happy. For example, players like Alan Harper and Kevin Richardson, who were too good to be sat on the bench every week. Howard was good at doing that and was a fantastic man-manager. Tactically he knew what he was doing as he knew the game, but there were a lot of tweaks that Colin did. They were a good team together.

'Howard was the man-manager, the motivator, a great one at that, terrific in the dressing room when he had to be. He was not a master tactician.

'His backroom staff were a huge influence on Howard's success as a manager. Mick Heaton and Colin Harvey were very different. Colin was very much into the tactical side of the game, almost on a daily basis taking you up individually into the coaches' room where they would put a video tape on of a game to show you things to improve on from the previous game. Colin would sit and talk and tell you what he wanted you to do. Colin thought deeply about the game. The promotion of Colin to the first team was pivotal to the upsurge of our form and the way we played.

'Mick Heaton, he was always Howard's big pal, a real important factor, but as a trio, they were a really good mix.

'Howard was an easy-going character who would be at his happiest winning football matches. I always thought that when the season was finished, and we went away on an end-of-season tour, he was happy being around his players. He loved sitting around a table relaxed and comfortable with a couple of beers talking football. That to me was Howard at his happiest.

'I can't recall ever seeing him angry. What would have made him angry would be players not prepared to do what they were capable of doing. When he thought anyone was underachieving, knowing that they were better than that probably upset him. I don't ever recall Howard raising his voice in the dressing room. If he was annoyed, he would make his feelings known in a calm way. He was never one to throw tea cups or slag anybody off or shout at people. He was always in control of the dressing room area.

'My favourite memory of the man was when he was switched off from the game. We would be on the end-of-season tour somewhere chewing the fat over a beer. As Reidy and I were more experienced, the younger lads never really got involved, but we would sit around a pool having a couple of beers.

'Howard was great with all of his players and anybody who might be a handful, but not in a disrespectful way. If any players were difficult, they wouldn't be there for long. We signed Pat Van Den Hauwe with a big reputation as a bit of a bad boy.

'Howard settled him in, becoming part of the group which Pat loved. He wasn't called "Psycho" for no good reason. Howard tapped into that angry side of him which became a positive, not a negative.

'I recall the first time that he left me out was away to Gillingham in the first FA Cup replay. I had never been left out before other than being injured, but when I was ready to play, and I thought I would play, I didn't play. He told me before he named the team on a one to one. He would give his reason as to why you would be left out. Of course, I was gutted, but what can you say? You don't want to upset the apple cart. You don't start throwing a tantrum a couple of hours before a massive cup tie, and as chance had it, we drew that game, I played well in the next replay, and Howard never had a cause to leave me out after that.

'Howard had to do that a lot with a lot of good players. He was always willing to give you advice. The best advice he gave me? Sign here son!

'I always remember in the dressing room a very famous team talk at home to Bayern Munich in the second leg of the European Cup Winners' Cup. As it happened, we went one down at half-time and we had played well. Howard at half-time was brilliant, he told us not to panic, told us to be calm. We were then to be kicking into the Gwladys Street, and Howard told us not to worry as the punters would suck the ball into the net, we will get a goal and go on to win which we did 3-1, and I was fortunate to be involved in all of the goals, creating two and scoring the other one, so for me it was an unbelievable night and for all Evertonians to achieve that first European final. To be part of the team that did that was just sensational. But we still had to go on and win it, and win it we did.'

Andy had played for nine clubs in his career including two spells at Aston Villa playing under some great managers. How did Howard compare with them?

'He's obviously up there with some great managers I'd played under. I was lucky that I played for my first manager, Jim McLean at Dundee United. Jim was not a man-manager; he was a tactician. He was purely all about tactics and teaching people and was great in that respect.

'I played for Ron Atkinson who was fantastic and the way he went about his management.

'Howard was the best. You don't achieve what he achieved and put together the team he put together. It's not all luck. Howard's record was success after success. He would be top with the rest behind him.

'His signings were a key part of his success. In those days, there were some amazing players that went on to achieve so much. When Howard brought in myself and Reidy, it was absolutely key to how the team went and how it progressed. I think without Peter and myself, I'm not sure whether the team would have gone on to achieve what they did. Reidy and I were of a similar age with similar experiences. We both had to cope with injuries throughout our careers; people were thinking that our best days were behind us. We were determined to prove everybody wrong and prove Howard right. So, Reidy has to be up there as does Neville Southall. Nev was an amazing signing for what Howard paid for him and for what he became, the best in the world. It was so important to know that you had the big man behind you when we were playing in every game which was reassuring.

'The news of Howard's passing was a shock to say the least. I remember going to his funeral and was overcome with the outpouring of love for Howard. It was an amazing turnout. The warmth that was spoken about him. Legendary football people turning up in their droves to pay tribute and their respects to Howard. It was an occasion befitting for what he achieved as an Everton coach.'

DARREN HUGHES

Debut: Tuesday, 27 December 1983, Wolverhampton Wanderers 3 Everton 0

Wolverhampton Wanderers: Burridge, Humphrey, Palmer, Blair, Pender, Dodd, Towner, Clarke, Troughton, Eves, Crainie

Everton: Southall, Stevens, Hughes, Ratcliffe, Mountfield, Reid, Irvine, Richardson, Gray, Rimmer, Sheedy (Steven 75)

DARREN HUGHES, nicknamed 'Yosser', always found his position to be a comfortable one, playing as a midfielder in his days as a youngster with Cheshire Boys. He was later asked to adopt the left-back role for Everton in an FA Youth Cup semi-final in 1983 at Sheffield Wednesday and from that day forward, that position became permanent.

He was serving his apprenticeship when the club were on the verge of great things. It must have been a great experience to be surrounded with the class of players who were around, to watch and learn from, and also to seek advice.

Darren had a taste of the sweet and sour of football, playing in the FA Youth Cup Final in 1983 to be on the losing side against Norwich City, but 12 months later won the competition against Stoke City, scoring what proved to be the winner with a screamer from 25 yards.

However, his opportunities were limited, and he appeared 11 times in the reserve league, scoring once. His minimal reserve outings were nothing to do with his ability;

a pelvic injury sustained at the end of the previous campaign held him back, and he made three first-team appearances in total, including the last two league games of the 1984/85 title-winning campaign. During that season he said, 'I'd love to stay at Everton even though I know it will be harder to break through now that the first team is at the top of the league.'

He was given a free transfer to Shrewsbury Town in the summer of 1985 and later had a steady career in the Football League including a good spell at Port Vale from 1987 to 1994.

Darren spoke about working with Howard Kendall, 'I was surprised how good he was at still playing football when I came to the club as an apprentice. He and his backroom staff were massively competitive when it came to anything in training which involved winning such as five-a-side and head tennis. Howard was never on the losing side but he cheated just a little [laughing].

'He was very strict with us [apprentices]. The regular first-teamers, he was as close as a clot without that exuberance.

'All of his staff had a role which they performed well. Mick Heaton used to do a lot of one on ones with me. Howard was quite hard because I think he could see my potential. We were in the FA Youth Cup Final two years running and even [youth team coach] Graham Smith was close to Howard too.

'Colin was in charge of the reserves and we seemed to go on an unbeaten run for ever and a day. Colin's promotion to the first team obviously influenced Howard by bringing some of the players through the reserves, who went on to be regular members of the first team.

'I was a young kid and obviously at that age I have to say I was quite scared of him [Kendall]. I could never relax around him because I was too young. I never really spoke with him all that much to be honest. I wasn't involved with the first team that much. I would travel to away games with them to get the feeling of being involved and experience what it was like. They were of course the days when only one substitute was required.

'Howard always gave good advice on the training pitch. I have never come across anybody that bettered what they did on a training field.

'Howard's standards were very high and demanding, in line with what the club motto stood for. He would lose his temper with any sloppiness. He couldn't and wouldn't tolerate it. He would scream out at anybody who placed a sloppy pass, or if anything wasn't done with the right intention. He liked everything to be as perfect as possible.'

Howard's hard work and perseverance paid off and brought Everton on a par with neighbours Liverpool, who had enjoyed success for most of the previous decade.

Darren says, 'I don't think anything gave Howard as much pleasure as winning the league which meant they were the best, and also beating their rivals at their own game. Out of all the silverware he brought to the club, it has to be the league that satisfied him most of all. Everton beat Liverpool at their own game.'

At the time of writing, Darren is involved in a painting company in the north-west.

ROB WAKENSHAW

Debut: Saturday, 5 May 1984, Everton 1 Manchester United 1

Everton: Southall, Stevens, Bailey, Harper, Mountfield, Reid, Wakenshaw (Bishop 75), King, Sharp, Steven, Richardson

Manchester United: Bailey, Duxbury, Albiston, Wilkins, Moran, Hogg, Robson, Moses, Stapleton, Hughes, Davies (Whiteside 63)

ROB ORIGINATES from Ashington, well known for being the home of the Charlton brothers, Bobby and Jack. Rob, like many a young lad from that area, wanted to be a footballer as a youngster. The Geordie boy chose Everton, rejecting interest from the two north London giants, Tottenham and Arsenal.

Learning his trade for the youth team, Rob played in midfield, a position he disliked, with Stuart Rimmer and Mark Farrington playing in the forward roles, but he was happy to be involved.

Rob's performances and indeed goals for the youth team, and later the reserves, caught the eye of his manager who had faith in the youngster, by throwing him in at the deep end into the first team that Howard Kendall was building. His debut against the Red Devils from the opposite end of the East Lancashire Road was nothing short of a memorable one, opening his account by scoring on the hour only to be denied the glory as Frank Stapleton equalised 14 minutes later and the match ended all square. He was replaced by another youngster that afternoon, Ian Bishop, who saw out the last quarter of the game. It was a debut that can only be likened to a *Roy of the Rovers* comic strip, and Rob was still involved the following season and made a small number of appearances as Everton lifted further silverware.

At the end of the 1983/84 season he was awarded a winners' medal in the FA Youth Cup after the victory against Stoke City in the final, also having the honour of being top scorer in the competition. Finally, he furthered his experience by playing in New Zealand in a short summer season for Hamilton Wanderers.

He also appeared as a substitute in the European Cup Winners' Cup, replacing Adrian Heath against UCD in the second leg of the first round at Goodison, with a further European appearance at Fortuna Sittard in the second leg of the quarter-final in March 1985.

Once the league and European Cup Winners' Cup were put to bed, another substitute appearance came in a victory over rivals Liverpool, replacing Ian Atkins minutes after the half-time interval, as the Blues did their first league double over their neighbours for the first time since 1964/65.

Rob was hungry to play first-team football and was later to find more opportunities outside of the top flight.

He said, 'Howard was a very approachable guy; as a first-team player you could do what you wanted within reason. The lads were able to go out and let their hair down, but as long as you would perform at the weekend, he was happy with that.

'He gave me my debut which I will always be grateful for. I wished I had more of a chance but was probably at the right club at the wrong time.

'Howard was one of the boys. He had a good group of lads who did the business for their manager. Results and trophies speak for themselves, don't they?

'A lot of the success was down to the backroom staff too. Mick Heaton was someone that Howard brought with him, who was a nice fella and a character. Also, we had Colin, Clinks [John Clinkard] as physio. Colin and Howard played together and respected each other. All I can say about the backroom staff, including the doctor by the way, they all wanted success.

'The training was always fun. You looked forward to it each day. We used to have practice matches and I was up against Kingy [Andy King] who would kick seven bells out of me and we would end up in a rumpus. The next day he would come in with a collar on his neck and Howard looked at me with this stare of I was in trouble. He summoned me up to his office after training.

'I went up to his office fearing the outcome that I'd injured one of his star players. Howard looked at me, saying, "Do you see what you did yesterday? Never change that, it doesn't matter who you're playing against. I admired you for standing up to him. That's what I want you to do every week." I did it to him once in training but he didn't like it!

'My biggest disappointment with Howard was not giving me more games. Right place, wrong time for me, as we had a fabulous team and I had massive respect for them. If what happened in Heysel never happened, who knows how far we would have gone?'

On Howard's best signing, Rob said, 'There was some competition for places at the time I was trying to break through. Howard brought some quality players into the club who made a difference. Inchy [Adrian Heath] was great, but things started to catch fire when Andy Gray arrived on the scene. Reidy was also a great signing but I'm going for Andy Gray because I felt as though he lit the torch where success started. Andy was also a massive influence on Sharpy too.

'Howard liked his players together as a group. I remember once we went to Crans-Montana [in Switzerland] where we played FC Sion. It was a testimonial and it was a blank weekend where we had no league fixture. Johnny Morrissey was included in the squad too. Howard had the group of lads together after the game with a meal and drinks, and it seemed to relax the players having the whole group together. I think Howard liked the idea of the sessions as it seemed to be a regular feature.

'He was always a man that would happily give advice, no matter how big or small. The best advice he gave to me was, if I was selected, he would always say to me, you're going to score. When I made my debut, they were the words he used which encouraged me. I did score which was gratitude from myself to him for giving me the encouragement.

'He repeated that when I played for Everton in the FA Youth Cup finals. He instilled the confidence in me with those encouraging words.'

Rob represented England in the FIFA World Youth Championship in the Soviet Union in 1985. They were in Group D with Mexico, China and Paraguay; Rob actually scored his country's first goal against Paraguay in a 2-2 draw in Baku in front of a 40,000-plus crowd. This was the only point England won in the group and they finished joint-bottom with Paraguay.

Rob was without doubt a goalscorer. In the 1984/85 season, while playing for the second string in the Central League, he netted 26 goals which was the most scored at that level since the Second World War.

After three league appearances Rob departed Goodison in the summer of 1985 and joined Carlisle United. He continued to pursue his career in the lower reaches of the Football League until taking to the non-league scene in 1988.

IAN BISHOP

Debut: Saturday, 5 May 1984, Everton 1 Manchester United 1

Everton: Southall, Stevens, Bailey, Harper, Mountfield, Reid, King, Wakenshaw (Bishop 75), Sharp, Steven, Richardson

Manchester United: Bailey, Duxbury, Albiston, Wilkins, Moran, Hogg, Robson, Moses, Stapleton, Hughes, Davies (Whiteside 63)

IAN WAS a local boy coming from the Cantril Farm area of the city. An Arsenal fan as a youngster, he declined an opportunity to sign for Liverpool, choosing Everton instead. He put pen to paper as a schoolboy in July 1981 after being spotted by a scout called Les McGrail.

In the 1982/83 season, Bishop was a regular in the youth side. He played 21 games that season, finding the net ten times, a good tally for a midfielder. He also made the reserves, feeling very comfortable in that side too. He was no stranger to applying himself in the Lancashire League where he netted a total of 11 goals over the season with seven in the last four games which wasn't a bad return considering his overall tally was two fewer than top scorer Rob Wakenshaw.

After his one and only senior appearance he moved down the divisions to Crewe, playing four games in a loan spell. He found himself in new surroundings with a permanent move to Carlisle United.

Bishop said, 'When Howard came and signed a bundle of players, it meant my path was blocked, despite me having nine months of my contract left. We only signed one-year deals then and Howard pulled me in and told me Carlisle wanted to buy me, and left the decision to me.

'He told me that I could stay, see out my contract and get released, but at that time I was probably 12th in line for a first-team place.

'I asked Howard for his advice and he told me that I was best going to Carlisle. Maybe the fact he included a sell-on clause meant he rated me, but maybe I wasn't quite ready for Everton just then.'

However, Bishop did find himself crossing paths with Howard Kendall again after his short reign in Bilbao ended with a return to the north-west of England and Manchester City. He was a huge crowd favourite of the Kippax followers, then experienced being shown the door by Kendall for a second time. Weeks later, the Maine Road fans held banners aloft showing their disapproval to the board who were letting their better players go.

Bishop was very well regarded as a player for the future while serving his apprenticeship. He was tipped by Gary Stevens, Stuart Rimmer, Kevin Richardson, Alan Irvine and Alan Harper, to name a few, and they were right, as he went on to have a long spell with West Ham United in the Premier League before returning to Manchester City in the late 1990s.

Howard Kendall (1946–2015), manager of Everton at Wembley Stadium in London on the day of the FA Cup Final, 19 May 1984. Everton beat Watford 2-0.

The Everton team pose with the trophy after beating Watford 2-0 in the FA Cup Final at Wembley Stadium, 19 May 1984. Back row (left-right): Derek Mountfield, John Bailey, Peter Reid, Alan Harper, Andy Gray. Front row: Trevor Steven, Kevin Richardson, Neville Southall, Kevin Ratcliffe, Graeme Sharp, Adrian Heath and Gary Stevens.

19 May 1984. FA Cup Final at Wembley. Everton 2 v Watford 0. Everton captain Kevin Ratcliffe holds aloft the FA Cup.

Defender Derek Mountfield holding the FA Charity Shield after their 1-0 victory over Liverpool at Wembley Stadium, 18 August 1984.

Howard Kendall in the stands at Goodison Park in Liverpool, Lancashire, UK, on Thursday, November 15, 1984.

(Left) Everton manager Howard Kendall pictured smiling in the dressing room with the Canon League trophy after Everton had won the First Division championship for the 1984/85 season after the home match against West Ham United. (Right): The team celebrate their 2-0 victory over Queens Park Rangers at Goodison Park that clinched the First Division title, 6 May 1985.

25 March 1984. Everton and Liverpool created history by competing against each other for the first time in a ever major final at Wembley. This was known to many as the 'friendly final' as fans mixed together.

Ron Atkinson and Howard Kendall at the FA Cup Final, Wembley, 18 May 1985

Everton clinched the league title for the eighth time in their history with a 2-0 win over Queens Park Rangers on 6 May 1985, eventually finishing 13 points above second-place Liverpool. Picture shows: Andy Gray fires in a shot at goal tipped over by QPR goalkeeper Peter Hucker.

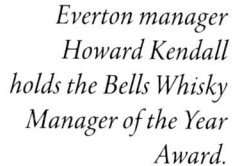

Everton manager Howard Kendall holds the Bells Whisky Manager of the Year Award.

Everton manager Howard Kendall in his office with Adidas award, 20 November 1985.

15 May 1985, European Cup Winners' Cup Final, Rotterdam, Everton 3 v Rapid Vienna 1, Everton's Trevor Steven's 73rd minute strike gives the blues a two-goal advantage. 'Goodnight Vienna'.

Pat Van den Hauwe grips the European Cup Winners' Cup trophy with a delighted Gary Stevens.

Bayern Munich defenders stand helpless as Graeme Sharp's header gives the Toffees the aggregate lead in the second leg semi-final of the European Cup Winners' Cup on 24 April 1985.

4 May 1987, Norwich – Everton manager Howard Kendall is surrounded by fans as he celebrates Everton winning the championship title.

20 May: Howard Kendall celebrates with the trophy during an open-top bus tour through the streets of Liverpool following their FA Cup final victory over Watford.

Captain Kevin Ratcliffe joyfully holds the big championship trophy after defeating Luton Town in May 1985.

Kevin Sheedy, Andy Gray and Trevor Steven homeward bound from Rotterdam with the FA Cup Final against Manchester United at Wembley three days later.

Footballer Ian Snodin pictured signing for Everton watched by manager Howard Kendall (right). January 1987.

PAUL BRACEWELL

Debut: Saturday, 18 August 1984, Everton 1 Liverpool 0 – Charity Shield

Everton: Southall, Stevens, Bailey, Ratcliffe, Mountfield, Reid, Steven, Heath, Sharp, Bracewell, Richardson
Liverpool: Grobbelaar, Neal, Kennedy, Lawrenson, Whelan, Hansen, Dalglish, Lee (Walsh 53), Rush, Nicol, Wark

PAUL BRACEWELL was born at Heswall on the Wirral but moved to Newport in Shropshire as that was where his father's job took him. While based in Shropshire, Stoke City noticed the potential in a young Paul where he trialled with the Potters before joining as an apprentice.

Howard Kendall was aware of Paul's ability and never thought twice about bringing him to Goodison. He signed before the 1984 FA Cup Final, but was away on England under-21 duty in the European Championship, coming back with a winners' medal as England defeated Spain in the final.

His winning streak continued as he came away from Wembley with a winners' plaque as Bruce Grobbelaar's own goal put the first prize of the new season in Kendall's trophy cabinet.

Paul was no stranger to Kendall having had the pleasure of playing with him in his days in the Potteries. Kendall's knowledge of Bracewell was enough to make sure that he was the club's first signing after the FA Cup success in May 1984.

Bracewell made his debut at Wembley, a stadium that became his second home during the 1980s. In what proved to be the club's most successful season in their history, out of a possible 63 games in all competitions, Paul played in 57 of them.

Paul's presence in the midfield complemented his teammates and vice versa. He suffered a horrific injury on the first day of 1986 in a 2-2 draw at Newcastle United after a collision with Billy Whitehurst, which cost him a place in the England squad that went to Mexico for the World Cup in the summer of 1986.

He then missed the whole of the 1986/87 championship-winning season, not returning to first-team action until a midweek FA Cup rout at Hillsborough as Everton pummelled Sheffield Wednesday 5-0 at Hillsborough in January 1988. Paul received the biggest reception of the night as he replaced Ian Snodin on 73 minutes to wear the blue shirt for the first time in two years.

Paul says about Howard Kendall, 'Howard was a proper football man who loved his football. His man-management was a real strong point. A man of integrity, honesty and a great man to work for. He would get the best out of you as he knew what made you and the rest of the squad tick. He won honours at Everton as a player so he knew what was required to win things and repeated the success as a manager.

'He would often make general comments about a player or players. If ever we were about somewhere watching a game or a team, live or on TV, he would mention players he rated in social terms only. Being in management, watching players and games, that was part and parcel of their role.

'In the dressing room he was very bubbly and full of enthusiasm. One of his strengths was getting proper people, proper men, getting them to work together to produce not only good football, but a winning team. He had a fantastic team spirit. There were so many players in the squad and the players knew that if they weren't doing it, somebody would take their place. Everybody wanted to win having the same spirit.

'My relationship with him was brilliant. My relationship goes back to the days when I was an apprentice at Stoke City. I eventually left for Sunderland with Howard buying me for Everton in 1984. When I got injured and was on crutches, he was still prepared to offer me a new deal but all I wanted to do was get fit. With him being so much a man's man, that's what made him so popular. Howard was one of the best. I'd seen the good times of winning things and the side of being injured. The care and attention he and his fellow coaching staff gave me is something that will always stay with me.

'Howard, and let's not forget Colin, they were both ahead of their time. They were a great partnership. There were loads of things that later on in life, you think back to what they did. I remember Colin sitting in a room after watching hours and hours of tape, the methods he used for training. The Bayern game where we played a 4-5-1 formation. These days he would have been known as a tactical genius. There were a lot of things that were at the forefront back then. Don't forget, Everton were at the forefront of football at the time.

'I think one of Howard's strengths was picking a team with balance. I know it sounds daft but people who played on the right side were right-footed, players who played with their left foot played on the left. He would have pace at the back, pace at the front, midfield players would get box to box and tackle. All together it was a nice blend. He put a team together magnificently while he was there. Not only did he know the team very well, he knew the individuals too which was a great asset in his man-management skills.

'He loved the lads getting together. Over the years we were taken out as a group for a Chinese banquet. Even though as manager he would mix, he still kept his distance – you knew he was the boss. He also had a method where if a player was fined, the money would be put into a pot or into a collection towards the Christmas night out where he was very good company but you never stepped over the line with him. Howard had a great sense of humour, always prepared to crack a joke, and took the lads to Magaluf at the end of the season for a break. Howard loved Majorca. Howard believed in rewarding you for your efforts all season with the end-of-season trip.

'When things weren't going the way he wanted it he would let you know individually and collectively. He was a winner that wanted to win games. Anybody that wants to be successful has to have that streak in him.

'I have so many memories of Howard that I will never forget. A funny one in particular was my first trip away which was in Greece. We'd just won the FA Cup. We went to the hotel feeling very nervous. Howard asked me if I was in the A or B team. I wasn't quite sure. I wasn't sure if he was referring to a five-a-side or head tennis team or whatever. I was taken out by Andy [Gray] and Reidy for a few cans which turned into a few cans more. I went back to the hotel later. Howard was stood in reception with a glass of champagne where he said, "I'll see you in the A team."

'I am involved in coaching these days at Tottenham Hotspur with the academy. The younger coaches obviously laugh these days, but although we talk about how the game hasn't changed, the team wears the same colour shirt, when people see the film *Howard's Way* and see the likes of Reidy and Andy that's what people talk about, and that will never change. You've got to be able to control and pass the ball, you've got to tackle and head the ball and most importantly, you've got to compete, and those were the things that we did in the Everton days.

'It was of course very sad to hear the news break that the Gaffer had passed away. I think Howard looking down would have been very proud [about the attendance at his funeral]. Funerals as we know are not great days but in terms of a celebration of his life it was a great day. It wasn't doom and gloom, it was very upbeat. People spoke of him with so much fondness because that's what he was. Whether you were a supporter or a player, a coach of the opposition or whatever, he will always be known as one of the true gents of the game. Everton was his club, and the fact that we went on to win trophies under him and bring success, and to be the most successful manager in the club's history would have given him so much happiness over the years.'

PAT VAN DEN HAUWE

Debut: Saturday, 6 October 1984, Arsenal 1 Everton 0
Arsenal: Jennings, Anderson, Sansom, Talbot, O'Leary, Caton, Robson, Rix, Mariner, Woodcock, Nicholas
Everton: Southall, Stevens, Van Den Hauwe, Ratcliffe, Mountfield, Reid, Steven, Heath, Sharp, Bracewell, Richardson

PAT VAN Den Hauwe's move to Everton came as a complete surprise to him. He had just finished a training session at Birmingham City when manager Ron Saunders told him he was Merseyside-bound, a move that turned out well for both parties.

Howard Kendall brought him in to challenge John Bailey for the left-back berth. Pat became the regular wearer of the number three shirt and his performances were encouraging. His character was of a very shy nature, but he earned the nickname 'Pyscho', which I don't think he particularly liked.

During his second season at Goodison he made the most appearances of the squad, scoring two goals. His first was at The Hawthorns as the Toffees eased to a 3-0 win, and a goal in the FA Cup came at home to Blackburn Rovers the following month. The goal he will be most remembered for is his strike after 55 seconds at Norwich City to win the First Division in 1987.

He cemented his love for Everton as a lifelong commitment when he had the club motto *Nil Satis Nisi Optimum* tattooed across his back.

Pat had five happy years on Merseyside before departing for Tottenham in 1989.

Pat says of Howard Kendall, 'When he first signed me, we met and had a beer in a bar in Formby. We never even discussed my salary, I just wanted to play for him and Everton.

'I have a photograph of him in my bedroom. It's a daily reminder of all the good times we had under him, and especially for me and my career, also a bit of endearment.

'In our squad, Howard got on with everyone, and it worked both ways because in return, everyone loved and respected him too. He was the type of person that you wanted to play football for, it was that easy. When you look back, the quality of players we had in that squad was unbelievable. Two players spring to mind in Alan Harper and Richo [Kevin Richardson] who came in when called for and did ever so well. Those two could have walked into any side in the top flight at that time. That must have been a headache to Howard, knowing he had two individuals who were quality and reliable, and when deputising, we never seemed to miss the guys who they were in for because they were that good, but somehow, they seemed to understand the situation.

'I wouldn't say he was laid-back, but comfortable. He wasn't one of these managers that had to raise his voice to get attention. In the five years I was at the club, I never once heard him raise his voice, not once. That included the training ground, and the dressing room on a matchday. He didn't have to, did he? We did the job for him.

'I've played for some great managers during my career, and it's very hard to talk about them and try to compare as they all had their own different attributes.

'Howard for me was outstanding in every way. Terry Venables was a really nice man, I had a good relationship with him too. Mick McCarthy at Millwall, another nice fella. Jim Smith at Birmingham City, well, he could get hot-headed. Ron Saunders was an old-school manager, very similar to Harry Catterick I'm told, who didn't particularly like the press.

'Every manager has their own methods and ways of doing things. Howard had a belief in his players which was a big strength. I can't think of any weaknesses in the man at all which goes a long way when a manager knows his players can go out on to that pitch and trust them.

'On the training ground at Bellefield as it was then, he was laid-back, and there were some sessions where we worked really hard, and towards the end of the week when we were preparing for a game, his sessions were relaxed – we would play head tennis, nothing too strenuous. We would do some sprints, ending with a quick five-a-side game.

'Even when it came to being a disciplinarian, he dealt with issues and that was that, which he kept in house. I personally never had a problem with him on that side of things even when I was sent off at Loftus Road along with [Queens Park Rangers striker] Gary Bannister for an altercation.

'If I had a problem with anything, whether it was at the club or of a personal nature, Howard was the first one that I would go and see.

'When I had an issue on the international front when I had a choice of playing for England, Wales and Belgium, I found it stressful, so Howard was the obvious choice to deal with that situation. He was very much a father figure in that respect.

'My father was Belgian, my mother was English, and Wales also came in. Howard explained things to me, Kenny Sansom was featuring regularly for England under Bobby Robson which would make that difficult for me.

Guy Thys was another who wanted me, but because Rats [Kevin Ratcliffe] and Nev [Southall] recommended me to coach Mike England, I chose Wales. I played at left-back and centre-back too.'

Howard was undoubtedly the club's most successful manager, winning trophies for fun, so I asked Pat which one the manager might have cherished the most.

'Howard had won the FA Cup in May 1984, six months before my arrival. I won the league and Cup Winners' Cup in my first season there, a Charity Shield the season after, so, Howard would have been delighted to have won the FA Cup because it was his first trophy for himself and the club who waited such a long time from their previous success.

'The Cup Winners' Cup must also have been special as that was the first European silverware the club had won. Then another league title followed in 1986/87. I think any piece of silverware is special as it shows a sign of success. I could not identify which one was more meaningful to Howard.'

As much as Pat's career was blossoming under the managerial genius of Kendall, Colin Harvey's input didn't go unnoticed.

Pat continued, 'Colin's influence as Howard's right-hand man was massive. They were two people who knew each other really well, always engaged in conversation, both having respect for each other.

'I mentioned earlier about Howard as a disciplinarian, it was more Colin than Howard. They had respect for each other. Like any great partnership in any walk of life, if you have a good working relationship, there's no reason why it won't work, and fortunately for us, it did.'

At the time of writing Pat was still involved with his beloved club, in the Everton in the Community department.

JOHN MORRISSEY

Debut: Wednesday, 7 November 1984, Everton 3 Inter Bratislava 0 – European Cup Winners' Cup second round, second leg
Everton: Southall, Stevens, Bailey, Ratcliffe, Mountfield, Reid (Harper 69), Steven, Heath, Sharp, Bracewell, Sheedy (Morrissey 78)
Inter Bratislava: Maluniak, Krupcik, Barmos, Fieber, Ducky, Sebo, Mraz, Brezik (Michalec 64), Moravec, Tomcak, Konik (Lehnert HT)

JOHN MORRISSEY was born on 8 March 1965 at the Park House nursing home in Waterloo. He is the son of the 1960s and 70s Everton idol John senior. Young John never shared the fame his father endured, making one start, his other as a substitute in the European Cup Winners' Cup.

For the second leg against Inter Bratislava in 1984, as John arrived at Goodison, he found out that he would be one of the five substitutes. He was totally taken by surprise when the boss told him to warm up in the second half and he finally made his bow on 78 minutes, contributing to the passage into the quarter-finals.

It wasn't due to John's lack of ability that he couldn't break into the first team on a regular basis. He was four months short of his 20th birthday when he made his introduction from the bench at Goodison, but there was too much experience ahead of him.

The skilful winger with a sudden burst of pace eventually left his boyhood club at the end of that season, seeking a new start in the Black Country with Wolverhampton Wanderers. Johnny's Wolves debut was on the first day of the season in 1985/86 under new manager Sammy Chapman, a 2-1 Third Division defeat at Brentford.

His home debut was a defeat by the same score against Newport a week later but he played in between in a 1-1 League Cup draw at Walsall which helped bring his Wolves appearance tally up to 11. Five were as a substitute and one brought him his only goal, in a 4-1 defeat at Bolton.

They were not happy days for John and he returned to the north-west a season after, dropping into the third tier with Tranmere Rovers. He went on to play over 500 games for the Prenton Park outfit. He scored an absolute belter for Rovers, against former employers Wolves in February 1992, in a 4-3 win.

John has no interest in his football career, therefore did not wish to contribute to the book. He likes to focus on the future, not the past.

IAN ATKINS

Debut: Wednesday, 26 December 1984,
Sunderland 1 Everton 2

Sunderland: Turner, Venison, Pickering, Bennett, Daniel (Atkinson 65), Elliott, Hodgson, Berry, Cooke, Proctor, Walker

Everton: Southall, Atkins, Bailey, Ratcliffe, Mountfield, Reid, Steven, Gray, Sharp, Bracewell, Sheedy

IAN ATKINS was signed by Howard Kendall in November 1984 for a mere £60,000 from Sunderland. There were several clubs hunting his signature too, including Sheffield United – with whom he held talks – Luton Town and Norwich City. It was just six weeks later that Ian returned to face the 'Roker roar' in an Everton shirt, replacing regular Gary Stevens at full-back.

Ian was capable of filling in for anybody in any position and made six appearances in 1984/85.

His preferred position was at centre-back, but the quality partnership of Kevin Ratcliffe and Derek Mountfield held strong which paved the way for Ian to leave the club in September 1985 and join Ipswich Town.

Atkins said, 'Howard was an absolute genius, someone that I can only describe as a natural. A natural manager, a natural communicator. Not every player loved him, but he knew what he wanted, and most importantly, he was good for the team.

He was spot on with everything. He had that air of casualness about him as well which made the players feel at ease. There was a natural instinct and Howard had it.

'He always knew his best team and always picked his best team. I remember playing in two successive games, winning both. If ever I was drafted in to do a job, I knew I'd be out as soon as the player you were deputising for returned. You knew the decision that Howard made was right, so how could you argue with him? Howard would play with the tried and trusted which you couldn't knock. Any football manager would have done the same. The team he built had some strays like Andy Gray and Peter Reid who had persistent injuries, but Howard knew he could rely on them both with their experience to help the squad gel.

'When the players that you deputised for became fit again, they were installed straight back in which was the right thing to do. Everyone had belief in what Howard was putting over. Howard for me was a person that never changed. He always seemed to be on the same level. He had success in adversity.

'I played for a few managers. Howard to me was the best. If someone wins the league championship title and the European Cup Winners' Cup, it's not done by luck. You may have a small element of it, but you have to have an awful lot of ability which Howard had in abundance. He knew his players inside out. He knew when things weren't right with you. He treated his players like puppy dogs.

'Everybody thought Pat Van Den Hauwe had a reputation of being a difficult player, but Howard knew how to handle him and brought the best out of him. There were a lot of strong characters within the group and Howard handled them all well. He could be sharp if someone upset him. He had a good manner where he wouldn't rub you up the wrong way, but motivated you which to me is an art.

'He would make a point to have a chat with you, also the social side kicked in. During Howard's reign in football the social side was a big part of the game which there was nothing wrong with. It had an effect on the team and the spirit amongst the lads. He was fantastic company. Howard was a person that embraced life, and the social side of it was very important. His social side never got in the way of managing.

'Howard liked to play a pressing game. When I look at teams today and what Liverpool did to win the league in 2019/20, we were doing that in 1985.

'He had us so well organised and dedicated. Everyone was so well drilled to become very hard opponents to play against where teams feared playing Everton.'

Ian played his part in the road to Rotterdam, making his European debut in the second leg of the quarter-final at Fortuna Sittard.

'It was the first time that I had been available for Europe and it was very enjoyable to get a game,' he says proudly.

'It was a bit frustrating playing in the reserves, but an understandable situation because of the way the lads had been playing. The prospect of playing in Europe was keeping me keen. That was one of the attractions of signing for a club like Everton.

'I will always have my memories of such a wonderful man. The fondest memory I have was half-time in the dressing room of the Bayern Munich game at home, despite not being in the starting line-up. Trailing by the one goal, Howard walks into the dressing room wearing a great big smile. He said, "Don't worry Akers, the Gwladys Street will suck three goals in this half." I still feel the tingle now.

'I had a very good relationship with the Gaffer. When I joined Everton, I had been out injured for three months. I was only able to train one day a week so it took me a while to get fit. During my first year I was never 100 per cent fit. If it wasn't for Heysel, I probably would have stayed longer and would have enjoyed more game time. When I left to join Ipswich, Howard told me that he would send me my league championship medal through and was true to his word.

'It was a massive loss to the football world when Howard passed away. I made the funeral in Liverpool which obviously was a sad day, but on the other hand a celebration of his life. The turnout on the day included people from different circles which showed the respect he thoroughly deserved.'

At the time of writing Atkins was still involved in football, scouting for Wolverhampton Wanderers.

NEILL RIMMER

Debut: Tuesday, 28 May 1985, Luton Town 2 Everton 0
Luton Town: Sealey, Breacker, Thomas, Nicholas, Foster, Donaghy, Hill, Stein (Moss 71), Harford, Nwaijobi, Preece
Everton: Southall, Hughes, Bailey, Harper, Van Den Hauwe, Richardson, Morrissey, Wakenshaw, Wilkinson (Rimmer 75), Danskin, Walsh

NEILL RIMMER was born in Liverpool in November 1967. He joined the club as an apprentice after being recommended by youth development officer Ray Minshull, signing professional forms in 1984.

Neill tasted success in the FA Youth Cup Final as Everton defeated Stoke City over two legs. He scored the first goal in the final, and also earned international recognition by representing England Youth in September 1984 against Yugoslavia.

He became a regular for Everton's reserves in the Central League at the end of April 1984.

It was very tough for any of the youngsters in those days to break into the first team due to the quality of the first 11. Having played mostly Central League football, Neill was given the opportunity to make his solitary appearance as a substitute at the end of the 1984/85 season, replacing Paul Wilkinson with the last quarter of an hour to play at Kenilworth Road.

Neill says, 'When you play for a manager, your opinion swings at times. If you're enjoying a good period, you think he's great, if not, you take it out on the manager wrongly.

With older eyes, I look back fondly on my time there with Howard as manager. He was the man in charge, a strong character, very much a big believer in discipline for us young ones as well which was a good thing.

'I remember a time when I was only really young and playing for the reserves. I boarded the team bus with the dress code back then a shirt, tie and suit. It was my first game and I had very little money, as I was still an apprentice. I arrived for the team bus in a pair of trousers and a jumper. Howard pulled me to one side and asked me where my suit was. I then went into a panic and within days I had a suit. I was well prepared for the following reserve game, I can tell you.

'Although he was a great believer in discipline, he was very approachable as well. It was a good lesson for me, especially early on in my career. I think when you've moved on and worked with other managers, you realise how good he was in every aspect as a manager.

'His style of management, as I've already mentioned, he was a disciplinarian. You certainly knew where you stood with him. I was very lucky in the sense that I lived in Ormskirk, and would travel in with Colin Harvey where I would try and pick his brains about things.

'When I played for the reserves, Howard would pop his head around the dressing room door. I was also involved with the youth team when we won the FA Youth Cup; he would again appear and say things if needed, good or bad, especially if we were struggling, and even give us a rollicking. He was never afraid to do that. Why shouldn't he? He was the manager of the club.

'When we won the FA Youth Cup, he made a fuss of the lads, praising us with plaudits. He always encouraged a lot of the young lads, as he told me that my time would come if I continued to work hard. Unfortunately, it never did.

'When I left Everton, I joined Ipswich Town and then went to Wigan Athletic later on, where I was made the club captain. One afternoon whilst playing for Wigan, Howard was in attendance. After the game, Howard came over to me and made such a fuss, giving me advice which he didn't have to, but that's the man that he was, also knowing that he'd never forgotten me which was a nice feeling as I was never involved much with the first team. So, for him to do that, it meant a lot.

'He was a manager who had an aura about him which made him stand out. It's something that all managers have I guess, now whether that comes with success, I don't know. As soon as he walked into a building, you'd immediately have that respect for him. It didn't matter if you were one of his favourites or not, it still was a respect thing. Apart from being a good manager, he was a gentleman. He cared about the club, the players and the supporters. He had this affection which was natural. The club meant so much to him, it shone through his personality.

'I think it's worth mentioning that Colin Harvey, who I'd also played under for the reserves, was a bit of an unsung hero. It wasn't a coincidence that things started to progress when he worked alongside Howard. There were also players who stepped up given the opportunity. The way Colin was, particularly with his attitude, a driving force if you like, blending in with Howard's personality, their partnership was perfect on and off the pitch.

'When I saw them in training sessions, they had players running around and also were prepared to get their knees dirty. They wanted to get stuck into the players, not someone who was prepared to stand on the sideline, but get involved physically which I think builds respect up with the playing staff. Both Howard and Colin had never lost their appetite for the game and they showed in sessions that they still had the desire to win. The both of them including Mick Heaton on a Friday in training were absolute geniuses at head tennis. They would take on anyone and never be beaten. When they did lose, which was very rarely, they took it so badly.

'That winning mentality must have been something they continued from their playing days. Their attitude I felt was something that rubbed off on the players in training. Howard just loved Everton Football Club; it meant a lot to him.

'He would get very annoyed if players failed to fully commit themselves in training. He would not tolerate a lack of effort from anyone. At the end of the day, in whatever capacity it was, you were representing Everton Football Club and he expected you to live by the standards of the club's tradition.

'I think as we're talking about the transition with the appointment of Colin Harvey, Howard on his arrival in 1981 built up a team to succeed. He brought some players in at the beginning who steadied the ship, then eventually he brought in players that went on to be very successful and great team players as well as individuals.

'With regard to his best signing, wow, that would be a difficult one considering the quality of the players he had in his squad. From a business point of view, Gary Lineker; as an influence about the club, for me, it's hard to say one. I always thought Trevor Steven made a big impact on things. Peter Reid and Andy Gray were more experienced pros that had been around and knew the game, bringing some influence on and off the pitch to the club. Again, they were the kind of players who had that aura around them. Players amongst the group respected them which brought confidence amongst the team as they performed on the pitch.

'Would Reidy and Gray have been as good without Howard? I don't know. Don't forget, players like Ratcliffe and Stevens were brought through the ranks under the supervision of Colin Harvey, which eventually gelled it all together.

'I was heartbroken years later to hear of his passing. I don't think anyone expected that news as he wasn't old.'

Neill later went into coaching in the USA, and has also been involved with the Prince's Trust, where he worked with youngsters, giving them an opportunity of a second chance in life.

JASON DANSKIN

Debut: Tuesday, 28 May 1985, Luton Town 2 Everton 0
Luton Town: Sealey, Breacker, Thomas, Nicholas, Foster, Donaghy, Hill, Stein (Moss 71), Harford, Nwaijobi, Preece
Everton: Southall, Hughes, Bailey, Harper, Van Den Hauwe, Richardson, Morrissey, Wakenshaw, Wilkinson (Rimmer 75), Danskin, Walsh

JASON WAS spotted by an Everton scout in the Winsford area. Ray Minshull went to cast an eye on the promising youngster, but returned for a second look with Jason's performance below par. Minshull was more impressed with what he saw on his second viewing.

Jason takes us back to his days at the club, 'If I'm honest, in the beginning, I was frightened to death of him [Howard Kendall]. Nothing to do with him being unkind, but I think when you're a young apprentice at a professional football club, you've got to take notice and hope that you become someone that is respectful of the personnel there.

'He and Colin Harvey I remember one day on the training ground having what was called a shadow game. He stopped the game as I had been seen to do something wrong, caught in possession or something like that. He told me that in your mind, you have to have a picture of the game, and know your next move. He explained that it was like being a snooker player where you know what your next shot is before you've potted the ball. He and Colin encouraged the likes of myself and Derek Walsh who played in similar positions to do these things.

'Even though he was a serious character on the training ground, he could be a funny guy too, especially away from that environment. He could be hard, and make no mistake about it, you knew if you weren't living up to expectation. He wanted everything right, always willing to offer plenty of encouragement. Tactics, he loved. We used to have reserves against first team matches, shadow play and set pieces. The latter he loved. He always insisted in his drills that Graeme Sharp would be at the near post to flick on, which he insisted a lot of at that time when I was there.

'People used to say that Colin was the brains behind everything. The appointment of Colin coincided with the turnaround of form that Everton were struggling with at that time. He created a good atmosphere at Bellefield, an always upbeat character. He liked a laugh and a joke in a training session, but was very serious when it came to work. He was always willing to offer valuable advice especially as he was a midfielder like myself. Colin and Howard both loved a five-a-side. Nothing with either of them was overcomplicated, they made it enjoyable.

'Terry Darracott was my coach during the time I was there, and I think his ways were to follow what the first team did.'

Jason's one and only appearance came at Luton when the league championship had already been won.

He continued, 'When the first team used to train, Howard would invite a few of the young lads over to make the numbers up. There would be Rob Wakenshaw, Ian Marshall who was in the year above me, then myself, Derek Walsh and Darrin Coyle would savour that too. I sometimes got invited to an away game as a squad member, in a way to get used to what was to come. Regarding the game at Luton; I think Howard told me on the day, whether that was to calm my nerves or not to dwell on things too much, but that's how he did things.

'I then had to alert my family members to make sure they shared the proud moment with me, and arrange some tickets for them to collect on the night of the game.

'I can't describe the feeling I had when I knew I was playing, unbelievable and proud. I remember leaving the team hotel heading towards Kenilworth Road, a journey that took five minutes.

'I played the whole 90 minutes with the game flying by. Sadly, back in the day, there was never any footage captured for me to cherish.

'The season after, I was on the bench with Paul Wilkinson when we played Exeter City in the FA Cup third round at Goodison Park. I was keen to get on, but the game was settled with a Gary Stevens strike ten minutes from time. Before the goal, Howard was sweating on a replay especially with it being a midweek game. I think if we had been cruising by three goals, Howard would have put me on.

'I was also an unused substitute at Tottenham Hotspur in the ScreenSport Super Cup the following month. I remember Neville Southall getting interviewed years later, being asked what his proudest moment was at Everton. He replied the game at Tottenham in the ScreenSport Super Cup because he was made captain, mentioning that Howard had included a few of the young lads like myself, and full debuts for Darrin Coyle and Peter Billing.

'It was an honour for me to go into work especially at that time, being around the place with some great people.'

DARREN OLDROYD

Debut: Saturday, 11 May 1985, Nottingham Forest 1 Everton 0

Nottingham Forest: Segers, McInally, Swain, Walker, Hart, Bowyer, Mills, Metgod, Clough, Birtles, Hodge

Everton: Southall, Stevens, Van Den Hauwe, Ratcliffe, Mountfield, Richardson, Steven, Harper (Oldroyd 83), Wilkinson, Atkins, Sheedy

DARREN WAS a young lad who was at the club during the glory years. He was inexperienced, but with the league championship already in the bag four days previous, and a European final only days away in Rotterdam, he was handed his debut in May 1985 as a substitute at Nottingham Forest.

'I remember Howard Kendall saying to me that he wanted me involved in a series of games that were coming up. I made my debut at Nottingham Forest. Two of the other games which were Luton Town and Coventry City away, I was injured. That was the story of my time at Everton. I was just injured all the time.'

Darren sadly declined to take part in this publication.

PAUL WILKINSON

Debut: Saturday, 30 March 1985,
Southampton 1 Everton 2

Southampton: Shilton, Mills, Dennis, Curtis (Collins 62), Wright, Bond, Whitlock, Lawrence, Jordan, Armstrong, D. Wallace

Everton: Southall, Stevens, Van Den Hauwe, Ratcliffe, Mountfield, Reid, Steven, Sharp (Wilkinson 88), Gray, Bracewell, Richardson

PAUL WAS born in Grimsby, and for a local lad, the Mariners were his team. He played local football, and back then was a midfielder. A forward in the team got injured which led to Paul being asked to take over as his height would be an advantage. Fortunately he scored in that game, repeating the same task the week after.

He joined Grimsby Town and for the under-18s, scoring became a habit which led to signing apprentice forms. As Paul says, 'It's all about being in the right place at the right time.'

Paul was attracting interest from clubs in the top flight and while on international duty for England under-21s at The Dell, Graham Taylor and Brian Clough, the managers of Watford and Nottingham Forest respectively, were watching with interest. Howard Kendall was also aware of the situation, wasting no time to seal a deal with Grimsby for his signature.

Paul Wilkinson had signed for Everton on 28 March 1985 for £250,000. Two days later, he was selected for the team's visit to The Dell, where he took up a place on the bench. Paul had previously made 71 appearances in the Second Division for Grimsby. He had also contributed towards Everton's League Cup exit in the same season, causing a massive upset, when his free kick found the head of Phil Bonnyman, who beat Neville Southall.

Kendall must have been impressed with Wilkinson as he added him to his squad four months later. The partnership of Graeme Sharp and Andy Gray was inseparable, with Paul a reliable replacement when called upon. Incidentally, Paul's first goal, which proved to be the winner in an Everton shirt, was against Liverpool eight days after Everton's European success in Rotterdam.

Paul says, 'When I was in talks with Everton, Howard didn't have to say a lot really. Everton, top of the league, one of the biggest clubs in Britain at the time and of course a fantastic opportunity for me.

'There was a lot of interest in me. I remember playing for England under-21s on a Monday night at Southampton.

'I had the next day off and was visited by the Grimsby manager at home around teatime. He said that Howard Kendall was coming to see me the next day and wanted to meet me and my dad. "The clubs have agreed a fee, we can't stand in your way, so it's up to you." I had heard before that Everton were watching me, more so after me scoring that goal against them. Colin Harvey and Terry Darracott used to drool over their fish and chips in Grimsby so I knew they had been over a few times monitoring my progress.

'The move to Everton was impossible to turn down and there was never a moment's hesitation. The day that I signed, I left my dad and Howard together in the hotel in Grimsby. I'd gone to collect some things to take with me for my journey to Liverpool. My dad was a very quiet man, but when I returned with my belongings, there were about six empty bottles of champagne on the table with both of them merry.'

Paul's debut was a long time coming. He appeared regularly for the second string before being handed an opportunity, albeit coming off the bench two minutes from time at The Dell as a 20-year-old to replace Graeme Sharp. The game was dramatic: a double from Kevin Richardson in a three-minute spell was followed by a penalty save seven minutes later as Neville Southall thwarted David Armstrong's weak effort, guessing right and going down to smother the ball. Joe Jordan added a late consolation for the Saints as the Toffees held on.

Paul made only four appearances that season, finding the net on two occasions. His first won't be forgotten by himself and those who witnessed it on the night as Everton defeated Liverpool. He added to his tally three days later in an early Sunday morning kick-off at Coventry City as Everton were preparing for their 62nd game of the season. The Sky Blues were staring relegation in the face, with the championship already wrapped up by Kendall's men. Wilkinson equalised for the blues before half-time but Everton eventually lost 4-1, keeping Coventry in the top flight for the following term.

Paul played his part as Everton won their second championship in three years and earned a winners' medal for his personal collection. He left in March before the title was won and joined another great manager, Brian Clough, at Nottingham Forest.

He continued to play for many clubs, retiring in 2000 after playing for Northampton Town before trying his hand at management in a caretaker capacity with Northampton, Grimsby and Truro City. His last post was with Bury when they were expelled from the Football League in 2019.

'Howard was a very good man-manager,' says Paul. 'A good people person who knew how to get the best out of his players. He was very astute at how to deal with having a very good squad of players. He gained everybody's respect in the way that he treated them. If he detected that you weren't yourself, he would take you in his office and talk to you to find the root of what was bothering you. I was in his office a few times as I wasn't a regular starter. If you weren't included in his matchday plans, sometimes he would tell you, sometimes he wouldn't, like all managers. You had to accept the news if you were left out. You have to remember at that time, every player was an international.

'The biggest compliment he ever paid me was that he came back for me again when I was at Middlesbrough. The best advice he gave me [laughing] was to watch Sharpy and Andy Gray.

'He had a good relationship with his assistant Colin Harvey and they had a very clever way of working together, which was probably his biggest strength, but were both different characters.

'Obviously, he was very good by the way he led by example in football terms where he was always around the lads, and everyone could see how he and Colin had been as players. You knew that you were around people who knew what they were talking about.

'Both Howard and Colin were leaders, so were very good. You knew what was expected, also they allowed the players to lead which was a big thing back then. His knowledge on the game was second to none. He brought players in that he knew were going to be like himself, a winner, and with that mentality he brought success to the club, which he and the fans thoroughly deserved. You don't get to the top without demanding the best.

'On the subject of training, his performance in training on a Monday was enough sometimes just to see what he could still do. Colin was equally as impressive too. I think if you had the qualities that Howard and Colin had to show the players what you can do, the players then have a belief.

'As a person, I always got on with Howard. One thing that I really regret was that I nearly came back to Everton when I was at Middlesbrough, everything was all sorted until Boro pulled the plug on the deal. It was disappointing for me because I would have loved to have gone back.

'As a player, I've been lucky as I've played for some great managers, Cloughie and many more, but for me, Howard would be at the top alongside Cloughie. Under Howard, I learned to become a winner. Everybody says that you are a born winner, but I think I learned how to win as well. It was a pleasure just to be around the place in the three years I was there.

'My fondest memory would be the night when we beat Bayern Munich. I hadn't been at the club long, but to see the joy on everybody's faces, even Howard – that night was probably one of the best performances I had witnessed in all of the time that I was there. To go on and win the cup a month later was even more poignant because of what we had achieved at that moment.

'It was devastating news hearing of his passing. I, like many, attended his funeral, and it was nice to see so many of the lads there. It was a fantastic send-off for someone that deserved every bit of recognition he got. He was loved by everyone.'

GARY LINEKER OBE

Debut: Saturday, 10 August 1985, Everton 2 Manchester United 0 – Charity Shield

Everton: Southall, Stevens, Van Den Hauwe (Bailey 88), Ratcliffe, Mountfield, Reid, Steven, Lineker (Heath 75), Sharp, Bracewell, Sheedy

Manchester United: Bailey, Gidman, Albiston, Whiteside, McGrath, Hogg, Robson, Duxbury (Moses 60), Hughes, Stapleton, Olsen

HOWARD KENDALL was keen to build on his success from the previous season. Gary Lineker was high on Howard's radar, and who could blame him? Lineker had been the top scorer in top-flight football with 24 goals for Leicester City in 1984/85, enjoying a partnership with Alan Smith.

A fee for Lineker was decided by an FA tribunal which brought him to Merseyside, finishing yet again as the division's top scorer.

In what proved to be his only season with the club, neighbours Liverpool snatched a league and cup double from Everton, depriving them of continued silverware with Gary leaving for the sunny climate of Catalonia and Spanish giants Barcelona.

Gary says of Howard, 'He was a huge personality, and I think about him with great affection and warmth. He was a person who was great fun, and most importantly, a wonderful football man who was tactically very astute.

'I only had one year with him unfortunately, and if I would have had more than the one year, I would have won more trophies. I have always said that Howard's side was the best club side that I ever played for.

'He was unique in many ways with his style of management. He was a players' man and at the same time he was tough, and could be ruthless, if necessary, but he was the kind of manager that you want to play for. He did things in his own way. If things weren't going well, the whole squad would be taken along to a local Chinese, and his style of management was encapsulated the day I actually signed for Everton. It was the time when my contract had ceased at Leicester City. In those days pre-Bosman, you weren't a free agent. So, if the clubs couldn't agree a price, they would have to go to what they called a tribunal which they used to have at Lancaster Gate.

'I went along, and it felt like you had been put into a dock. I stood there in front of this small committee of three people from the FA. Gordon Milne, the Leicester City manager at that time, stood up and said how great he thought I was; I'd scored so many goals, and had won the Golden Boot with Leicester, I'd broken into the England team and was going to be an international superstar.

'It was Howard Kendall's turn to stand up and put over his point. He started to say, I'm taking a bit of a punt on this lad and can't see him playing much in the first team, certainly not in his first season. He continued to say that he was taking a chance as I was very raw and green. I'm sat there thinking what have I done, why have I signed?

'At the end when it was time for the committee to make a decision, I think Everton were prepared to pay £500,000, Leicester wanting over a million. It eventually got agreed at £800,000.

'My head was down as we walked out of Lancaster Gate, thinking not only does he not really fancy me, he's paid over the odds for me as well. That made me feel really bad. As we continued to walk away, he put his arm around me and said, "Don't worry about all of that bollocks I said back there." He told me that I was going to be his big player and score all of these goals for him. He then bought five bottles of champagne that we shared between us on the train journey home.

'I was completely sloshed when we arrived back at Lime Street station, then he took us to a Chinese restaurant near Liverpool, and I don't remember much of that evening.

'He was always a happy character, especially at the training ground and in particular on a matchday. Football ran through his veins.'

Gary won't like to be reminded that his Everton league debut came at his old hunting ground, Filbert Street. Firstly, he walked into the home dressing room by mistake, leaving him red-faced. Then he had to face defeat as the league champions were turned over after taking the lead through Derek Mountfield, only for Bobby Smith to equalise a minute before the break. The man who became his successor at Leicester was Mark Bright, who netted a brace in 16 second-half minutes to clinch the three valuable points with a 3-1 win.

Lineker got off the mark for his new club with a 75th-minute goal which clinched the game at Tottenham on the August bank holiday Monday. His next two blue outings produced five goals, with a hat-trick at home to Birmingham City, and two in a 5-1 away win at Sheffield Wednesday.

The end total that season was 40 goals in all competitions. Adding to his tally was a further six goals when representing England in Mexico at the World Cup.

'I was very fortunate to have a really good relationship with him [Kendall],' Lineker continued. 'I was surprised that he let me go to Barcelona. I've said many a time that I would have been delighted to have carried on at Everton and won trophies, but he accepted a large offer from Barcelona, and when a club comes to you to say that they have accepted an offer for you, you kind of think that you are being shown the door which is certainly what I felt. But, for me, it was. Barcelona was not an unattractive club with all due respect. It was a massive decision I had to make which ended with me leaving.

'I was very fortunate to have worked with some great managers in my career. I have already mentioned Gordon Milne, not forgetting another guy called Jock Wallace at Leicester City who was a tremendous help to me. For me, the big three were Howard albeit only for a year, Terry Venables at Barcelona and later Tottenham, and obviously Bobby Robson. The three of them all had one thing in common, and that was they were all in love with the game, they lived for it and managed with their heart on their sleeve. So, Howard would compare very favourably despite me spending more time with the other two. With what he achieved with Everton, he has to be right up there.

'Handling his players, Howard did it in different ways. There were certain individuals that he could give a little bit of a rocket to, but mostly he would do a bit of mickey-taking. There was a lot of that at Everton anyway with Southall being very sarcastic, Kevin Ratcliffe, Peter Reid who were massive characters too. I think the fact is that Howard brought in these kinds of personalities – a lot of his managing was done within the squad, which was part of his cleverness. He could wield the stick if he needed to, but like most good leaders, he was better with the carrot and could make you feel loved which I think is important.

'Those who remember Howard during his playing days would appreciate his contribution as a player, and funnily enough, he never spoke of his own playing career; he didn't have to. We were familiar with it and what a terrific player he was, but he would mention it occasionally when he was bringing himself up against some of the players, but only in a fun way using his humour. He also had Colin Harvey alongside him, who was also a very good player and good in the management team.

'When I think about players who were similar to Howard in his playing days, you have to remember that the game has changed a little bit since then. Perhaps if you look at one or two of the young players coming through, possibly Declan Rice or Kalvin Phillips who can get up and down the pitch.

'Nowadays, you're either a holding player or you're a forward midfield player, and that's where the game is in that sense. Howard was a box-to-box player, similar to Bryan Robson. Jude Bellingham is another that springs to mind. As the game has changed, the players' roles also become different.

'Howard had a very good backroom staff who were immensely influential to him and the success during that period. I'm always wary about the number two syndrome. People always say the manager's very successful and that was down to the number two whether that's Colin Harvey or whoever. Essentially, it boils down to the number one, and obviously his number two is important and it's like all good leaders bringing the best people around them which is what Howard did. So, Colin Harvey was terrific, again a likeable guy but someone you wouldn't want to upset. I thought Howard and Colin pivoted really well and worked well together.

'Make no mistake, Howard was the man in charge, and I've heard right through my footballing life that managers who have done well, people say, "Well, it's really the number two that does all of the work." No, it's not like that. Yes, they do a lot of important work, but they are very much the manager's teams.

'I will never forget the day when I was informed of his passing. I heard the news through my agent, who called me to break it to me. My agent was quite close to Howard from way back. I was deeply saddened with the devastating news; I had a huge amount of respect for Howard. I had bumped into him two or three times post football, post my playing career, and he was always fantastic company. It was a really sad day, especially for those that had played under him and clearly his family as well. I couldn't attend the funeral sadly as I was away at the time.'

Lineker finished his playing career in Japan in the early 1990s, and by the end of the 20th century he was the main presenter for the iconic Saturday night football show *Match of the Day*, a role he held until stepping down at the end of the 2024/25 season.

IAN MARSHALL

Debut: Tuesday, 20 August 1985, Everton 2 West Bromwich Albion 0

Everton: Southall, Stevens, Van Den Hauwe, Ratcliffe, Marshall, Harper, Steven, Lineker, Heath, Bracewell, Sheedy

West Bromwich Albion: Godden, Nicholl, Cowdrill (Anderson HT), Hunt, Bennett, Forsyth, Whitehead, Varadi, MacKenzie, Statham, Valentine

COLIN HARVEY introduced another one of the pupils from the youth setup, a member of the squad that won the FA Youth Cup in 1984, rounding off a great season for the club with the seniors taking the FA Cup at Wembley. Both trophies were paraded around the famous Goodison pitch before the opening game of the 1984/85 campaign.

Ian Marshall broke through the following year and appeared 17 times for the first team in all competitions before moving to Oldham Athletic, becoming a regular starter.

Ian says, 'Howard was my first manager and obviously a very influential figure on my development as a footballer and how I see the game.

'His style of management, I always thought he was 30 years ahead of his time. He made you feel welcome, he liked a laugh and a joke but was stern and tough when he needed to be. He was a great coach and very much a father figure to me. He helped me an awful lot, guidance wise and many other things.

'He was always happy and jolly, and fun to be around, but very serious when it came to football. I've played under managers who were very offish with you, but Howard was the opposite. Even with the younger lads, he would take time to help them. I was also in that category as a young lad, he used to collect the fines which paid for the Chinese meal with the lads in Southport. It was an old-school camaraderie with a great team spirit and a fantastic time to be in football.

'He was indeed in his element when he was winning the league titles. I've never been a manager, but I can imagine the adrenalin when you're winning games.

'You would also know if things weren't going too good too. I think like most managers, it's got to be when your team doesn't perform. Howard was one of these guys that accepted defeat only if the lads gave 100 per cent. When the team was going through a very difficult time on the pitch he kept anything which was controversial away from the dressing room. The players were aware of what was going on with the protests against Howard and the chairman, but Howard handled it well, as a true professional would.

'He handled his playing squad very well. I don't think there were any difficult players amongst the group. I think if there was anyone that was difficult, Howard would do the easy thing by moving them out of the club. If players didn't fit into his plans or agree with his philosophy, and wanted to pursue their careers elsewhere, he'd move them on.

'He was never one to add pressure on you. If you didn't perform too well, he would totally understand and ask you to move on to the next game. He knew if you were having a bad time, but he was more concerned with helping you improve your game.

'On and off the pitch, I had a good relationship with him. I came through as an apprentice, and he gave me the opportunity to make my debut. I was with him from the age of 16 to 20. All of the advice that he gave me was always of a positive nature.

'I've worked under some fantastic managers in my football career: Joe Royle, Martin O'Neill, John Lyall and Sam Allardyce. I've always said that Howard was top of the tree. He guided me a lot and told me how football should be played.

'The Colin Harvey appointment to the first team as Howard's assistant was massive and a masterstroke. I thought Colin was a great man, probably more disciplined than Howard. Colin proved when Howard left that he couldn't continue the success Howard brought, but, like all partnerships, the two complemented each other. Colin must have had a lot of influence on the success when he joined up with Howard.

'Howard admired the Liverpool team because of what they'd achieved over the years. That's how much admiration he had for football and the club's local rivals. He admired great football players and would comment on when they were doing great things.

'Years later after I'd left the club, not seeing him for a long time, he would always greet me with a big smile, and I'd have a brief conversation with him. He'd never forgotten me, which was nice.'

NEIL POINTON

Debut: Saturday, 9 November 1985, Everton 6 Arsenal 1
Everton: Southall, Harper, Pointon, Ratcliffe, Stevens, Heath, Steven, Lineker, Sharp, Bracewell, Sheedy
Arsenal: Lukic, Anderson, Sansom, Davis, O'Leary, Caton, Williams, Allinson, Nicholas, Woodcock, Rix

NEIL WAS with Nottingham Forest as a schoolboy but was released and he joined Scunthorpe United. Middlesbrough were also showing an interest in Neil before Everton came in with an offer, and an opportunity to play in the top flight.

Scunthorpe had a reputation during the 70s after bringing through Ray Clemence and Kevin Keegan, who both went to Liverpool. In the 1980s, Howard pulled off a coup by signing full-back Pointon from Scunthorpe for £75,000.

Howard was looking for cover for Pat Van Den Hauwe, and not once did Neil look uncomfortable in that role, considering that he had been plying his trade in the lower depths of the Football League prior to his big move to Everton. In his first season, Neil was involved 22 times in all competitions.

In 1990, Howard Kendall was managing Manchester City having returned from Athletic Bilbao and reunited with Neil, signing him for £300,000.

Neil says, 'Howard set me on what was a magnificent career for myself. He gave me the chance to play at a higher level with better players. He always seemed to have confidence in what I could do and I have nothing but total respect for how he spoke to me as a manager.

'I would also like to put on record that the lads at the club from day one were just brilliant. They were mickey-taking, very much down to earth with no heirs and graces. The first players I think I met were Sharpy then Inchy and Gary Lineker. The rest of the lads then came upstairs into the canteen area where I was waiting to have my medical with John Clinkard.

'Howard's style of management was second to none. He could put his arm around you, rollick you too. He had that thing where he taught you as well. On a Monday morning, he could call you into his office to have a word about something I may have done wrong during the game at the weekend. He would have the video analysis in front of him that he had watched over the weekend and pointed out your mistakes and how he wanted you to rectify them.

'When I signed, which looking back was my fondest memory, Howard told me that I wouldn't be in the first team for at least a year. He told me that he'd signed me as backup and was one for the future. Because I'd played in the lower leagues, he told me that my physical side was good, but he was looking to improve me technically. He told me that I would have to push Pat Van Den Hauwe to make him a better player and I could learn from watching him.

'At Bellefield, Howard had a set routine where he'd be there before the players. He would have a run then a jacuzzi, there was always a cold plunge with the baths. He would go upstairs for breakfast, chat with the catering staff then wait for the players to arrive.

'Colin Harvey would do his bit with Howard viewing. Nine times out of ten, Howard would take his tracksuit bottoms off and join in as would Colin. They still had the quality too on the ball. Their legs may have gone a bit but their brains were still geared up for football.

'Howard loved the gatherings he had with his players on and off the pitch. Howard would sometimes talk about his days when he played with Colin and Bally [Alan Ball] in midfield, and how games would pan out which was part of your education.

'Howard loved nothing more than sitting in a bar with his squad of players to get that bonding, and things would come out after a few drinks. He would talk about his own career only when asked. He would mention the players he came up against like Billy Bremner, and players like that.

'He would be so relaxed and happy, especially at the end of the season where he would look back, that was his relaxing time if he had a couple of weeks off. He was still planning for the following season as I remember when we went on tour to New Zealand and Australia in 1987.

'My personal relationship with him, no complaints. It was total respect from my point of view. I think Howard also had respect for me when he signed me later for Manchester City. He told me that I didn't get the rub of the green at Everton, but I would be his first choice at Maine Road. He told me to take all the experiences and disappointments I had at Everton and make this work for me at City. He's the best manager I'd ever played for, not disrespecting anybody by the way. He was like my dad where he would give me good advice, told me when I did something wrong and how I could improve myself and would help me when certain things were going wrong. The top man for me.

'Howard was very proud of the side that he assembled in 1984/85 when they were one game away from doing the treble – he said that was the best side he had ever put together. It probably was, and still is. When he brought in some of the players such as Trevor Steven and Neville

Southall and a few more he brought in, they weren't big names. The team eventually came to fruition and dominated for a number of years.

'Let's not forget the influence Colin Harvey had on the success too, and his relationship with Howard's management. I think Colin was the blinkered one by saying, "This is what you need to be, this is what you need to do, that's how we train, that's what Everton is all about."

'He was determined to sustain the standard of the football club, which he had loved all of his life.

'Howard was the relaxed one who saw things in a different way. I remember the FA Cup game away at Sheffield Wednesday when we were 5-0 up at half-time. With the game going to three replays, Colin was the one that made you believe that you could eventually win that tie. He would drum it into you.

'Howard had a good eye for a player. I'd have to say Peter Reid was his best signing as he was a natural leader. Reidy was a driving force. Reidy never believed that the team could lose no matter what the score was. He always drove you forward. He always helped to encourage you, as well as rollicking you when required.

'I remember the game at Anfield in 1985/86 when we were walking out of the tunnel. Peter was shouting at the top of his voice, "We're having these, nothing is going to stop us, they are scared of us." He was no different when we played at City together years later too.

'Howard was always ready to give out advice. The best advice to me was, we played Arsenal away and Paul Merson made a great run across which led to Howard pulling me on to one side on the Monday and saying, "Trust in your ability. You are quicker than him, but you tried to stay up with the rest of them. If you'd trusted your ability, you would have cleaned it up."

'He could be very disciplined when he needed to be. There was an occasion when I was at Manchester City. I never got fined at Everton but did at City. We were in Ireland but going to Bilbao on a pre-season tour. Niall Quinn, Mark Brennan and myself had gone out and got back just as the coach was leaving for the airport. We all got fined £1,000 each.

'He was a character of good temperament, but would let you know if you got on the wrong side of him. He wasn't too happy when Peter Beagrie went through a glass door of a hotel on a pre-season tour of Spain during the Everton days in 1991.

'That was Howard's third spell in charge at the club. He told me off when we went to Hawaii and I had too much to drink. I was being sick all night and Howard was in the room directly above me. He told me his thoughts the following morning.'

When Everton clinched the league title crown in 1987, Neil qualified for a medal after making a sufficient number of appearances. His only goal that season came in a 4-0 rout of Norwich at Goodison on the first Saturday in December, the third of the afternoon.

When the trophy was presented on 9 May having celebrated by beating Luton Town, Evertonians were already believing the future was looking very optimistic. But nobody would have known at that point there was going to be an announcement in the coming weeks regarding a change in manager.

'It was a sad day when Howard left to go to Spain and join Bilbao,' said Neil. 'I don't think he would have left if Everton would have been able to continue in Europe at the top level. Things were taken from his hands.

'When we were in Hawaii there were a few rumours circling that he was leaving to go to Spain. I never knew anything, maybe some of the older players did, but said nothing to me.

'Attending the funeral of the great man, I remember the number of players that attended. Players from other clubs showed that he had respect.'

DARRIN COYLE

Debut: Wednesday, 5 February 1986, Tottenham Hotspur 0 Everton 0 – ScreenSport Super Cup semi-final, first leg
Tottenham Hotspur: Clemence, Stevens, Roberts (Hughton 71), Mabbutt, Miller, Perryman, Chiedozie, Falco (P. Allen HT), C. Allen, Crook, Waddle
Everton: Southall, Stevens, Pointon, Marshall, Van Den Hauwe, Reid, Steven, Coyle, Wilkinson, Billing, Richardson

DARRIN COYLE joined Everton in December 1985 for £20,000 from Linfield after Terry Darracott had monitored his progress following a recommendation by Jim Emery, the club's scout in Northern Ireland.

Terry went to watch the youngster play against Ballymena, and with his mind already made up, he was then left with the job of persuading Darrin to come over to Liverpool.

Darrin did agree, but was mostly involved in the Central League which led to a couple of appearances in the first team, albeit in the non-glamorous ScreenSport Super Cup against Tottenham.

Sadly, he suffered a leg break in a 'mini derby' for the reserves against Liverpool, damaging his tibia and fibula, which saw him sidelined for nine months. His road to recovery was never the same, so he decided that he wanted to return to his homeland.

Darrin says, 'Howard was a person that you could describe as a players' manager. Considering his position, he was very much down to earth, and a person you felt comfortable with when having a conversation, but when he spoke, you listened. He was a man who was well respected by each member of his playing staff. He was very open with the players, engaging with the training sessions, someone who was very much hands on. His assistant, Colin Harvey, was also very much hands on and in many ways they were very much alike.

'Colin was more abrupt with the players, and kept everyone on their toes. Howard would have influence, and when he spoke, you listened.

'I also have to mention that the success at the club had been achieved before I arrived, and from working with the players, each and every one of them had talent. I rated Paul Bracewell highly, and in my opinion, he was probably Howard's best signing. Sadly, Paul sustained an injury at Newcastle United when he and Billy Whitehurst collided. Paul sat out with his injury for a good while, and you could tell how much his presence was missed off the pitch.

'I can only describe Howard's man-management as fantastic. He had a very good relationship with all of his players, and I'm not sure if modern-day managers have that same relationship. That, I can only describe as one of his strengths. He knew exactly what was needed with a player, if it was an arm around the shoulder, or a telling off. I can't remember him ever having a fall-out with any of his players as he was so close to each and every one of them.

'His team talks were always very calm. He was a very deep thinker, and tactically, very, very good. He did his homework by learning about the opposition for the coming games. He certainly knew how to motivate his players and get the best from them. A manager can be a great tactician, but he still needs to know how to motivate his players, and to play together as a team. He certainly ticks the boxes as a top, top manager.

'When you assess the squad he had during the days of silverware, it was a team full of internationals, and the position I was fighting for, you had two or three players also in for that jersey. For example, as a defender, you had Gary Stevens, such an athletic guy who rarely picked up an injury, with Alan Harper ready to deputise when needed. Of course, I was still raw coming from Irish league football.

'He was definitely one of the best managers that I had played under. I have to say that back in the day, players had a bit more freedom socially which has changed in the modern day, because he was trusting with his players – that was probably the reason why he got the best out of them. In all honesty, I never really played under that many, especially at that level.

'I played at Linfield in Northern Ireland before I came across to England. My father [Ron Coyle] was the manager and had a reputation for being pretty ruthless. He had a different style to what Howard had; he managed by fear if I'm honest. If you lost a game at the weekend, you knew what was coming when we went back into training on the Tuesday night, it would be a very physical session. My father was a deep thinker, and you knew exactly what was coming. He was very methodical in his training. The difference between my father and Howard was that Howard was more laid-back.

'Howard had a great influence on my career, and even though it was a different type of football to what I was used to, the equivalent from the English top flight was much faster than the Irish league. It was one-touch football, and I was also playing with some great players, mostly internationals.

'I was loaned back to Linfield, with the Irish league being very physical, and I got back into the physical side of it with heavy tackling, hoping to bring back my confidence which I'd lost through being out injured. The directors of Linfield had noticed a difference in my style of play upon my loan return to Ireland. My first touch had improved, and at Everton it was very much a pass and move technique we'd played. It's a well-known fact that if you play with better quality players, it improves your game too.

'My father built up a friendship with Howard which stemmed from me joining the club. When it was my father's testimonial as he was finishing in management, Howard came over to speak at an event in Belfast.'

PETER BILLING

Debut: Wednesday, 19 March 1986, Everton 3 Tottenham Hotspur 1 after extra time – ScreenSport Super Cup semi-final, second leg

Everton: Southall, Billing (Van Den Hauwe 100), Pointon, Marshall, Mountfield, Richardson, Harper, Heath, Wilkinson (Sharp 54), Coyle, Sheedy

Tottenham Hotspur: Clemence, Thomas (Bowen 39), Hughton, Allen, Miller, Stevens, Mabbutt, Falco, Galvin, Chiedozie, Waddle

PETER WAS another player who made the break from non-league football into the big time, having been an unemployed youngster making use of his Saturday afternoons while playing for South Liverpool. When the opportunity arose to sign for Everton, Peter played mostly with the reserves. His big chance came in the ScreenSport Super Cup, a competition for the teams who would have been playing in Europe but for the ban after Heysel, a poor substitute, if one at all.

Peter's career was more productive elsewhere once he left Goodison, and he found his level in the lower leagues.

Peter recalls, 'Howard was a man that I can only describe as way ahead of his time during that successful period at Everton. I remember going there from South Liverpool and seeing the difference in his training methods to what I was used to, and the way he used to talk about things.

'He was brilliant with the players who had nothing but ultimate respect for him. The noticeable thing that caught my eye was his interest in keeping a team spirit. He loved taking the players out to let their hair down by having a meal and a few drinks. He also took the players away occasionally for a break in the sun.

'The training was always competitive on a daily basis. Howard himself would get involved by showing his appetite that he was also a winner. He had the hunger and desire to win, no matter what they were doing in that session. He loved his head tennis and would accompany Colin Harvey and a couple of other coaching staff members, and they would never lose.

'That's probably why his team on the field were so successful, that urgency to win. Many a time, if things weren't going the way he'd planned, especially in training, he would let you know about it. He just wanted everything to be perfect. With that mentality, winning trophies paid off for him, his players and staff. When you're in the game it's all about winning and Howard created that winning mentality.

'My strengths were that I had pace, was physical in the tackle, decent in the air and could also move from the full-back position to centre-back. I would look at the team sheet every week when it was put up on the noticeboard and I would ask myself how I was going to break into that side with the quality amongst it.

'Going into Bellefield, the group of lads were very relaxed, but once the training started, it was business as usual. Howard was amazing for the age that he was where his technical ability stood out. When he struck the ball you would think, WOW.

'My relationship with the Gaffer was very different to the other squad players as I wasn't a regular, so wasn't involved with Howard all that much. Coming from non-league, the whole thing was a culture shock for me.

'I was only ever involved in the ScreenSport Super Cup competition, only as a fringe player, but I did play one game in the top flight which was against West Ham. I think we were second in the league with West Ham third. It was a totally different atmosphere from what I'd experienced before. It was only five days before Everton played at Wembley in the FA Cup Final too. We beat West Ham that night, 3-1. Despite not being a regular first-teamer, Howard always kept us involved. It was down to you to prove your worth, and if you were good enough, he would have played you in the first 11.

'He was a person always willing to help. The best advice he gave me was when I left Everton. There was interest from Crewe Alexandra, so Howard told me that the drop in divisions, to the fourth, would be the best thing for me to 'learn my trade', and if I was good enough, I could work my way back to the level where I had gone to.

'Howard was the best manager I'd ever played under by a long way. Colin Harvey played a big part in Howard's success too, don't forget.

At the time of writing, Peter was earning a living from being a taxi driver, and was also doing a bit of TV work for IMG, mainly at Liverpool and Everton, compiling match statistics for Premier League fixtures.

BOBBY MIMMS

Debut: Saturday, 29 March 1986, Everton 1
Newcastle United 0
Everton: Mimms, Stevens, Van Den Hauwe (Heath 45), Ratcliffe, Mountfield, Reid, Steven, Lineker, Sharp, Bracewell, Richardson
Newcastle United: McKellar, Anderson, Bailey, McCreery, Clarke, Roeder, Stephenson, Gascoigne, Whitehurst, Beardsley, Stewart

BOBBY HAD taken the biggest risk of his life by going into football before taking his O-levels, and he signed for the Toffees from his native Yorkshire home Rotherham United, as cover for the mighty Neville Southall. It would have taken an earthquake to have shifted Southall from performing his weekly duties, but an accident while representing his country in Dublin led the way for Bobby to deputise in the big man's absence. When Bobby pulled on the green shirt for the first time, Everton had lost their first game in 18 the week before at Luton Town. He went on to keep six successive clean sheets in the league.

I can't recall Bobby ever being faultless while performing for Everton, but taking over the gloves of Southall was never to be on a permanent basis.

He looked back, 'When I joined Everton, they had just won the league championship and Cup Winners' Cup. I then went out on loan to a number of clubs. I got into the team through Neville suffering an injury whilst on international duty.

'Because of the quality players within the squad, there were players like myself that weren't featuring on a weekly basis.

'Howard always made you feel part of the squad because the sessions were not split up. Everybody was in it together which kept you interested and the feeling of being wanted. He also had this demeanour about the place. I have probably picked up on that and taken into my coaching career.

'Howard was a nice and amenable man who made everybody that came into his company welcome, which was the first thing I noticed about him when I walked into the club. From a footballing point of view, he knew the game inside out. He had a good eye for a player, and from my time there, it was a squad with quality players and with the help of Colin, they assembled a good side.

'Howard and Colin's relationship was a good cop/bad cop scenario. Colin was the snapper and would have a word with players if that was required, where Howard would cajole people and keep players in check. Howard may have been laid-back but he knew what he wanted out of the team, also individuals in training sessions and matches. He was a person that was ahead of himself and had gone away from the tutorial way of management, probably the first of a new breed.

'Just like the team, everybody had their own job to do. Colin was a good number two to Howard as they worked really well together. They both had a great knowledge of the game. They would watch games on TV together, and just listening to them in conversation would make you learn things from them. Their knowledge complemented each other also having a different style. Mick Heaton was another who was very influential in his own way.'

On 26 March 1986 while on international duty for Wales, Neville Southall landed awkwardly, resulting in an ankle injury which kept him sidelined for the remainder of that season. Three days later, Mimms made his debut in front of the Goodison crowd as Everton secured a 1-0 victory over Willie McFaul's Newcastle United. He kept goal for 12 games in 1985/86, keeping six consecutive clean sheets in the First Division from 29 March to 30 April. Unfortunately for Bobby, the first goal he conceded after that run was the night the season went horribly wrong at Oxford United. The Blues were vying with Liverpool for the title. With their rivals also in action that night at Leicester City, the Toffees' defeat and the Anfield team's win gave the Reds the advantage to take the title away from Everton.

Mimms continued to keep goal for a further 16 games the following season until Southall returned on 25 October 1986 as Watford visited Goodison. Bobby felt aggrieved by the return of the legendary Welshman and made his feelings known to the manager.

'When I did get left out of the side after Nev returned from injury, I went to see Howard and gave him my transfer request. I handed him the envelope and he said, "What's that?" I replied, "My transfer request." He opened it, looked at it, and threw it in the bin. Howard was a top man, and he knew exactly how to deal with his players. I think Howard was one of the first managers at Everton to start collecting a squad. A lot of new players came into the squad and as soon as somebody got injured, there was somebody ready to go in.

'At Bellefield, Howard was quite a chilled character, quite relaxed, although very competitive. Howard and Colin would both participate in games and would coach from within.

'In the dressing room on a matchday, Howard would get around players individually and talk to them.

'Outside of the dressing room and away from the club, Howard was great company. He liked a drink, but most importantly, he liked being around his players and being part of the group. Whichever way results were going, good or bad, he would take the players out for a Chinese, wanting to get them back on board.

'Regarding his emotions, I can't say that I ever saw him angry. He was at his happiest when he was around his players talking about football. He loved talking about the game and the fixtures that were coming up, or games that had been on TV the night before.

'Howard as it's well documented had a real love affair with Everton. He loved being at Bellefield, and Goodison spoke for itself on a matchday as you could imagine, the place was buzzing. I was lucky enough to have been at the club during its successful period.

'As a comparison to other managers, Howard was very similar to Terry Venables who I played under at Tottenham. They were two individuals that could trust their players. He had a very reliable captain in Kevin Ratcliffe, who carried the orders from Howard on to the pitch.

'The team Howard built, all of the players he brought into the club had an impact. Kevin Ratcliffe was already there from being an apprentice; he was the best centre-half that I ever played with through his pace and reading of the game. He commanded the team as well as the captaincy.

'Gary [Lineker] came in and scored his goals. Paul Wilkinson was another that scored his goals and did what he had to do when he was called upon. Howard developed a squad that was competitive.

'It was a sad day when Howard decided to further his career elsewhere after bringing the success to the club. There were rumours in the press, but when it happened, I was very surprised because of knowing what the club meant to him. He came back a couple of times later which says it all. I was disappointed to see him leave to take on his role in Spain as were a few of the lads.

'Colin took over and nothing actually changed around the club, so from that point of view, things were not as disastrous as they could have been.

'I have some very fond memories of the man and a funny memory too. It was the day we won the league championship at Carrow Road in 1987. In the dugout they had those cinema-style seats that would spring up once you stood up. Every time Howard stood to shout orders, the seat would flip up and he would fall on his backside. We were in stitches. Howard didn't see the funny side of it though.

'It was a total shock to hear of his passing, He was far too young to leave this earth. I attended his funeral to show my respects and it was just amazing how the city came out to show their respects. There was a very eerie feeling around the city, and irrespective of blue or red, people respected what he had achieved and what he had done for football in Liverpool in that period.'

PAUL POWER

Debut: Saturday, 16 August 1986, Everton 1 Liverpool 1 – Charity Shield

Everton: Mimms, Harper, Power, Ratcliffe, Marshall, Langley, Steven, Heath, Sharp, Richardson, Sheedy (Adams 56 (Wilkinson 83))

Liverpool: Grobbelaar (Hooper 56), Venison, Beglin, Lawrenson, Whelan, Hansen, McMahon, Johnston, Rush, Mølby, MacDonald (Dalglish 65)

PEOPLE WOULD assume that when you reach the age of 32, sustaining a career in football at the top level would be considered impossible. Paul Power had only played for one club – Manchester City – before his move down the M62. He actually signed as cover for Pat Van Den Hauwe and Neil Pointon but went on to play 40 league games from a maximum of 42 in 1986/87.

For those who doubted Howard Kendall's latest signing, he proved to be a class act and ended up with not just the league championship, but on a personal level, the player of the year award, an honour he received twice in his time at Maine Road. His initials are PP but he was known to his team-mates as Peter Pan.

Paul looked back on his time with Kendall, 'Thinking of the great man, I actually think about a manager that most inspired me as an individual player. I've worked under some good managers, Tony Book for one, Malcolm Allison, John Bond, all good managers. Howard was a little bit different because he could manage any department within the football club. He was comfortable in the players company, tell a joke, but the players would tell him to f*** off as his jokes were crap anyway. He could talk to players individually or collectively; it was that easy for him.

'When he spoke about the directors, he was never in awe of them. I could imagine it being the other way round where they would be in awe of him.

'If there was a word to describe his style of management, it would be friendly. He rarely fell out with anybody. I've worked under managers who I won't name, and the way they would speak to some experienced players and internationals, it was despicable. Howard was never like that. He would have words, but would never fall out with them and vice versa. It was mutual respect between each other. The players knew that whatever decision Howard made, it was always for the good of the football club. When I first signed for Everton in 1986, I was 32 years of age. Howard wasn't that much older than me!

'We as a group went out all of the time. It wasn't just me; it was all of the lads. I remember once getting beat by Wimbledon away in an FA Cup tie. We were expected to beat them but we didn't. Most other managers would have demanded that we be in for training the following morning and run the socks off you. Instead, Howard said, "There's no training tomorrow, everybody meets at a Chinese restaurant in Southport."

'There were games going on amongst the lads, to keep morale going, and if any players had been fined for whatever, the money was used to pay for the meals and drinks, etc. He also loved being around his staff: Terry Darracott, Colin Harvey, Mike Lyons. All of them liked a drink. Howard was always happy when he was around his friends.

'Howard would take all the lads away for a week's break at the end of the season to Magaluf, which was his favourite holiday destination. He was always proud of what the club stood for, their standards.

'Howard always told you when you went out on your own not to forget that you were representing Everton Football Club. Don't do anything stupid, but he trusted you.

'I never saw him angry. He dealt with players without the anger. I've seen him frustrated after a poor performance. I do recall one Monday morning; we always had an 11-a-side game and Howard and Colin would join in. Howard was hoping to put things right from the game at the weekend previously, or maybe a view to making changes for a midweek game coming up. There was one occasion when Howard and I were on the same side. I was playing wide on the left; he played the ball to me and I went on the overlap. I shouted "Yes Howard" as I was going to play the ball down the line to him. On the way back he said, "It's Boss, not Howard, OK? I'm not your best mate."

'He had a way of telling you what he wanted without belittling you or coming the heavy hand. He was very diplomatic.

'Did I share a good relationship with him? Yes, absolutely. I was there for two seasons, then Howard left for Bilbao. I had one good season there when we won the championship. I got injured towards the end of that season then struggled to get into the team after that.

'I would play with Lyonsy in the reserves as well as train with the first team to help bring the lads on such as John Ebbrell, Eddie Youds, Mark Wright and a few more. Howard would sometimes give me orders to conduct a training session. He would give you that responsibility. Howard would encourage you to further your career.

'I remember one time I was in the dressing room at half-time having a cup of tea. He came over to me and tapped my knee. His remark was, "That's the best performance

I've ever seen by a left-back at this football club." He had a way of making you feel like a million dollars. If he thought you'd played well, he would tell you. If you played poorly or did something wrong, he would put it right on the training field. He would stand with you and explain how he wanted to rectify things where you would be made to understand.

'If he left you out of the side, he would break the news to you individually. You wouldn't be expected to come in and read a team sheet without your name being on it. He would get you in his office on the Friday, and if you were absent from the squad, he would tell you to your face, also the reason why you weren't included.

'Comparing him to other managers in my career, if I was going to write a book – and because I wore the number five shirt at Wembley for Manchester City, I would write my five favourite managers – Howard would be number one. Gordon Taylor would be number two. I worked with Gordon at the PFA.

'Howard was unbelievable. His knowledge of the game was second to none. I never knew how to defend as a back four until I went to Everton. Kevin Ratcliffe and Dave Watson were the two centre-backs, defending as a line, when to drop and when to hold. I never understood any of that until I went to Everton. I have worked with some great coaches over the years. That was the biggest lesson I learned from him.

'In his company, he never ever spoke about his own playing career. Everybody knows about Kendall, Ball and Harvey. I had the pleasure of working with two of them, and Bally was at Manchester City as manager around the same time.

'Going back to the players, he would actually ask players their advice. He wanted to buy Neil McDonald from Newcastle United. When I was injured in my second season, he would send me out to watch players. He asked my opinion about Neil McDonald. He was never above himself to ask players their opinion on certain players.

'For those who never saw Howard play, he was very similar to Peter Reid. Kevin Ratcliffe was the captain but to all intents and purposes Reidy was captain because he led by example and was utterly reliable. If and when Howard signed a player, he was reliable.

'Howard liked a player that played with the same commitment as he trained, someone that would put in a full shift.'

Nobody could deny Paul a league championship winners' medal. He weighed in with four goals, the first one coming at Maine Road against his former employers at the end of November 1987 in a 3-1 win. It was the second Everton goal that afternoon. He accepted a pass from Graeme Sharp on the edge of the 18-yard box and unleashed a drive with his left foot beyond Perry Suckling.

Paul had nothing but respect for the fans who worshipped him from his Manchester City days and he refused to celebrate his strike. That didn't stop Kendall and co. celebrating on the bench though.

NEIL ADAMS

Debut: Saturday, 16 August 1986, Everton 1 Liverpool 1 – Charity Shield

Everton: Mimms, Harper, Power, Ratcliffe, Marshall, Langley, Steven, Heath, Sharp, Richardson, Sheedy (Adams 56 (Wilkinson 83))

Liverpool: Grobbelaar (Hooper 56), Venison, Beglin, Lawrenson, Whelan, Hansen, McMahon, Johnston, Rush, Mølby, MacDonald (Dalglish 65)

NEIL WAS another player who came from Stoke City; he had been spotted by the Potteries club while playing in a junior match. At this time, Neil was studying a career in electrical engineering as everyone's dream of being a professional footballer doesn't always come true.

In his last season at Stoke, Neil appeared 38 times in all competitions, scoring four goals. Making his debut in the Charity Shield alongside Paul Power and Kevin Langley, Neil was introduced as a substitute just before the hour then was later replaced by Paul Wilkinson from the substitutes' bench, something that's not common in football.

In September 1986, Neil received his first England under-21 cap when lining up for a game in Sweden.

Neil failed to establish himself as a first-team regular at Goodison, and with limited appearances he was loaned out to Oldham Athletic before making the move permanent.

Neil says, 'When you mention Howard, for me, he's the one name that made my career as a footballer. That's how big of an impact he had in shaping my career. I was at Stoke City at a relatively young age, going into the first team and becoming a regular. I was only there for under a season. When arriving at Everton, Howard told me he had scouts looking at me at every single game. He got to know everything about me, and to go to Everton in the summer of 1986, Everton for me were probably the best team in Europe. The season before I arrived, they had won the league and Cup Winners' Cup, and the season later just missed out on the league and the FA Cup. For a 19-year-old lad, going to Everton was a dream come true which was made by Howard.

'Every time I hear his name or see a picture of him, he's the one that put me on that platform to grasp the chance to go on and have a good career. Had I not gone to Everton, who knows what would have happened. He was a fabulous person, a fantastic player and a fantastic manager; his record speaks for itself. To think what he achieved after a poor start, he's probably one of the best managers that they have ever had, and also the last manager to bring a league title to the club.

'Comparing him to any other manager in my career, it's probably biased to say, but of the success, I only have to look in my trophy cabinet at home with the equivalent of a Premier League medal. I think all of the players will be forever thankful to Howard for that.

'If you asked any Everton player about his strengths, nine out of ten would say his man-management. It's quite a loose throwaway term. What is man-management? It's hard to put it down in words, and ask some of the staff that worked alongside him. He had this way where he could interact with his players. You knew he was the boss, you knew when it was the right time to have a laugh and a joke, when to get your head down and work. He got that right off to a tee; he was absolutely brilliant at it. He loved nothing better than to be sitting around a table at the end of the season with the players having a beer, a laugh and a sing-song.

'Some people might say that a manager shouldn't do that, getting that close. I would say that was right, he probably shouldn't, but he was that good at how he managed it that he could do it, because he never really got too close to the players where he became friendly and familiar other than the end of the season where he was just one of the boys. As soon as that was over and went back into pre-season training, he was then the Gaffer. That for me was his biggest strength. All of the players loved him whether you were in or out of the team or on the bench. He kept everybody involved. It made everyone feel part of the squad. It was really difficult to dislike him, he was such a fantastic guy. I was a young lad looking up to all of these heroes. Howard kept everyone and everything together. Everyone talks about that spirit, the dressing room spirit, the camaraderie, there was nothing better than that anywhere apart from Goodison at that time. Howard was the one that set that environment.

'He was the boss in the dressing room, it's as simple as that. He was never one to waffle. He was an intelligent footballer who took his knowledge into his management. He knew what to say, to keep it concise, to get his point across whether it was a pat on the back, or something that would shake up the team or as an individual.

'He told you exactly what he wanted, there was no ambiguity there – if you didn't do it, he would tell you. Those are the type of managers that players respond to the best.

'At the training ground he was slightly different because it's a non-matchday. Matchday is business day, isn't it? At Bellefield, there was a laugh and a joke every single day.

Howard loved to train and play, and even then, whilst playing, you could see what a player he must have been in his time, as was Colin. You wouldn't even know they were coaches; they were that good.

'In his playing days, Howard was a maestro that belonged to a great, well-known midfield. He was also an elegant player, a classy player that could pick out a pass, very comfortable on the ball. I think he just liked a player that could do that. Paul Scholes was similar.'

I asked Neil what made Howard happy. 'Obviously, success. I wasn't there when he endured a tough time, but have read about it. To achieve the success he did, starting in 1984 through to 1985, 1986 and 1987, that magnifies how much it meant to him. He had been on the opposite side of it where results weren't going his way. Lifting silverware at Wembley and running around Goodison twice with the league championship trophy must have meant an awful lot to him. Aside from that, happiness is success on the pitch where he did a fantastic job, and afterwards enjoying himself being with his players. He loved being in Majorca with the lads, with a glass of wine in his hand and a smile on his face on the back end of a successful season.

'Howard loved team bonding too. Every dressing room's banter is good but at Everton, it was everyone. Everybody was in it together and it was one of the reasons they were so successful. It's an old cliche but it's not all about ability and talent, it's about how the players are with each other. It's well documented that we used to go out together and it would not be five or six but 20-odd of us and Howard would encourage that with a Chinese meal. The squad list would go up for a Chinese meal as well as a game, we had sing-songs with staff and players alike, but everybody knew where the line was with the manager. People who didn't know who we were could walk in and think that we were 25 rowdy blokes having a great time. Howard, Colin, Mickey Lyons and Terry Darracott were also part of that. Mick Heaton too, God rest his soul.

'Howard would show his anger if you were underperforming. He knew that you were always prone to making mistakes, and I was told on my arrival by Adrian Heath that one thing the manager and fans will love you for is 100 per cent effort. They will forgive underperforming and mistakes, as long as you're giving absolutely everything.

'At half-time when things weren't going too well, Howard could be quite snappy but never shouting and bawling.

'Regarding my relationship with him, I was a young player going to play for a manager that was known worldwide in football. I was never going to be "pally-pally" as some of the senior players were at the time. I can't pretend that I was very close because that wouldn't be right for a young player like myself who had only been in the game for just over a year. I was concentrating on getting my career going and getting as many minutes on the pitch as I possibly could.

'Some people say that Colin Harvey didn't get the credit he deserved; I think he did. I think certainly that everyone that worked with him would happily say how much he did contribute to the success and he was a big help to Howard.

'Colin was sort of the bad cop a lot of the time where Howard was the good cop. Colin was the one that would crack the whip if training wasn't right. Colin had a nasty bark about him which made people jump when he had to.

'Howard was very good at dealing with the media and the press, but Colin was very good at the technical side of the game, spotting where things had gone right or wrong.

'Colin would take you in the office on a Monday to point out the smallest detail of a mistake. Everybody talks about [Brian] Clough and [Peter] Taylor ten years prior to Howard and Colin, but they weren't too far behind them.'

Everton were denied the opportunity to play in the European Cup as circumstances at the Heysel Stadium in May 1985 led to English clubs being excluded from European competition for several years.

'The European ban on the club was very harsh,' says Neil. 'I think as a group we all felt the disappointment. Howard never spoke about it; he didn't have to. I feel that the ban from the biggest competition had a massive impact on his move to Bilbao. It must have been a bitter blow to him to lead the team to the top of the tree only to be denied the opportunity to play in the top European competition.

'Howard's signings? You'd have to look at the likes of Peter Reid, Kevin Sheedy, Trevor Steven, those players that had a massive impact at the club. Peter Reid would probably be the big one for me. What a player to play alongside. He was inspirational. He would put his body on the line to win an 80-20 against him. He'd been footballer of the year, played in the 1986 World Cup in Mexico, and was the driving force of the team when he was fit and available. It sounds unfair to select one player from a team that had so much success with the squad that they had, but he was the heartbeat of the team.

'Howard was always offering advice to each and every one of his players. I can remember when I signed, Paul Power signed at the same time. We had our medicals and signed contracts at the same time and we both had some time with Howard. I can remember sitting in one of the restaurants at the ground having a bit of lunch. He said, "The people that come into this stadium are probably different to what you'll see." I asked him what he meant. Howard replied, "The success that these people crave for is something you will understand when you hear the passion there is."

'Of course, you don't understand until you experience that moment when you get that opportunity. I can remember it most in my first derby game. I remember Sharpy saying to me, "Wait until ten seconds before the kick-off when you hear the roar, you'll get what it's all about, also what Howard had told you." The referee checked with both goalkeepers before blowing his whistle and this roar came from nowhere. I then realised what Howard was talking about.

'It was a surprise and a shock I guess to find out Howard was leaving a club he played for and managed to undertake a new role, on foreign soil, which I did in the summer of 1987. We were away on an end-of-season tour. There were rumours, which is always the case. You hoped deep down that it wouldn't happen, but you were resigned to the fact that because he'd been so successful, he probably would go with a big offer from a big club. I don't think it came as a shock or a surprise because you could see that he wanted to manage at the highest level and take the best opportunity he could. It wouldn't have been fair to have begrudged him that opportunity as he'd done so well.

It was a massive shock when I heard that Howard had passed away. I travelled from Norwich for the funeral. It was a real emotional day, and it's easy for me to sum up the day. I remember virtually every single player being there which pretty much sums Howard up as a person, manager, as whatever. Those people just had to be there to pay their respects because of what he'd done for them, whether it was in a big or small way. Everybody owed him something, we all did because he helped us be successful and we helped him be successful.

'After the funeral we returned to Goodison where we raised a glass to him; he loved nothing more than that. It was such a good day, but a good day in inverted commas. We lost one of the best in Howard, and if he could have seen that he would have been exceptionally proud of his players. It was a fantastic tribute to a fantastic person and manager.'

KEVIN LANGLEY

Debut: Saturday, 16 August 1986, Everton 1 Liverpool 1 – Charity Shield

Everton: Mimms, Harper, Power, Ratcliffe, Marshall, Langley, Steven, Heath, Sharp, Richardson, Sheedy (Adams 56 (Wilkinson 83))

Liverpool: Grobbelaar (Hooper 56), Venison, Beglin, Lawrenson, Whelan, Hansen, McMahon, Johnston, Rush, Mølby, MacDonald (Dalglish 65)

BEFORE BECOMING a professional footballer, Kevin Langley was a painter and decorator playing in his local area. His father made a phone call to Wigan Athletic asking them to cast an eye over the youngster, and the rest as they say is history.

Langley's Everton career kicked off at the stadium where he had played his last game for Wigan the previous May, winning the Freight Rover Trophy against Brentford.

A sum of £120,000 changed hands between Everton and Wigan and Kevin became a regular in the first 11. He hit the ground running, finding the net three times in his first nine appearances, with his first goal coming in the second game of the season at Hillsborough, securing a hard-earned point and elevating Everton to third place in the table.

His first goal at Goodison was eight days later, sealing the points in the 82nd minute and restoring a two-goal cushion in a 3-1 victory against Oxford United.

However, he later lost his form and within seven months he had left Goodison for nearby Manchester City in the Second Division.

Kevin looks back, 'When I was at Wigan, I came in one day and the manager [Ray Mathias] said to me that a club had made an offer for me to which I asked who. "Crewe Alexandra," came the reply. I said, "Well, you've obviously accepted it so OK. "I'm joking," the manager replied. "You'd better sit down; you're going to get a phone call from Howard Kendall." I could not believe my ears. The phone rang and it was Howard.

'The first time I ever met him it was at the Bell Tower on the East Lancs Road. I took my wife to be with me; Howard was absolutely brilliant. One of the first questions he asked me was, "Do you drink?" "Yes," I replied, to which he answered, "You'll do for me, lad."

'Howard was always one to offer advice, from day one. In pre-season I remember Oldham Athletic came to Bellefield for a behind-closed-doors game. Everton and Oldham's first teams competed on one pitch with the reserve sides playing against each other on another. I was playing for the second team but was called over to play the second half for the first team. At the full-time whistle Howard came over to me, telling me that I did really well. That sort of attention is good for your confidence. I wasn't one for finding the net often, but I scored three times in my first nine games for the club.

'Howard was obviously a person that brought success to the club, but behind every top manager is an assistant which in this case was Colin Harvey. In fact, at first, I thought he WAS the manager because he did so much. He gave me advice on a regular basis and lots of encouragement.

'Colin was very influential in the dressing room. Before a game he would speak to individuals and go over set pieces.

Howard was always suited, would be quite relaxed and basically encourage you. Nothing with Howard's talks was complicated.

'In training at Bellefield, Howard and Colin both made the sessions enjoyable. Terry Darracott and youth team coach Graham Smith would also be involved, especially when it came to playing head tennis. They were teammates from their playing days and best friends. I could only describe them as a good cop, bad cop. They were the perfect partnership.

'Howard and Colin participated in everything, and both loved to play head tennis with Howard always wanting to win. Five-a-side, again, he wanted to win. Being a winner was in his make-up, which was proved in the time that he was there, with no manager ever coming close to his achievements.

'Coming from the third tier of English football with Wigan Athletic to a team of Everton's quality, despite the difference in leagues and the standard, Howard always made you feel like an equal.

'I felt that Howard restricted me in a lot of ways on the field as to how I played on the pitch. I was pulled to one side by Howard moments before we played Arsenal at Goodison as I was up against Kevin Richardson. Howard told me that he didn't want me to have more than two touches of the ball and he didn't want me in front of the ball. If he saw that, he was going to withdraw me.

'Like all human beings, Howard could show an angry side to him. He didn't like to lose games but then who does? To be fair, when I was there at that time, we didn't lose many games, did we? He gave me a telling off once for losing my marker [Alan Dickens] down at West Ham who scored and they went on to win the game.

'If individuals needed telling off, he would do it, that's only because he cared. He wouldn't waste his energy on you by yelling at you if he didn't need to. It was his job to make sure you were doing a job you were getting paid for.

'The flip side: when we won, especially away from home, there was nothing he enjoyed more than a sing-song back to Merseyside.

'Nobody can argue that he was a great manager. You only have to look at the trophies he won in his time at Everton which has made him the most successful manager in the history of the club. As much as I loved playing for him, I'm not trying to compare, and I know it sounds daft, but Harry McNally at Chester I adored, he was a top man. He was a fair man, and when you did something wrong you knew about it. Howard and Harry were two different people with different personalities, but a pleasure to play for.

'In the transfer market, how many managers would have brought in old heads like Andy Gray and Peter Reid? For me, Colin Harvey was a great signing in terms of appointing him as his number two, but what a player Paul Power turned out to be. He, for me, had to be his most influential signing.

'Being a manager like any other role in life has its advantages and disadvantages. Managing a successful side, how do you keep your players happy? He always made sure the squad were a tight-knit group who did everything together. Eating out at a Chinese restaurant, having a few drinks together, that's what Howard introduced and liked with the results paying off because of that.

'I recall one moment when I had a spell playing as a regular, and one morning on my day off, I received a phone call from Howard telling me that Peter Reid and Paul Bracewell were on the verge of a return and that I would have to take a step back. That's very hard to take, but Howard knew his strongest players making his starting 11. He had a hardcore squad of about 17 players. At one stage, there were players like Gary Stevens, Neville Southall, Pat

Van Den Hauwe, Derek Mountfield, key members injured, but the players that he'd signed, when drafted in, did a great job. I can't think of anyone ever letting the boss down.

'I signed for the club after they had reaped the glory in 1984/85, but I was part of the squad that won the championship for the second time in three years. What an achievement that must be to be top of the tree after a nine-month haul over 42 games as it was back then. Winning the league championship has got to be the top priority for any manager, that is the one you want to win. You also have to give credit to the backroom staff who didn't get the recognition they deserve. What a great team the boss had behind him.'

DAVE WATSON

Debut: Saturday, 23 August 1986, Everton 2 Nottingham Forest 0

Everton: Mimms, Harper, Power, Ratcliffe, Watson, Langley, Steven, Heath, Sharp, Richardson (Wilkinson 85), Sheedy

Nottingham Forest: Sutton, Fleming, Pearce, Walker, Metgod, Bowyer, Carr, Webb, Clough, Birtles, Campbell

GARY LINEKER went through the exit door after Everton suffered heartbreak by conceding the double to Liverpool in 1985/86. The 40-goal wonder was not replaced by another striker, Howard Kendall choosing instead to fill the centre-back role solidly with the arrival of Norwich City captain Dave Watson for £900,000, a club record at that time.

Derek Mountfield had cemented a good relationship with his idols on the Gwladys Street terrace, where he once stood as a fan, with Watson not being very well received by the Evertonians. But Kendall was never a bad judge of a player and 'Waggy', as he was known in the blue camp, never failed to live up to his reputation and time was the healer as he won the fans over.

Dave appeared 35 times in the league as the First Division championship was restored to its rightful place in the trophy cabinet at Goodison. He found the net three times, all in the second half of the campaign and all at home, against Sheffield Wednesday, Southampton and West Ham, the latter a resounding 4-0 win.

It was on Monday, 4 May that Dave returned to Norwich to help his new team-mates clinch the important victory to wrap up the league title.

He served Everton well, later becoming the club captain, and he remains the last Blues skipper to lift a trophy – the 1995 FA Cup Final victory over Manchester United.

Dave spoke of his memories of Howard Kendall, 'I think of a great football man who, as an ex-player himself, knew how players want to be managed. He could relate to the working-class lad and relate to anyone. He could manage any type of player. He had a great understanding of man-management, which was his massive strength.

'His style of management was a great demand on the players for 100 per cent work ethic and team spirit. He's a person that loved a great atmosphere about the place which he would create. He would buy players that can make these things happen. I would describe him as a very passionate man, who loved to see passion around him when he's at the training ground. He loved characters; he loved a sense of humour about the place.

'At the training ground he worked with Colin, who took a lot of the work off Howard. Howard was well organised and always had a smile on his face and even if we were beaten on a Saturday, he had this knack of making you feel good after a defeat. Normally, you would be moping about for a couple of days, but he would get you out of that mope by taking the lads out for a meal as he could sense when they were feeling low.

'We as a group would respond magnificently from that. Howard would have been in those situations I'm sure a few times himself as a player.

'Colin by the way was very different to Howard when he took over after Howard left for Spain. Colin was very intense. He demanded the best from everyone every day, which was great from a coach, and Howard would be able to soften things up with a bit of a smile. Howard would be able to have a talk and a laugh with the players, whereas Colin was the intense one.

'It is a little bit difficult to change over from being the intense one to having a laugh and a joke. I think that Colin found that a little bit tough really. Overall, what Colin has done for Everton and the number of kids that he has helped come through; he had been unbelievable for them. His desire rubbed off on people.

'Everyone would love to be in Howard's company. Wherever you were you would get round Howard because he always had stories, not stories that were boring, stories that would make you laugh. He had such an infectious laugh himself.

'Magaluf was a place Howard loved. It was time for us all to enjoy ourselves having worked our socks off all year. If you'd had a productive season, going away was magnificent. If your season was trophyless and the team were burnt out, it was still a great way to keep the team atmosphere and spirit.

'When all of the lads would go into Bellefield for training, we would sit down and have a cup of tea with him. He was the heart and soul of the conversation all of the time.

'Howard by the way would show touches of class in training, similar to Peter Reid. Reidy is a winner. Everything he did from playing cards on the bus to what he did on the pitch, he wanted to win, a typical predator. When players were in trouble and had to go in to see the manager, Reidy would instil confidence in you to take away any concerns.

'Howard never spoke about his own playing career, but spoke of players he rated by bringing someone like Andy Gray in that's injured, a character and a battler, that got the rest of the squad motivated. Andy was the ideal person that was great for the dressing room.

'Howard obviously identified players; Paul Power is another example. A player who was at the end of his career, and probably someone that no other club would touch.

'Wayne Clarke was another Howard brought in, with Stuart Storer. Clarkey goes on to score a very important goal away to Arsenal which set us up for clinching the league.

'Winning is what football is all about. Howard was in his element after we'd won a game, making a very happy man and knowing the lads had given everything to win. Howard could take a defeat as long as everyone gave their best. He would let you know too if he wasn't happy. A manager at times has got to do something different. Every now and again he has to throw a bomb in. Howard would of course lose his lid sometimes, mostly down to frustration at things not being the way he wanted them to be.

'I shared a fantastic relationship with him from the day that I signed up until he died. We would often bump into each other at dinners, etc. He's a man that will remain with me for the rest of my life.

'Howard was always upbeat. If ever you were going through a tough time, he would get you over it. If ever you had any personal issues, he would like to find out and help you. I endured problems myself when I first went to Goodison. It took time to adjust, but Howard was always there to help me. He would also tell you not to let the football take over your life. If you go home after a game on a Saturday and have lost, you were expected to come back in on the Monday morning firing on all cylinders again. If you lost, it was let's go again.

'Also, if he left you out of his team, he would call you in the office and talk to you. One time he called me and Derek Mountfield in together and told us as much as he would love to play the two of us together, he couldn't. He told me that I was included in the team but also consoled Derek with words of, "Well, it could have been you," which still made Derek feel wanted.

'I had played for several managers throughout my career, and every manager has his own style. Howard got it right because he put a team of players and a team of coaches together. Colin was a great, great, great number two for Howard because he was the most disciplined man in the world. He demanded more so than Howard that things were done right where players would arrive on time and work as hard as they possibly could. Colin was the main man to be fair as far as the training went. Howard would be assessing things from the side. When you're training with the manager stood watching, you're always aware of what he may be thinking. That had more of an effect on the players than Howard participating in training sessions.

'He had a great way of handling his players. If someone came in and had bad press and Howard was aware of it, he would call that person concerned into his office. He would break the ice by giving them a little can of lager or something as well as a chat. It wouldn't be a rant and a rave. Howard would I'm sure been in those situations himself as a player where he thinks he's going into an office to get a rollicking, and maybe the manager he was under saw how he handled that situation.

'I can remember players coming in stinking of alcohol. I won't name the player out of respect, but one morning Howard joins in with the training as we were grouped in a circle and shouts of "STOP". Howard says to the player, "You stink of alcohol." "Gaffer," says the accused, "I was out last night having a curry."

'Howard said, "I can tell the difference between a curry and a pint of alcohol," which then brought out a laugh amongst the lads and got the atmosphere going in the place.

'I can't remember too many players being punished heavily with a fine unless you got sent off and there was a clause in your contract to say you would be fined.

'For his funeral to be held at Liverpool Cathedral says it all about the man; the turnout, the sheer numbers were expected anyway. The number of faces there – not just football, celebrity stars too. Even outside, people came to pay their respects in the same way. There were even Liverpool supporters there too which showed how loved he was.

'Reidy read the eulogy which he did well. Funerals are not great occasions but from a send-off point of view, it was magnificent.

'I will always be grateful for knowing this man and will hold nothing but good memories. Funny memories are something that will stay with me for ever too. The funniest memory was when we went out to Mauritius and a few kit skips went out with us. In the skips there were bottles of Moët & Chandon. When we arrived, Howard demanded that the skips were put in his and the kit man's room. Howard would help the lads out too with the contents of the skip.

'On a boating trip, we were on this very small boat. One of the lads jumped out over the side but was able to stand up in the water to his chest. Howard jumped over the other side thinking that the depth would be the same but to his surprise sank right down and he nearly drowned.'

Dave retired from playing aged 39 and had a spell managing Tranmere Rovers, as well as working as a coach at Norwich, then later at Newcastle. He also worked as a volunteer with the National Trust.

WARREN ASPINALL

Debut: Tuesday, 16 September 1986, Liverpool 3 Everton 1 – ScreenSport Super Cup Final, first leg
Liverpool: Hooper, Venison, Beglin, Lawrenson, Whelan (Mølby 71), Gillespie, Dalglish, Nicol, Rush, MacDonald, McMahon
Everton: Mimms, Billing, Power, Ratcliffe, Marshall, Langley, Adams, Wilkinson, Sharp, Steven, Sheedy (Aspinall 42)

WARREN ASPINALL was a local boy from Wigan who played at Springfield Park from the age of 13 to become an apprentice with the Latics. He progressed through the ranks, eventually breaking into the first team, which was managed by former Everton player Bryan Hamilton. Howard Kendall wanted to make Aspinall a part of his plans, persuading Wigan to part company with him for a fee of £150,000. Warren played most of his games for the Toffees in the Central League and scored five goals in a 7-0 rout against Middlesbrough in October 1986, the first player to score that many since Rob Wakenshaw hit six two years previously.

In his first campaign, Aspinall made nine appearances as a substitute before heading back to Wigan on loan until the end of the season.

He never returned to Goodison, and instead found himself at Aston Villa, helping them clinch promotion out of the Second Division in 1988.

Warren recalled his transfer to Everton, saying that in talks with Kendall, the manager wouldn't let him leave the room until he put pen to paper on his contract, 'He wanted me to learn off the best, which was Gary Lineker at the time. I still had the chance to live at home which was OK. I was always going to learn from working and playing with world-class players.

'I came on for Gary Lineker; it was his last home game of the 1985/86 season for Everton. I remember touching the ball and nutmegging Alvin Martin, who at that time was a very good defender. It was a good end of the season despite finishing second in the league.

'I was loaned back to Wigan as they were going for promotion. We were denied promotion on the last day of the season on goal difference, as there were no play-offs in those days.

'Just being involved with the lads, especially the week of the FA Cup Final, was probably my most memorable time at the club. I wasn't playing, but it was still nice to be involved with the build-up. They were things that you dreamed of when you were a little lad. I had to be pinching myself that I was around with so many players who were immense and to be of that stature.

'Howard was amazing and a good man-manager. He liked to socialise with the players too. The players respected him, and would one day work with you, and the next he'd be having a drink with you. He had that perfect balance.

'Colin Harvey wasn't the same as Howard in that way. In training the two of them were by far the best head tennis players in the club. They would play with Terry Darracott and Peter Reid. Howard on the training ground showed that he still had the class that made him such an important cog in the Holy Trinity in his playing days. He was in a league of his own when it came to head tennis in the training sessions.

'He was a very approachable manager. His door was always open if you wanted to speak with him. He liked a laugh and a joke, but you always knew that there was a line not to be crossed. Off the pitch he looked after his players; for instance, every couple of weeks he'd take us to a restaurant in Southport, using the money that was raised from the fining of players! His methods were for the spirit of the players and the team bonding.

'Howard was a man that always made you feel wanted no matter what. I was called into his office after the last game of the season in 1986. He told me that England wanted me to go to China, but he wanted me to go to Magaluf with the boys for an end-of-season get-together. As I thought about it, Howard told me I was going to Magaluf, which left me with no choice but to go.

'Whilst in Magaluf, I was out with the players on a night out. Howard loved the players to socialise and loved morale amongst the group. I went out for a meal with Peter Billing, Darrin Coyle and somebody else, I can't remember who. I was wearing a pair of cream trousers that night. Peter Reid was out, but sat down having a drink. I went to break wind but followed through. I went to the toilet to wash my trousers and dried them with the hand dryers. By the time I went back into the restaurant, the lads had left with the bill for the meal unpaid.

'Fortunately, I emptied my pockets and just had enough money to cover the bill.'

IAN SNODIN

Debut: Saturday, 17 January 1987, Everton 2 Sheffield Wednesday 0
Everton: Southall, Stevens, Pointon, Ratcliffe, Watson (Snodin HT), Power, Steven, Heath, Sharp, Harper, Sheedy
Sheffield Wednesday: Hodge, Morris, Worthington, Smith, Madden, Snodin, Jonsson, Megson, Chapman, Bradshaw, Shelton (Chamberlain HT)

IAN SNODIN was involved in a tug of war with Liverpool for his signature from Leeds United. Howard Kendall and Kenny Dalglish tried their best to convince 'Snods' that their club was the best place for this young Yorkshireman.

Whatever Howard said worked, with Ian putting pen to paper to seal his commitment. The decision proved to be the right one with a league championship medal appearing in his cabinet months later.

Unfortunately, injuries took their toll, but years later he was recognised as a club ambassador.

Ian says, 'I think of Howard first and foremost as a manager, my manager, and secondly, even bigger a compliment, a friend. We became friends after he finished his managerial career. He lived in Formby, I was in Birkdale, and not being too far apart from each other, we spent many a time together. I found him to be a fantastic human being to be around, not just in the dressing room but sociably as well.

'His man-management was as good as I've ever known. Billy Bremner was the best manager that I'd had for my career as he'd had me from a 15-year-old. I think Howard took over from Billy when I'd left Leeds United.

'I could not have wished for a better man-manager than Howard, even though he left six months after I'd signed.

'He knew when to give you a rollicking, and also when to have a laugh and a joke. That for me is a sign of a fantastic man-manager.

'If I wasn't involved, especially through being sidelined with injury, he made sure he always spoke to me every day. There are no darker days than when you're out injured and in the treatment room on a daily basis. He always made sure that I was mentally OK. He always made me feel part of everything despite not being able to participate with the group.

'When I was injured, Howard would request that I go and watch players he would be interested in signing. The biggest compliment I could pay him was that he took me into his office and explained that if I never recovered from my niggling hamstring injury that had been operated on four times, I was going to be made youth team coach. Thankfully, I recovered, and Dave Fogg became the youth team manager. I'm sure there are managers then and now that will only concentrate on the players that are available. Howard sent me and my family away for a week's holiday abroad to keep my spirits up.

'I can only describe my relationship with the man as nothing but fantastic. I think the fact that I signed for him in 1987 and turned down Kenny Dalglish and Liverpool helped. I think that must have been a massive plus for him because in my eyes, Everton were as big a club as Liverpool back then. I think the reaction surprised Howard when I told him that I was going to sign for him and not Liverpool. That, I guess, made me a little favourite with him. I don't think I could have gone wrong with him personally as a friend.

'I mentioned the fact that he could dish out a rollicking when he needed to. As a disciplinarian Howard was a no-nonsense fella and was very strict when it came to lateness. He did not take kindly to any player who would turn up late for a team meeting, catching the team bus, things like that. If you were late, no question, you would be fined.

'If you failed to react to his rules, he would make it clear as to who was in charge and put you back in your place.

'He was someone that I could never really fault on anything. He would always be upfront and honest with players by telling you if you were not to his standard on the pitch for the 90 minutes you had played. I saw Howard as the whole package, and the whole package is what I enjoyed on and off the field.

'He loved the team bonding sessions, which were mad. They were very much part of his man-management that was a big strength on his part. I'd never witnessed anything like it in my life. If there were any issues, it would give anyone the opportunity to clear the air. We would always win the game after we'd had one of those team bonding sessions.

'I had never in my life been out for a Chinese meal until I joined Everton. The first time I went, Neville Southall and myself had chicken and chips!

'In the dressing room, Howard's team talks, I remember probably my first one. I was used to Billy Bremner going around individuals giving instructions telling you what to do and revving you up. He probably would have spent from 2pm until 2.50pm giving you instructions, preparing the players for the game ahead.

'The first one I'd been involved with at Everton, I wondered where the manager was. Colin Harvey would go through in detail as to who you had to pick up from free kicks and corners, that sort of thing. Howard would appear about 2.45pm and give a little bit of a team talk, and when the bell rang to order you out, Howard would pat you on the back wishing you all the very best. All he would say was, "The same as last week, boys." Then again, what did he have to say to a team like that? He didn't have to say anything as the team were good enough.'

Many years later, Ian holds a memory which he regards as a very special moment, 'I will never ever forget the interview I did with him at Formby Hall. It would have been one of the last interviews that he ever did. Howard brought me to this fantastic football club, and I will always be grateful to him for that opportunity.'

Howard repeated the success of bringing the league championship trophy back home for the second time in three years, but which of those successes did Ian think gave the manager the most pleasure?

'I think Howard would have got most pleasure from the success before I joined because of the massive pressure he endured before things started to change for the better. That team would have given him more satisfaction and rightly so.

'When he won the league the second time around, he'd brought in Dave Watson and produced a masterstroke by bringing in Paul Power and Wayne Clarke.'

Following that second trophy, the announcement that Howard was to depart Goodison shocked the football world. Ian recalled, 'It was a total surprise when it was announced about Howard's departure to Bilbao, which was very much a hidden secret. I found out from the radio which came as a massive shock to me. I honestly thought that when I signed for Everton, he was going to be my manager for many years to come.'

If Howard's move to Bilbao came as a shock, so did the news that he had passed away.

'Learning of his passing came right out of the blue. On the Thursday, Howard had asked me to stand in for him, as he wasn't feeling too great, for a dinner he was supposed to be attending at Wavertree Town Hall. I told him to ring me the following day to give me the details of what time I had to be there, etc.

'Howard rang me and said that he would call me the following day to see how the event went.

'On the Saturday, I was going in to do the *Saint and Snods* show for the radio at 12pm. The life on my mobile phone battery was very low and it eventually died as the train was coming into Moorfields for me to catch. I wasn't able to charge my phone until I reached the Radio City Tower. When I had got some charge on my phone, I had several missed calls from the media guy at Everton, finally getting me five minutes before I was due to go on air, and he told me the news that the Gaffer had died.

'I was in a state of shock knowing that I'd only spoken to him the day previously, and I sat there looking at Ian St John saying, "No, no."

'Saint sat worryingly looking at me wondering what was going on, then asking me what the matter was. I put down the phone shedding tears and said to Saint that Howard Kendall had died. I was due to go on air but obviously wasn't feeling up to it. I went into a room for about 15 minutes, composing myself and my thoughts.

'The first guest on the show was Dave Prentice from the *Liverpool Echo*. I eventually went on air around 20 minutes later.

'At his funeral, I thought the turnout was absolutely incredible, and much deserved for the man that gave so much to the club, and the city. So many players and managers from other clubs showed the total respect that everybody had for him. It was definitely one of the saddest days in football and my life.'

JOHN EBBRELL

Debut: Tuesday, 3 March 1987, Everton 2 Charlton Athletic 2 after extra time (Charlton won 6-5 on penalties) – Full Members' Cup quarter-final
Everton: Southall, Van Den Hauwe, Pointon, Mountfield, Watson, Harper (Langley HT ET), Steven (Ebbrell 76), Heath, Wilkinson, Snodin, Adams
Charlton Athletic: Bolder, Humphrey, Reid, Peake, Thompson, Miller, Bennett (M. Stuart 92), Lee, Melrose, Shipley, C. Walsh

JOHN EBBRELL made his Everton debut in the Full Members' Cup, a competition that came in for the benefit of teams who were prevented from playing in Europe on account of the ban after Heysel. It was a far cry from Europe as it held no attraction whatsoever, which the attendances indicated.

Irrespective, the opportunity for John to make his first-team debut meant the competition was relevant, and it was a chance to show his manager what he was all about as Howard Kendall had been very much aware of his talent from a very early age.

John says, 'He was a great man, very astute, who brought some great characters into the dressing room, and was to manage that very well. He built a successful team and club in his first spell there. He was very demanding in wanting to play a certain way, demanding nothing but 100 per cent in training, which led into matches, where there was a logic to it with him and Colin. He always wanted you to enjoy what he was doing. I still have a phrase from Howard that

I use myself now in my management. So, to me, that's a sign of a really influential coach over a long period of time.

'Looking back, he saw something in me, pushing me as he was aware of me from the age of 14 or 15. So, from a selfish point of view, he looked out for me and got me integrated into the first-team squad as soon as he could.

'When he walked into a room, for me I was young when he was in his prime, you knew he'd walked in because he had that presence. There's a great picture of him walking out for the FA Cup Final against Watford where he just looked the part.

'He was a man of few words at times and put you in your place if he needed to. He had a tongue that was never rude, but you understood that you were there to work and do what he wanted and that was that.

'Howard was human like us all and he had his strengths and weaknesses. I thought he was really good on matchdays, in the dressing room I felt he always tried to get the players to relax, taking any restrictions, worries, concerns away. Sometimes, it would literally be two lines before you went out which might be motivational, it might be a little joke, but I felt he wasn't a coach before games who filled your head with too much tactics as you'd already done the work. You knew how you were going to play. If there was anything that needed addressing at half-time, whether that was telling a couple of players to pipe down, he had that authority to make sure that they shut up. He also had that, does the striker need to get hold of it more, do we need to get the full-backs on a bit more, what's the weakness in them?

'He added a few things but they weren't massive things, but actually in the second half, he'd made that difference because you could see the reaction.

'In his second spell, I once won the Barclays Young Eagle of the Month award, and we were out at Bellefield where we formed a circle with a few of the players who came out early and Howard stood at the back near the entrance of the building, when a shout cried out, "Eagle, Eagle." He called me over, hugged me, and said, "Young Eagle of the Month, son." He was so pleased for me and you could tell. He was never one to give lots of praise, and when you were on the receiving end of some, it meant a lot because you knew that you had to earn that.

'I was away a lot at the age of 14 and 15, and when I returned, he had me training with the first team in my school holidays. "How are you son, are you OK?" he would ask. The fact he had me training with the champions and the best team in the country, I would go back to Lilleshall feeling like one of the best players in England. That's how he made you feel which gave me great confidence.

'I had nothing but total respect for the man, and would have run through a brick wall for him. He just had that charisma that you wanted him to. He could make you feel six feet tall within seconds, if you wanted to be on the right side and not hear the worst which he could, but you needed to be at the top of your game.

'When I started to play for him in his second spell at the club, he very much left me alone. I can remember him very rarely overly criticising me. I can very much remember him standing on the touchline at Goodison after 15 minutes with his arms outstretched, "Any chance of a tackle, John?" That made me go and get tight to people. For him to say or demand that from me was unusual. You always knew where you stood with him.

'It's very difficult to put your finger on how he pulled it all together, but he had some really good players, a really good coach with him in Colin, and you could feel that something was igniting, but he was the one that brought it all together by managing it, and kept it all going and evolved it. Gary Lineker came for one season and did brilliantly. He replaced Andy Gray who had also done very well and was a favourite of the fans. Andy was a catalyst in the dressing room and was loved by everybody. Howard moved him on to bring in Gary Lineker, then we had an unbelievable season and won nothing. Gary then left after one season, and you are left to think, what's next? Who then comes in? Wayne Clarke. You start to ask yourself how does Howard have this vision to sign one good player after another? How can you let the best striker [Lineker] in England go and yet win the league the year after? Howard had this ability to really bring it together.

'Later, in his last spell, we had no money and the club were going nowhere. We were at a pre-season function, and Howard was required to give a speech where he had to introduce all of the players. It was pretty much man for man the same, and the same squad from the previous season where we had finished 14th or 15th. For someone who had been there for quite some time, it was quite soul-destroying really. The way he introduced us all, you would have thought we were all new signings and we were going to be unbelievable this coming season. It was unbelievable to hear considering there were so many cynical people in the room, but they started to applaud and were positive about it. He managed to turn a situation that so easily could have been quite toxic into something quite vibrant.

'On the training ground, he loved nothing more than to join in as did Colin, and they both hated getting beat. That was the DNA of the football club.

'When I first became a scholar in 1986, the DNA of the football club was there for all to see. It was well engrained at that point. The intensity that we had to train with, the pressing that was demanded by every player, the speed that you had to play with. You had to think quick under Howard.

If you couldn't do it, you couldn't do it. The training allowed you to practise the things that I've just talked about. He was an unbelievable volleyer of a footballer. He had vision and could pass but when the ball was in the air, he would volley it, he would love to get the proper posture out and volley a ball 60 yards on to someone's chest. Pure quality.

'He was as you'd expect on discipline. I saw a tackle recently which took me back to the days when I was at Everton and at Bellefield, and in particular there was a Lancashire League game where Howard would watch from the top of the roof. Those games back then kicked off at 11am, so he would take that game in before heading off to Goodison for the first-team fixture.

'One of our players in the game went right over the ball, taking his opponent out, me thinking that was a bad tackle. Howard came into the dressing room at half-time tearing a strip off the culprit. Howard made a point that we were competitive and that we compete, but it wasn't in our game to hurt players. There was always a line with Howard. He had some moral lines which surprised you. If he didn't like something, it never mattered who you were, club captain or best player, it would not be tolerated, John Ebbrell academy apprentice, if he had standards, it didn't matter to him who you were.

'Howard was a man who was good under pressure which was one of his skills. I was too young to remember the real pressure he was under three or four years before I became part of it.

'I always got the impression that he loved the players to go out together, because he wanted to make it apparent that we were together on a Saturday as well. He would back his players if it was defendable, and I think that he always wanted to try and take any pressure off the players. Whatever he said in the dressing room, he very much wanted to keep it there and support the players.

'He had some very bad times at the club in his early days, and I think he tried to create an environment where the players knew the demands and felt comfortable that the manager would back them as long as they tried to do all of the right things.

'As regards to an influence on my career, I speak to a lot of the lads that were at the national school of excellence when I was there, and some of their stories from their clubs were horrific in terms of their time as not to be given a chance to express themselves. When I returned to Everton, it was the complete opposite. Colin and Howard had actually visited Lilleshall to put a session on, and also checking up on me as to whether I was fine and good.

'Whenever I came back in the school holidays, he always wanted me in around the first-team training, and when I came back for good as an apprentice, in that first season, I played every game in the reserves which was unheard of back then as a first-year YTS as it was in them days. I also travelled a few times with the first team, and I also went on the end-of-season trip when they had won the league for the second time, visiting New Zealand, Australia and Hawaii.

'My only regret is that I never played for Howard in his absolute prime. As everyone knows, the success he brought was not done alone. Howard had a great team of backroom staff, in particular Colin Harvey. Anybody who has ever worked under him will tell you that he is a great coach.

'I remember going to the game with my dad when Everton were on the verge of success. They played a pressing game but with intensity, and I think when Colin was in charge of the reserves, they had around 15 games where they were on a good run. When he was promoted to the first team, he brought that pressing game with him into training and matches. It stayed with the club for years after that, and I loved playing with that speed and intensity. You had to be incredibly fit to do it. They had in the ranks Gary Stevens, Peter Reid, Paul Bracewell, Kevin Ratcliffe, Trevor Steven and more who were great athletes, who could play that way, and press like crazy.

'When I was training with that group, the speed was ferocious, and they all had the desire to win, every single one of them. Every session there would be a forfeit, the players would be arguing in the right way. They trained the way they were going to play on the Saturday.

'I learned so much from Paul Bracewell and Peter Reid. Not that they stood and explained things to me, they played around you and you had to work it out. You were playing with them and they would be barking out as to where you needed to be, which was great learning for me.'

John later moved into coaching and management. Did he ever take any of Howard's methods into that stage of his career?

'To me, management and leadership overlap, and I think Howard had leadership qualities. He was a character, and especially when he let his hair down, you couldn't help but love him. I'm sure the players that were part of the success before I broke into the first team will have better memories and be able to talk around these things. So, my methods of Howard's management are all about leadership. Whenever possible he looked the part and spoke really well. If he had to raise his voice at anyone in the dressing room, you would just stop whatever was happening. There was a real logic to what he was saying, and again he got players to relax which I think is key.

'Fear was never a thought for any Everton player around that time. It was a case of we're going anywhere and will have a right good go. He gave that belief that you could go anywhere and compete which is a great skill, isn't it?'

In the glory days, the squad largely selected itself. There were players who were great when recalled, but how did Kendall keep the players involved?

'Back in those days, squads weren't big anyway, but I would say that Everton had a really small squad. The team that won the league in 1984/85 more or less picked itself all of the time. Alan Harper and Kevin Richardson would play enough games but be disappointed that they were not in the first 11 a bit more. When there were injuries, those two players were so versatile, they played enough games to qualify for a league championship medal.

'I felt that Howard was probably keeping 14 players bubbling along, then he would have some younger players that he bought and took a chance on like Kevin Langley, Warren Aspinall, Neil Adams, Paul Wilkinson and Ian Marshall. He bought players that were on the fringes but were quite happy to be at a great club like Everton. Those players would be learning from the likes of Sharp, Bracewell, Reid and Trevor Steven. Howard was able to give those players a little opportunity, but everyone knew more or less what the first 11 or 12 would be. I think the Gaffer was comfortable with that.

'Howard's departure to Bilbao was a bit of a shock. As I mentioned, we'd been on an end-of-season tour. As we were going out on the tour, I remember my dad saying to Howard, "You will look after him won't you, he's only 17?"

'On the return to the UK, I was thinking how lucky I had been having such an incredible experience. Howard was met at the airport and was taken straight to another check in desk, 25/30 yards away. It was only through reading in the newspapers that Howard had gone as I was too young to ask questions at that time.'

WAYNE CLARKE

Debut: Sunday, 8 March 1987, Watford 2 Everton 1
Watford: Coton, Bardsley, Rostron, Richardson, Simms, McClelland, Blissett, Barnes, Falco, Porter, Sinnott (Gibbs HT)
Everton: Southall, Stevens, Van Den Hauwe (Wilkinson 86), Ratcliffe, Watson, Reid, Steven, Heath, Clarke, Snodin, Power

WAYNE CLARKE joined Everton, his third club, having previously been with Wolverhampton Wanderers and Birmingham City. The signing of Clarke was another masterstroke from Howard Kendall as his goals in the latter stage of the season helped Everton over the line to win the championship and earn himself a medal. He will always be remembered for that strike at Arsenal at the end of March where he chipped Gunners keeper John Lukic from distance and put the Toffees at the summit, where they remained until that memorable day in May, clinching that important victory at Norwich to secure the title.

Wayne played in ten of Everton's last 13 games of 1986/87, scoring five goals. Three of them came against Newcastle United on Easter Monday in a second-half hat-trick. He was absent after injuring his shoulder against Manchester City in a goalless draw on 2 May, forcing him to miss the game two days later when the championship was confirmed at Carrow Road.

When asked for his thoughts on Howard, the word 'gratitude' was one of the first he used. He continued,

'When you're in football, you want to play for the best and you want to win trophies, and this was my opportunity at doing that. So, I'm grateful to Howard for showing interest in me, and I'd like to think that I have repaid his faith in me. I only played ten games at Everton for him but it should have been more. I scored five goals in ten games which shows I produced which was pleasing as well. The one at Highbury, which went down as a turning point, has gone down on record for Howard recognising that.

'He had injuries, and I think he offloaded Paul Wilkinson. Sharpy was out injured, and he wanted me to do a job for him until the end of the season. It was a crucial time of the season as we fought closely with Liverpool, and thankfully I got off to a fairly good start.

'Howard was a person I never really saw lose his temper. He dealt with players in a quiet, methodical way. If ever you were on the bench or sat in the stands, you went in to clarify things with him during the week. He was a great man-manager, and everybody wanted to play for him at the time.

'Don't get me wrong, he would fine you for dissent and lateness, but nobody really dared to step out of line. Whatever fines were issued, the money went into a pot anyway which paid for a meal out for the lads.

'I know he watched me for about six months before he bought me. He would do his homework before signing players. He wanted the right characters to fit into the team.

'Colin Harvey was a great support to Howard as he was a great coach filled with football knowledge. I'm sure Howard would have been the first to say that Colin was a great lieutenant to have in his ranks. I'm sure Colin made a good few decisions along the way during those successful years.

'In the dressing room before games, Howard was very calm. He told his players exactly what he wanted from them. If things were going well – great. If they weren't, he wouldn't fly off the handle. He would put his point over, and if anybody had anything to say, he would welcome questions. He was very methodical and rational.

'In training he was great. You could tell he'd been a good player in his day because in the five-a-side and practice matches we had, he stood out with the passing ability and touch he had. He reminded me of Luka Modrić. He would get the ball and give it. He was a good passer of the ball as well. Modrić got forward more than Howard did. I had never seen Howard play; I'm only surmising from the training sessions that Howard played in.

'Howard loved winning games which is a habit as is losing games. In that era, we were winning more games than we were losing which is a great habit to be in. I will also say as well, if we were having a dodgy spell he would remain calm, and if we had a blank weekend, he would take us all away to get the camaraderie going again. That was part of his man-management, it brought everyone together. His motto was, you work hard, you play hard.

'My relationship with him was nothing but good. He signed me twice [for Everton and Manchester City], so he must have thought a lot of me to do that. I'm just disappointed that I didn't spend more time with him.

'When I did sign for him at Everton, my wife wanted to discuss things with me. Howard said to me that he'd never done this to any other player. If a player refused to sign on the dotted line straight away, he would turn away and the player would lose out. At the end of the season, looking back, I could have missed out on all of the success if Howard would have stuck to his guns. He must have thought something of me to do that.'

As Everton won back their league championship in 1986/87, Wayne registered ten goals in 24 First Division outings, including that Easter Monday hat-trick against Newcastle.

Howard took a strong team to Bloomfield Road on Monday, 18 May for the testimonial of former Everton man Eamonn O'Keefe. Days later, the squad travelled to New Zealand to participate in the Winfield Cup. What did the players know about the news which was soon to be broken about his exit from Goodison to Bilbao?

'There were a few whispers towards the end,' says Wayne. 'I think he did all he could for Everton and wanted a crack at the European Cup because the English clubs were banned from Europe. I don't think he even said his goodbyes to the players.'

Life after the glory of Goodison was never captured again once Wayne left Merseyside. In the latter stages of his career, he continued to play, albeit in the lower leagues. He did return to Goodison years later where he would entertain the guests in the hospitality lounges.

'After I'd retired I went back to do a corporate day which was David Moyes's last game, versus West Ham. I was talking to the guests praising David Moyes for what he'd done at Everton but went on to say the best manager at the club was obviously Howard Kendall. He was stood at the right of me unaware he was there. He took the microphone off me and said, "This young man scored the most important goal for us in the run-in to the championship." He didn't have to say that but he did.'

Wayne today is retired and is now a grandparent to two adorable girls. He never engages in the modern game, showing more interest in his local church which he attends every Sunday, and occasionally volunteers with functions including church fairs and fetes.

COLIN HARVEY

COLIN HARVEY was very much a big part of the success as much as the players. Great teams have always had ambitious men behind the scenes. Brian Clough and Peter Taylor at Nottingham Forest are a prime example, and it was no different for Howard and Colin, two former team-mates who had tasted success in their playing days together in L4 during the late 1960s.

As Howard held the reins for the first team with results disappointing, Colin was experiencing the opposite with the second string in the Central League. His work did not go unnoticed and in the winter of 1983 he was promoted to first-team coach. With this move, and the arrivals of Peter Reid and Andy Gray, things were starting to take shape. Was this combination a coincidence?

Many an Evertonian will have their own story, but without the partnership of Howard and Colin, the silverware would never have arrived. Amen.

Colin says, 'We were friends for a number of years, going back to the days when we were youth team players for our respective clubs, Everton and Preston North End. We'd played against each other many a time in the A, B, and C levels. When Howard made the switch to Everton in the 60s we became friends which lasted for a very long time. Howard was pound for pound one of the best tacklers that I had ever seen. He was a very good as a passer of a ball. Roy Keane was a better player, but that was the style that Howard had.

'Arriving in the summer of 1981, he played a couple of first-team games, playing the role of player-manager. A while later, he asked my opinion. I told him that he would be better off concentrating on managing rather than the playing side of it.

'His man-management was spot on. In my time, he was the best in terms of dealing with players and knowing exactly what he wanted from them.

'Howard loved and believed in his team bonding sessions; he thrived on that situation because team bonding was something he believed in so much. It took a while for it to come to fruition. Howard wanted the players to get on together and enjoy one another's company.

'One of the advantages of the bonding sessions was that Howard detested lateness. If players arrived late for training or a team meeting, he would fine them. The money was put into a kitty which paid for the meal and drinks when the lads went out.'

Long before the success and the glory days that would eventually unfold, the dark days in the winter of 1983 showed signs of desperation with the fans venting their frustration and calling for the manager and chairman to go. I asked Colin how it affected Howard.

'It was pressure, as things weren't going too well on the field. The distributing of leaflets to get rid of Howard and the chairman was getting to Howard and rightly so; there was a stage where he was thinking about calling it a day.

'Thankfully, things started to improve on the pitch, and there was nothing Howard loved more than showing his delight when the team were winning. That is what a manager expects every Saturday.

'It was very seldom that he was angry. He could deal with players without falling out with them. It's not easy when you have to leave players out of the team and have to tell them, but that comes with the territory of being a manager.'

What about the recruitment of players?

'Harry Cooke, who was the chief scout, would watch and recommend players to us. I was with the reserves back then, but Howard and I would go and watch players that Harry would recommend.

'Probably one of Howard's best decisions, not a signing, was when Kevin Ratcliffe was at left-back which wasn't working. I told Howard after a discussion that Kevin was more suited to centre-back. Kevin then moved to that role and as they say, the rest is history. He became the most decorated captain in the club's history.

'I couldn't select Howard's best signing because it would be cruel to select one player in a team full of talent.

'With his team talks, Howard had his own style of doing things. Mike Tyson has a good saying, "You can prepare all you want, but as soon as someone hits you in the face, it all goes out of the window." Team talks are the same, you can beat your chest and want to tear down the dressing room door, but as soon as you go a goal down or something doesn't go right, it all goes flat.

'I do remember a very famous team talk, which has been documented, at Stoke City in the third round of the FA Cup. Stoke, at the Victoria Ground back then, had this old-fashioned dressing room where, as you opened the window, you could see the crowd.

'Thousands of Evertonians filled the away end that afternoon, and the noise from the fans came through the window into the dressing room. Howard told the players that a team talk wasn't required, just go out and do it for them.

'One of his biggest strengths, I may add, was the way he dealt with players. He had a way about him. What he said went and that was the way it had to be. There's only one boss at a football club and that's the manager.

'He was also a manager that worked on things to perfection if you like. We would work together a lot in training to get things right for matchday. If something broke down in a training session, we would work on it until we got it right. Howard and I would both join in with the sessions.'

In 1983, Colin was appointed to the backroom staff as Howard's number two. How did that come about?

'I seem to remember it was when we were beaten by Liverpool and after the game, we went for a drink together. He was as down as I had ever seen him before. I told Howard that we have to start again on Monday, which Howard agreed, but told me that I was going to join him to work with the players.

'I had worked with so many players that I'd worked with in the youth and reserve teams and knew them well who I'd recommend to Howard as I had the belief in those individuals.'

Everton of course flourished in 1985, but the tragedy of Heysel that May changed the future of football for English clubs with UEFA imposing a five-year ban from European competitions. How did Howard feel with Everton being one of the affected clubs?

Colin said, 'Obviously, Howard would have been upset as would the players. When you've won the league, you want a crack at the best trophy in Europe to play the best teams which wasn't to be. I think the denied opportunity forced him to go to Bilbao.

'I, was as shocked as most people when he rang me and told me that he was leaving Everton. The team were away in New Zealand I think, and she said when he returned, he would be going to Athletic.'

MICK HEATON

THE RELATIONSHIP between Howard Kendall and Mick Heaton went back a long way to their days at Ewood Park, the home of Blackburn Rovers. Mick had already come to the end of his playing career and was starting to coach when Howard arrived. When the two of them got together, it seemed like the partnership was destined to be, uniting their ideas to become a team.

Like any great partnerships in life – Laurel and Hardy, Morecambe and Wise, McEnroe and Fleming – that can only bring success. That's exactly what Howard and Mick did at Goodison, not forgetting the promotion to the first team of Colin Harvey in those formidable years of the 1980s.

Howard, Mick, Colin and Graham Smith would meet every morning to discuss what games they'd seen, whether it was opposing teams to play in the coming weeks, or just to keep things ticking over like clockwork. They were always involved together in training sessions at Bellefield. Some days one of the coaching staff would take charge while the other coaches would assess the ongoings, then in turn they would rotate the role of controlling the session. Teamwork was emphasised as an ingredient to success. There was never a truer word spoken.

Mick passed away in tragic circumstances in April 1995 in a car accident. I was able to speak with members of his family to assist me with information on his behalf about his relationship with Howard.

Mick's family said, 'Howard was only to be described as good company, and a great person to be around. There was no denying that they had a great working relationship, bouncing off each other with different ideas, not being rigid in what they were doing, hoping to improve situations, or even add to each other's ideas.

'The dressing room team talks were always down to the manager, but Mick would always be at hand and put his input forward, approaching players whose heads needed lifting to gee them on.

'Towards the end of Mick's time at Everton when success was frequent, he felt undervalued by Howard, not earning the recognitionof the other members of the backroom staff. Mick was very much for the players and he showed a caring touch by building the confidence up amongst the group when he sensed anxiety in the dressing room.

'The dark winter of 1983 when fans were unanimous that Kendall and the chairman should leave, it would have meant departures too for the remaining backroom staff. How would they get through this darkness? They both believed there was something that was possible which would change for the better which wass proved right.

'Trophies and success came in abundance with nobody expecting to achieve what they did so quickly after that dark period. The first trophy was always going to be important, which led to further success, adding more silverware along the way. Achieving what they did in that time, every trophy was appreciated and it's very difficult to distinguish which honour gave Howard and the staff the most pleasure. The first one is always special, isn't it? It proved to be the start of things to come.

'Howard, his backroom staff and players were a team off the pitch too, which included the wives and girlfriends, especially when Wembley was then looked upon as Everton's second home. Everybody felt equal, sharing the warmth like any close-knit family when brought together.'

Mick and his wife lived in the Lancashire village of Tarleton. So close were the 'Everton family' that Trevor Steven, Graeme Sharp and Gary Lineker would go out and dine with the Heatons.

Everton were cruelly denied the chance to participate in the European Cup. What effect did it have on the backroom team?

'The ban from Europe of English clubs due to Heysel probably had a bearing in Howard's departure. Mick, the staff and also the players were denied the chance to show what they could do at that next level. Despite the disappointment, there was nothing anybody could do to rectify things.

'When Athletic Bilbao beckoned Howard to take over in the summer of 1987, Mick felt that was the time for him to call it a day even though Howard wanted him and Colin Harvey to join him in the Basque country.

'Mick felt down and out at that time with himself. It was a moment Howard was unaware of. If he'd have known, things may have been different, but we will never know. They remained friends for the rest of their lives as Mick would very often visit Howard in Spain, even to the end with Howard attending Mick's funeral.

'The departure of Howard to Bilbao came as a total surprise to the players despite there being rumours, but Mick was aware as he'd been asked to continue their professional relationship by accompanying him as they'd fitted in so well together at Blackburn and Everton alike.'

GRAHAM SMITH

GRAHAM JOINED Everton in a part-time capacity in 1977. He graduated from university in 1974, doing a couple of years' teaching, and got asked to speak to Ray Minshull.

Before that, he was playing non-league football for Skelmersdale United. Their manager told him one day the reserve team trainer hadn't turned up and asked if he would take the young lads.

After a couple of weeks, he received a letter through the post from Ray Minshull inviting him in for a chat. The rest as they say is history.

Graham became part of the coaching staff with the first team when Colin Harvey inherited the job, accompanying Peter Reid, Terry Darracott and Mick Lyons. He was also a very valuable member to Howard too.

As a coach, Graham and his youth team were always successful in pre-season tournaments. He recalls a competition in the Netherlands where opponents Groningen brought a ringer in by the name of Ronald Koeman, someone who would later become very familiar to Evertonians. The Toffees beat Groningen in the final with the young Johnny Morrissey scoring a hat-trick. Graham took a lot of pleasure from the success in Europe with the youngsters. He also had success in the Lancashire League.

He takes pride, and rightly so, in bringing through players like Steve McMahon, Paul Lodge and Kevin Ratcliffe, as well as Eddie Youds, John Ebbrell, Tony Grant and David Unsworth who later developed through the ranks. Colin Harvey takes all the credit for that, but they made the transition from the youth team.

Another occasion was the 1983 FA Youth Cup Final against Norwich which spanned three games as the first two legs were level on aggregate at 5-5. Everton won the toss for the third and final match, and that was about all they would win as Norwich won 1-0 in front of a big crowd of around 25,000 fans.

Under Graham's leadership, Everton bounced back 12 months later to win the competition by defeating Stoke City over two legs.

Graham gives his account of the great man, 'He was probably the best manager that I have ever worked with, taking nothing away from others. What he lacked in some things, he made up for in other ways. He was never the best on the grass, coaching, but he was astute enough to put people around him who were. Throughout his career, he brought in, or appointed good number twos, and the best one of all, in my opinion, was Colin Harvey.

'Howard trusted Colin, who led the grass work, leaving Howard to carry on with everything else such as the media, and everything that goes on behind the scenes.

'He was a fantastic person in the dressing room, and I was lucky enough [to be in there], as he always invited me, which was a standard thing with all of the staff: if you wanted to go in, you were always welcome in the first-team dressing room.

'Even when Everton reached the final of the FA Cup at Wembley, or the European Cup Winners' Cup Final in Rotterdam, I was invited along with other staff members to sit on the bench. He was good at bringing his staff together, but more importantly, the way he brought teams together.

'What made him special was the rapport he had with the press. He very rarely got bad press. He also had a good relationship with the players; they certainly knew who was boss, there's no doubt about that. He was very patient with his players and very good to his staff too. He always invited all of his staff to end-of-season tours. What Howard had, I can only describe as a gift. It was like I'm the boss and you'll do what I say, and he would also take any feedback on board and would use it if he had to.

'To give you an example, we were playing Leicester City in the next round of the FA Youth Cup, so I went to watch the opposition. Leicester produced this free kick in the game which I told Howard about. He told me to put the idea to the first team. I thought what, me? Howard meant what he said, too. He was always open to new ideas. I put this free kick to the first team which they used a few times.

'As good a manager as Howard was, let's not forget Colin Harvey's input in all of this. Colin was full of ideas. He was the tactician as well as the coach in terms of he'd study games, take the games home and watch the videos for hours, returning to Bellefield the next day and have ideas as to what we didn't do last game, and what they could do in the next game, and he would know everything about the opposition we would be playing against.

'Howard's style of management, I would describe as a critical friend in a lot of ways. He was fair, but the players knew how far to go with him. A good story is when Peter Reid came back from the World Cup in 1986 looking a stone lighter. Howard bought him two crates of Guinness to build him back up. If someone was out of order, there would be a knock at the door at the end of training, "You want to see me, Boss?" That player would be dragged over the coals as it were.

'Howard's strengths and weaknesses? I wouldn't say his coaching was a weakness, because he'd passed all of his coaching badges and had a wealth of experience. His coaching was good, but Colin's methods were better. Howard had confidence in Colin. I played myself against the first team in training, and again, Howard would never correct Colin on his thoughts and ideas, and let him get on with it and maybe discuss it afterwards. That to me, is a good sign of man-management, especially when you trust someone to do something without having to stand over him. Howard might have said "That worked well" or whatever, but those occasions were few and far between. They would both discuss what they were going to do in the morning before a session, so they were both singing from the same hymn sheet.

'I had a good relationship with Howard, but at the end of the day, we all got sacked by him [chuckling]!! Again, he went into it with his hands tied. Years later he apologised to me, regrettably saying that one of the biggest mistakes was letting me go which was a nice thing to say and hear. It takes a lot for someone to do something like that. It takes a man to admit his mistakes.

'I always tried to pick his brains whenever we went out socially, and one thing that struck me was, he would talk about managers that he'd played under. He told me things he'd learned from Harry Catterick, Denis Smith at Stoke City, and Jim Smith [Birmingham City]. Howard said he would try and select the best bits from each manager, and use them himself. That is something that I adopted too as it all made sense.

'When Howard arrived at Goodison to take the manager's role, he was still playing briefly when he first took over. I remember a game with the youth team against Lancaster University, and Howard playing in a central midfield role. The kids were all nervous, but he put them at ease by giving them advice throughout. I listened to all of the instructions he was offering to each and every one which I also took on board as I used them in my sessions.

'I also worked under Billy Bingham and Gordon Lee, not forgetting Steve Burtenshaw, but one thing that Howard did more or less from day one, he said, "We all play the same way." If the first team played 4-4-2, the reserves did the same, and the youth team the same. That made sense because each player knew their positions when they moved up and down the squads. They knew what was expected of them, positionally, technically and tactically. He took it beyond that, which made sense tactically. We practised all of the set pieces, defended corners the same way, we all did a front-post corner the same way. The first team you have to understand had more variations because they were getting spied on every week by opposing teams.

'I always used to go to all of the reserve games as well, just to see if their playing system was the same as I was using in the youth team. I wanted to make sure that I was aiming to get the youngsters up to the same methods, and what was wanted from each position in the reserves, as the system was used right throughout the club.'

How did Howard handle the role of player-manager?

'I can't ever remember him struggling in any of those games he played in, but I think there came a point where he must have felt as though he wasn't contributing a great deal because he had that self-honesty. He was one of those people that would look at himself first which is a lesson that I have learned. I, too, had that self-critical reflection when I was in charge of the kids at Everton. Coming back from an away game after a defeat, I would look at things such as, should I have changed the shape of the team, did I make the right selection which brings you then to looking at the performances of some of the players, did he play as well as he should have done, did the striker hold the ball up enough, etc. You end up going through all of that process. That is one thing that I took from Howard, so it's something he must have done with his own players.

'One thing I remember him saying to me was, "Never let the players get you sacked."

'Howard had this belief in the way he wanted to play. I don't mean the school of science, but he loved the passing game. He had other options too where he could play the ball up to Sharpy and Andy Gray with the wide men helping provide the crosses for them both. Howard's style was to have a direction and purpose to the game. There are two things that you can do: if the chairman is on your back, also the fans, you work harder in training, and you stress to the players that Evertonians will forgive you for anything if your touch is off and you're missing chance after chance, they will forgive you for all of that as long as they can see that you are working hard to put it right.

'He eventually got it right and winning the FA Cup in 1984 was a fantastic occasion for the club and the fans. The one trophy that I think gave Howard the most pleasure was winning the European Cup Winners' Cup. That for me was when he'd made his mark. He's won the FA Cup to get into the Cup Winners' Cup, but when you get success in the domestic cup in this country, you want to test yourself against the best teams in Europe who were also the winners of their own cup. That was the tragedy of Heysel as well as people losing their lives and the way that football was scarred from that. I think that denied Howard the chance to work in what was then the European Cup.'

I asked who Graham felt Howard's most influential signing was.

'That's a good question,' he says. 'Influential in a lot of ways was Andy Gray because he was an absolute born leader, and he demanded that the players work around him as well. He was a large enough character on and off the pitch, and undoubtedly made Graeme Sharp a better player as Sharpy played alongside him every week. Sharpy learned how to back into and jump into players early, and take off early.

'Peter Reid was another great signing the boss made. He came to Everton with not the best of fitness records, didn't he? He had loads of injuries such as a broken leg.

'Kevin Sheedy – you can add him to the signings the boss made, not forgetting Trevor Steven. But for me, it was Neville Southall who was the most influential signing. I remember when I was over in America coaching and people approached me fascinated with Nev, asking how he was the best. They knew he was the best in England, and the reason he was the best was simple, because he worked the hardest. He used to work his socks off in training. He would say to me, "What are you doing this afternoon with the kids?" I'd reply, "I'm just doing some bits and pieces." Nev replied, "If I come out this afternoon after my lunch, and the kids train at one o'clock, would you do half an hour shooting with me?" I agreed to do that.

'If a youngster involved in the session would score past Nev, and he thought he should have saved it, he would then kick the ball the whole length of the A team pitch at Bellefield outraged, knowing he should have saved it.

'Howard had no time for players who didn't try. The first team had been at Norwich, so he decided to come down to watch the youngsters away in an FA Youth Cup tie at Millwall. Teddy Sheringham was playing for Millwall, we won 4-2 in front of a crowd of four or five thousand, and I have to say, even at that level, it was the most hostile environment I've ever experienced in my life! Our team bus got bricked coming away.

'He came into the dressing room after the game and commented on the shape that I'd set the team to play, also saying how much he loved the way the players worked hard on and off the ball.

'In the first-team squad you had to be proficiently technical and have the temperament. I always remember one thing he said to me, when we've got the ball, we work hard to play with it, and when they've got the ball, we work hard to get it back, and I have always kept that mantra.'

JIM McGREGOR

JIM STARTED his career as a physiotherapist at the age of 21. He was an assistant physio at Clyde on a part-time basis, attending training on Tuesday and Thursday evenings and also working with the reserve setup.

In 1966, Jim saw an advert in his local professional journal as a Third Division club in England were looking for a qualified young physiotherapist. There was no mention of what club it was, and eventually he found out it was Oldham Athletic. He was fortunate after applying to get an interview. The manager of the Latics was the great Northern Ireland international Jimmy McIlroy. Ken Bates was the newly installed chairman who had great ideasabout improving the facilities by changing the dressing rooms around, and made a great big medical room and wanted someone who was medically qualified to work in it. Jim was successful in getting the role and was the first person ever to be a full-time physiotherapist at the club.

Things changed for Jim in 1975 as Everton were seeking a replacement for Norman Borrowdale. He attended an interview at Littlewoods, conducted by a PR manager who knew nothing about football or the job in hand. He just wanted to get to know the interviewees and their backgrounds. There were an incredible number of applicants, over 100, with Jim's chances looking positive, reaching the last three candidates. At that stage, he was invited to the Atlantic Towers hotel for lunch with Everton manager Billy Bingham and Stuart Imlach, who was the club's first-team coach. Jim was then taken to Bellefield and on a tour of Goodison Park. A few days passed, and to Jim's delight, he received a phone call with the news to say he had been successful with his application. He served Everton until Manchester United showed an interest in appointing him, with perks including a free car and free health insurance for the family. It was an offer too good to refuse.

Jim gives his take on Howard Kendall, 'When I think of managers, you always seem to compare managers to other managers and other people that you've worked with. For example, when I was at Oldham, I compared Jimmy Frizzell to Jimmy McIlroy. In my Everton days, I compared Howard to Gordon Lee. At Manchester United, I compared Sir Alex Ferguson to Ron Atkinson. That's how I looked at things in lots and lots of ways.

'Howard and Gordon were complete opposites. Gordon was a lovely fella, perhaps the nicest manager that I'd ever worked with. He was so straight and honest, but sadly very naive about life in lots of ways because he probably hadn't lived the life of what you'd call a normal footballer, but also very straightforward. I have to say that he was never a well organised person either. He would be very late putting up the team sheet on the board, also forgetting many things of importance, and not the smartest of dressers. Sometimes he'd be late for training with things at times chaotic, but a football man through and through.

'When Everton appointed Howard Kendall after Gordon's sacking, Howard was the complete opposite. With him, everything had to be in order. He would put the team sheet on the board at a certain time every Friday morning. His training sessions were mapped out long before it actually happened with his coach Mick Heaton. Nothing was ever off the cuff, and he himself was absolutely immaculate. When he came out to train, his socks were turned over to perfection, his boots would be spotlessly clean, everything he wore had to be spotless.

'Gordon Lee would turn up for training with creased training gear, not really worrying about his appearance, whereas Howard was the total opposite. I could arrive an hour late for training and Gordon wouldn't have known. Again, with Howard, he was the complete opposite, he wouldn't miss a trick.

'Unfortunately, I didn't work with Howard for too long. Gordon Lee was sacked after the season had finished in the May, with Howard appointed with immediate effect. I left to join Manchester United in the October that same year, and not forgetting the players were then away from duty until the pre-season.

'When the players resumed training in the July, we then went on a tour to Japan, so got to know him more than the average manager. We'd been away on tour for about six to eight days, and not forgetting, I was with him every single day, morning, afternoon and evening. So, I got well acquainted socially far more than I ever did with Gordon because as Howard liked to go out to bars for a drink, Gordon was teetotal. Howard and his staff liked to be together where after a few drinks, tongues were relaxed and he was excellent company.

'I only knew him for six months whilst at Everton, and he never spoke about his career which was surprising. He was the youngest player to play in an FA Cup Final in 1964 at that time, and also had the pleasure to be part of that great Everton midfield known as the Holy Trinity. I can always remember Fergie talking about his time playing for Glasgow Rangers.

'When I look back at managers that I have had the pleasure to have worked with over the years in my career and compare them to Howard, Billy Bingham first of all was, like Howard, very well organised but never went out with his staff. He sat with the players on an away trip in the hall over dinner, maybe having a glass of wine, but never mixed socially.

'Big Ron [Atkinson] loved a night out, and socially, an amazing guy, fantastic fun, a great mixer, loved to be the centre of attention, unlike Howard, who did not. If we went to a function, Howard would like to sit on his own, whereas Ron would be up on stage singing songs.

'As far as managerial differences are concerned, big Ron was NOT as organised as Howard. Howard was more like Sir Alex Ferguson, who was also very well organised training wise, in fact, in many ways, spot on with everything.

'Howard in his appearance was very smart and immaculate with everything in place. That for me, was the biggest attribute about him, his appearance.

'You, like many other Evertonians, will remember the signings Howard made upon his arrival known as the Magnificent Seven. I was involved with every one of those medicals and something that I was involved with at every single football club that I worked with throughout my career. As well as the club doctor and specialist, I examined every single player.

'I can remember the medical with George Wood, the Everton keeper. I ran into Gordon Lee, crying out that George was blind and needed specs, but Gordon assured me that George was a good goalkeeper.

'Going back to Howard, regarding injured players on their way back to fitness, he would ask me to report to his office on a particular day, or he would come down to the medical room or into the dressing room requesting updates on injured players. He was never pushy regarding their return, but was always interested in their progress.

'In the short time I knew Howard, our relationship was spot on. When the offer came from Manchester United for me to go there, I don't think that he was that disappointed, because maybe he wanted his own backroom staff. When I left, he brought in John Clinkard, and his own recruitment was then complete.

'Years later when we were invited back to the Everton Christmas dinners, I would sit with Howard and we got on great.'

JOHN CLINKARD

JOHN CLINKARD, 'Clinks' or 'Magnum' as he was known to his familiar friends, was no stranger to football. He played for Oxford Boys, had a trial with Chelsea, signed on briefly with Oxford City, and later played for Cardiff Corinthians in a Welsh league.

John's association with Everton started as he was a friend of Terry Darracott. At the time he was working for Fulham, at a rehabilitation centre in Slough.

'It was run by the NHS and was a unique place where I would treat all of the athletes from Loughborough College as well as the national gymnastic and rowing squad,' he said.

'I would also treat the players of Reading FC when they had undergone cartilage operations when Maurice Evans was the manager. I would treat Terry Darracott who had an arthritic knee and at the time was at Wrexham, that's how our friendship began. I treated Terry for around eight weeks. I was working part time for non-league club Wycombe Wanderers on a part-time basis on Tuesday and Thursday nights.

'Terry asked me one day if I ever wanted to get into the professional game, which I did, and he told me that if and when the opportunity arose, he would put a word in for me. Bless him, he did. Everton's physio before me was Jim McGregor, who left for pastures new with a role at Manchester United.

'In this time at Fulham under the management of Malcolm Macdonald, I was in the dressing room after a game at Huddersfield Town when a knock came on the door with a request for me to take a phone call. I asked who it was and "Terry Darracott" was the reply. Terry asked me if I would be interested in the Everton vacancy as Jim McGregor was leaving, to which I enthusiastically said "yes".

'Howard, I'm told, asked Ron Atkinson if he could have some of the applications he didn't use and my name came up. I did apply for the Manchester United job half-heartedly. I received a reply saying that they would keep me on file. Howard, on receiving my application from Ron Atkinson, had seen all of my references, etc.

'The interview with Howard for the Everton job was on a late Wednesday afternoon as I had work to do that day at Fulham. I took a train to Liverpool Lime Street where I eventually met up with Howard and the club doctor, had a bite to eat at the Queens Hotel and was offered the job there and then. One of my references was from a guy called Fred Street who was the physio at Arsenal and the English national team. I knew Fred from when I was at Arsenal on a day's experience.

'Howard asked me an unusual question. "Have you ever been booked?" "Yes," I replied, "at Blackburn Rovers." "I know," said Howard. "I was there sitting in the stands."

'Howard was a very special man and a brilliant leader. You knew that he was the boss, and you would also socialise with the man. You would have your fun together and nights out, excellent company, always one for enjoying himself. When we were working, he was the most professional man that I had ever worked for. He was a man that knew the game inside out which led the club to success. When he was doing his interviews on TV, he always came across as the perfect gentleman.

'I was a relatively young person when I started at Everton and inexperienced in pro football, but I improved in that field as he taught me lots of good and important lessons. We used to have a staff meeting which was all of the coaches and even Harry Cooke, the scout. We would discuss what the latest information was, and where we were, and what we were about to do that day.

'Howard would want an update from me with players that were sidelined through injury, and how far they were from resuming training. He was always one that demanded that you do your homework and keep on top of everything that you were supposed to do. In the eight years I was employed at Everton, and when I left to go to lesser clubs, and I mean that with the greatest respect, I found myself frustrated at the lack of professionalism with some of the younger players, who didn't seem to appreciate the fact that football was their profession, their bread and butter.

'Howard was a man who was always fully in charge and was well respected by the players. Even though you would be in his company socially, you still knew he was in charge. There was always that fear factor which there has to be when you are the boss. I will say too that he was always up and in early for training no matter what, with a twinkle in his eye after a night out.

'Sitting alongside him in the dugout on a matchday as I did, when things weren't quite right on the pitch, he would leave his position in the stands to make little alterations that needed to be made with Colin. Then you would see tactically that they could sort problems out which fascinated me.

'His team talks in the dressing room, he didn't elaborate, he didn't have to. It was just a case of telling players to tweak things that needed doing. He wasn't one to rant and rave; he didn't have to as the players knew what they had to do, knowing they were both capable and good enough. He could be quite ruthless too, when he had to be.

'I was focused on my duties to be honest, but I do remember that famous team talk at the Victoria Ground in the FA Cup when he opened the dressing room windows! That is a very well-known and documented story anyway.

'Howard made a great appointment in promoting Colin from the reserves to assist him in his duties. Colin was a tremendous guy who I can honestly say I had a good relationship with. I treated him like an older brother. Colin was another who always did things right, and a person that cared. By that, I remember when we would be overseas on a pre-season tour, the players would be having a mid-afternoon rest. Colin and I would clean the players' boots. I have never known that to happen anywhere else. He didn't like the thought of the players going out wearing dirty boots. Also, when we were away, he would always be up early and go for an early morning run and a swim.

'Howard and Colin achieved success together. They were massive characters and very important people that made things happen.

'One thing I will say regarding both of them, they always made the training sessions enjoyable. Everything regarding the sessions was always with a ball. The banter also helped considering the characters we had.

'When Howard endured the dark days when there was pressure from the fans and the media, when things were going against them regarding results, he tried to keep everything normal as he didn't want it to affect the players. He was for sure a man that would protect his players. There was no hiding place for anyone at the club at that time, but as I say, he kept everything as normal as he could.

'It was very difficult to see why the team was struggling with so many good individuals in the dressing room. When we went out together for Chinese meals, he would welcome anyone to get things off their chest just to clear the air, but whatever pressure he was under, nobody could see it. Howard dealt with it in his own way.

'We always knew that we had a good side, and I could not believe how things changed. It is incredible to think how we struggled before the tide turned. It all came together at once surprisingly, and who would have believed only months later, a piece of silverware would be brought back to Goodison? It was incredible to think that season [1983/84] we reached the twin towers of Wembley twice! It was like the phoenix rising from the ashes, wasn't it? Everything at once clicked into place.

'Once Peter Reid got fit and established, things started to improve which may come across as a coincidence, but that type of character repaid Howard for bringing him to the club and having faith in him despite his injuries.

'Winning the FA Cup in May against Watford, the first trophy in over a decade, meant everything to Howard, a sight that was visible on his face as the cameras captured at pitchside as the players went up for their medals and Rats collected the trophy.

'A season later, he doubled the tally, adding another with it being the league championship. It was very difficult to identify which of those trophies gave him the most pleasure. He and his players worked for the success and eventually got it. It also proved that Everton were without doubt the best team around at that time in England. They of course continued their success further with another league championship a couple of years later, and narrowly missing out on two further FA Cups in that period.

'It was so cruel that Howard, the players and everyone connected with Everton should be denied a go at the big European trophy years later with the ban of English clubs from Europe after the devastation at the Heysel Stadium, which changed Everton's future.

'I have so many fond memories of the man, and a story I'd like to share. This is going back to the very early days. This was at Sunderland, nearing the end of the season. It was a nice sunny day. Howard that day wore a tracksuit top, shorts, socks and trainers which was very unusual as he always wore a suit.

'The old dugouts at Roker Park were very similar to the ones we had at Goodison with the perspex glass at the back. There was a bunch of Sunderland fans behind us banging continuously on the perspex. They were starting to annoy us, as Everton were under the cosh in the first half and trailing by a goal. We looked behind us to see one fan in particular, middle-aged, just staring at us both. Just before half-time, before going down the tunnel, Howard had a go at this individual by telling him to pack it in.

'We came back out for the second half with Howard still in his shorts, and three or four minutes into that period, he said, "My leg is stuck." I asked him what he meant. He replied, "My leg is stuck to the bench." He couldn't move his leg at all. My first thought was it was a medical problem, but as it happened, the angry fan must have jumped over the wall and managed to get into the dugout to apply super glue to the bench which Howard sat on. It took me about five minutes to free Howard, then we looked at this fan who wore a huge smile on his face.'